ECCE ROMANI

A LATIN READING PROGRAM

II·A
HOME AND SCHOOL

SECOND EDITION

ECCE ROMANI

A LATIN READING PROGRAM

II·A

HOME AND SCHOOL

SECOND EDITION

Longman

Ecce Romani Student Book II-A
Home and School, second edition

Longman, 10 Bank Street, White Plains, N.Y. 10606

Associated companies:
Longman Group Ltd., London
Longman Cheshire Pty., Melbourne
Longman Paul Pty., Auckland
Copp Clark Pitman, Toronto

This edition of *Ecce Romani* is based on *Ecce Romani: A Latin Reading Course*, originally prepared by The Scottish Classics Group © copyright The Scottish Classics Group 1971, 1982, and published in the United Kingdom by Oliver and Boyd, a division of Longman Group. It is also based on the 1988 North American edition. This edition has been prepared by a team of American educators.

Photo credits: Credits appear on page xi.

Acknowledgments: Reiterated thanks are due to the consultants who contributed to the 1988 North American edition of *ECCE ROMANI*: Dr. Rudolph Masciantonio, Ronald Palma, Dr. Edward Barnes, and Shirley Lowe. In addition to the authors and consultants who contributed to this new edition and who are listed separately, thanks are due to the following people: to Mary O. Minshall for providing original material for the Frontier Life essays; to Ursula Chen, Julia Gascoyne Fedoryk, and Franklin Kennedy for their help on the Teacher's Guides; and to Marjorie Dearworth Keeley for help with the preparation of the manuscript. Finally, thanks are due to Longman Publishing Group's production team: Janice Baillie and Helen Ambrosio; and its editorial team: Barbara Thayer and Lyn McLean, for all they did.

Executive editor: Lyn McLean
Development editor: Barbara Thayer
Production editor: Janice L. Baillie
Production-editorial and design director: Helen B. Ambrosio
Text design: Creatives NYC, Inc.
Cover design: Circa 86
Cover Illustration: Yao Zen Liu
Text art: Yao Zen Liu
Maps: Laszlo Kubinyi
Photo research: Barbara Thayer

ISBN: 0-8013-1206-X

12345678910-DOC-999897969594

REVISION EDITOR: GILBERT LAWALL
University of Massachusetts, Amherst, Massachusetts

AUTHORS AND CONSULTANTS

Peter C. Brush
Deerfield Academy
Deerfield, Massachusetts

Sally Davis
Arlington Public Schools
Arlington, Virginia

Pauline P. Demetri
Cambridge Rindge & Latin School
Cambridge, Massachusetts

Jane Hall
National Latin Exam
Alexandria, Virginia

Thalia Pantelidis Hocker
Old Dominion University
Norfolk, Virginia

Glenn M. Knudsvig
University of Michigan
Ann Arbor, Michigan

Maureen O'Donnell
W.T. Woodson High School
Fairfax, Virginia

Ronald Palma
Holland Hall School
Tulsa, Oklahoma

David J. Perry
Rye High School
Rye, New York

Deborah Pennell Ross
University of Michigan
Ann Arbor, Michigan

Andrew F. Schacht
Renbrook School
West Hartford, Connecticut

Judith Lynn Sebesta
University of South Dakota
Vermillion, South Dakota

The Scottish Classics Group
Edinburgh, Scotland

David Tafe
Rye Country Day School
Rye, New York

Rex Wallace
University of Massachusetts
Amherst, Massachusetts

Allen Ward
University of Connecticut
Storrs, Connecticut

Elizabeth Lyding Will
Amherst College
Amherst, Massachusetts

Philip K. Woodruff
Lake Forest High School
Lake Forest, Illinois

CONTENTS

REFERENCE MATERIALS

MAPS

■■■■■ CREDITS ■■■■■

Special gratitude is extended to Jenny Page of The Bridgeman Art Library, London, for her invaluable assistance in locating illustrative materials sought for *ECCE ROMANI*.

The publisher gratefully acknowledges the contributions of the agencies, institutions, and photographers listed below:

Chapter 28
(p. 6)   (a) Bronze head of a Roman woman, first quarter 2nd Century A.D., Louvre, Paris/Bridgeman Art Library, London; Bronze head of a Roman man, lst–2nd Century A.D., Louvre, Paris/ Bridgeman Art Library, London

(b) Sardonyx cameo thought to be of Emperor Julian and his wife (361– 363 A.D.), British Museum, London/ Bridgeman Art Library, London

(p. 7) Bas relief sculpture of a hair-dresser, circa 50 A.D., Landesmuseum, Hesse/Bridgeman Art Library, London

(p. 8) "A Roman Boat Race" by Sir Edward John Poynter (1836–1919), The Maas Gallery, London/Bridgeman Art Library, London

(p. 9) Woman Having Her Hair Dressed by a Maidservant, South West corner of South Wall, Oecus 5, 60–50 B.C. (fresco) Villa dei Misteri, Pompeii/ Bridgeman Art Library, London

Chapter 30
(p. 27) "Marius Triumphing Over the Cimbri" by Saverio Altamura (1826–1897) Museo e Gallerie Nazionali di Capodimonte, Naples/Bridgeman Art Library, London

(p. 28) "Caius Marius Amid the Ruins of Carthage" by John Vanderlyn, The Albany Institute of History and Art, Albany

Chapter 31
(p. 32) Roman butcher's, stone frieze, 2nd Century B.C., Musée de la Civilisation, Paris/Bridgeman Art Library, London

Chapter 32
(p. 39) Preparations for a banquet: fragment of marble, limestone, and glass mosaic pavement from Carthage, Roman c. 180–190 A.D., Louvre, Paris/Bridgeman Art Library, London

(p. 45) "Psyche and Charon" by John Roddam Spencer-Stanhope (1829–1908), Roy Miles Gallery, London/Bridgeman Art Library, London

Chapter 33
(p. 53) Roman tableware. Photograph courtesy Elizabeth Lyding Will

(p. 58) "Orpheus Charming the Animals," Roman mosaic, Blanzy, Musée Municipal, Laon, France/Girandon/ Bridgeman Art Library, London

Chapter 34
(p. 61) Counters and dice, Gallo-Roman, second half of 1st Century B.C., Musée Alesia, Alise-Sainte-Reine/ Giraudon/Bridgeman Art Library, London

(p. 64) Dionysiac Mystery Cult, c. 60–50 B.C. (fresco) Villa dei Misteri, Pompeii/Bridgeman Art Library, London

Chapter 35
(p. 78) "Cicero and the Magistrates Discovering the Tomb of Archimedes" by Benjamin West (1738–1820), Christie's, London/Bridgeman Art Library, London

(p. 81) Statue of Julius Caesar of the Trajan Era, Campidoglio, Rome/Bridgeman Art Library, London

Chapter 36
(p. 90) "Neaera Reading a Letter from Catullus" by Henry J. Hudson, Bradford Art Galleries & Museums/ Bridgeman Art Library, London

(p. 93) "Penelope and Her Suitors" by John William Waterhouse, City of Aberdeen Art Gallery and Museums, Aberdeen, Scotland

Chapter 37
(p. 103) Stone relief of Roman classroom scene, photograph courtesy The Mansell Collection

Chapter 38
(p. 110) "Ariadne in Naxos" by Evelyn de Morgan (1850–1919), The De Morgan Foundation, London/Bridgeman Art Library, London

Chapter 39
(p. 124) Antony and Cleopatra by Rockwell Kent in *The Complete Works of William Shakespeare* ©1936, Doubleday and Co., Garden City

(p. 127) Augustus (63 B.C.–A.D. 14) and his wife Livia (39 B.C.–A.D. 14) seated classical marble statues, Ephesus Museum, Turkey/Bridgeman Art Library, London

(p. 129) Detail from "Vergil Reading the *Aeneid* to Augustus," by J.A.D. Ingres (1780–1867), courtesy of The Fogg Art Museum, Harvard University Art Museums, Cambridge; bequest of Grenville L. Winthrop

Chapter 40
(p. 138) "A Roman Scribe" by Sir Lawrence Alma-Tadema (1836–1912), private collection/Bridgeman Art Library, London

Chapter 41
(pp. 145–146) Drawings by Mary O. Minshall

Italy

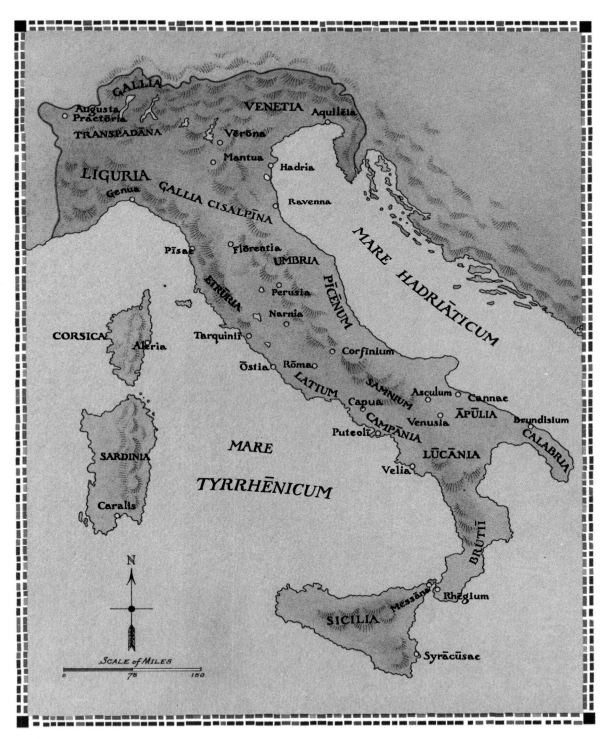

Italy

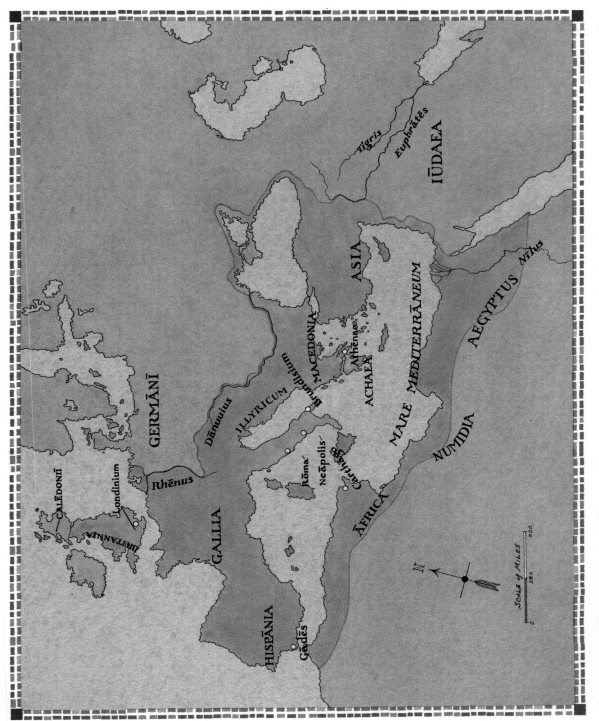

The Roman Empire, A.D. 80

PREPARING TO GO SHOPPING

Māne erat. Aurēlia in cubiculō sedēbat. Crīnēs eius cūrābant duae ancillae, quārum altera speculum tenēbat, altera crīnēs pectēbat. Phrygia, quae crīnēs neglegenter pectēbat, dominam vexābat; Syra, quod manus tremēbat, speculum nōn bene tenēbat. Aurēlia igitur, neglegentiā eārum vexāta, subitō, "Quam neglegentēs estis!" clāmāvit. "Abīte! Abīte! Vocāte Cornēliam! Eam mēcum in urbem dūcere volō."   5

Statim exiērunt ancillae.

Mox in cubiculum iniit Cornēlia. "Cūr mē vocāvistī, māter?"

Aurēlia respondit, "Pater tuus amīcōs quōsdam, in quibus sunt senātōrēs praeclārī, ad cēnam hodiē invītāvit. Porcum servus iam ēmit, sed ego in animō habeō ipsa in urbem īre ad mercātōrem quendam cuius taberna nōn procul abest, nam glīrēs optimōs ille   10 vēndere solet. Sī tū vīs mēcum īre, mē in ātriō exspectā! Intereā servōs iubēbō sellās ad iānuam ferre."

1 **crīnēs, crīnium,** m. pl., *hair*
2 **speculum, -ī,** n., *mirror*
   neglegenter, adv., *carelessly*
4 **vexātus, -a, -um,** *annoyed*
8 **in quibus,** *among whom*

9 **porcus, -ī,** m., *pig*
10 **cuius,** *whose*
   glīs, glīris, m., *dormouse*
11 **sella, -ae,** f., *sedan chair*

2 **pectō, pectere, pexī, pexus,** *to comb*
11 **vēndō, vēndere, vēndidī, vēnditus,** *to sell*

Exercise 28a
Respondē Latīnē:

1. Quid faciēbant duae ancillae?
2. Quam ob causam Phrygia Aurēliam vexābat?
3. Quam ob causam Syra speculum nōn bene tenēbat?
4. Quōcum Aurēlia in urbem īre vult?
5. Quōs ad cēnam Cornēlius invītāvit?
6. Quid servus iam ēmit?
7. Quid Aurēlia emere vult?
8. Quid Aurēlia servōs facere iubēbit?

Quam ob causam…? *For what reason…?* Answer: **Quod…**

BUILDING THE MEANING
Relative Clauses I

A very common type of subordinate clause is the *relative clause*. Relative clauses are descriptive clauses that modify nouns. You have seen clauses of this sort since the very first chapter of this course:

> Cornēlia est puella Rōmāna **<u>quae</u> in Italiā habitat.** (1:1–2)
> *Cornelia is a Roman girl <u>who lives in Italy</u>.*

The relative clause (underlined) gives information about the noun phrase **puella Rōmāna,** describing this Roman girl as one who lives in Italy. Relative clauses are introduced by *relative pronouns* (e.g., **quae,** *who*), which relate or connect the statement made in the subordinate clause to a noun or noun phrase (e.g., **puella Rōmāna,** *a Roman girl*) in the main clause. This noun or noun phrase in the main clause is called the *antecedent* because it goes (Latin **cēdere**) before (Latin **ante-**) the relative clause.

FORMS
Relative Pronouns

Here are all the forms of the relative pronoun:

	Singular			
	Masc.	**Fem.**	**Neut.**	**Meanings**
Nom.	quī	quae	quod	*who, which, that*
Gen.	cuius	cuius	cuius	*whose, of whom, of which*
Dat.	cui	cui	cui	*to whom (which), for whom (which)*
Acc.	quem	quam	quod	*whom, which, that*
Abl.	quō	quā	quō	*(see note below)*

	Plural			
	Masc.	**Fem.**	**Neut.**	**Meanings**
Nom.	quī	quae	quae	*who, which, that*
Gen.	quōrum	quārum	quōrum	*whose, of whom, of which*
Dat.	quibus	quibus	quibus	*to whom (which), for whom (which)*
Acc.	quōs	quās	quae	*whom, which, that*
Abl.	quibus	quibus	quibus	*(see note below)*

Be sure to learn these forms thoroughly.

NOTE:
Translation of forms of the relative pronoun in the ablative case will depend on the function of the ablative case in the clause. For example, **quibuscum** means *with whom,* and **quō** could be ablative of means or instrument and mean *with which* or *by which*.

Exercise 28b

On the chart of relative pronouns locate the following forms that appeared in the story at the beginning of this chapter. Some of the forms appear more than once on the chart. Identify all the possibilities that each form could be. Then identify the gender, number, and case of the pronoun as used in the story:

1. quārum (line 1)
2. quae (line 2)
3. quibus (line 8)
4. cuius (line 10)

BUILDING THE MEANING
Relative Clauses II

The form of the relative pronoun that introduces a relative clause depends on two things:

1. the *gender* and *number* of its antecedent
2. the *case* required by the function of the relative pronoun in its own clause

The following passages from the story at the beginning of this chapter illustrate these points:

> ... duae ancillae, **quārum** altera speculum tenēbat.... (28:1–2)

The fact that **quārum** is feminine in gender and plural in number relates it to its antecedent, **duae ancillae** (feminine plural). The fact that **quārum** is genitive shows how it functions in its own clause, namely as a partitive genitive (see Chapter 25) with **altera,** thus *one of whom*.

> Phrygia, **quae** crīnēs neglegenter pectēbat.... (28:2–3)

Here the relative pronoun is feminine singular because of its antecedent **Phrygia,** and it is nominative because it serves as the subject of the verb of its own clause, **pectēbat.**

> ...amīcōs quōsdam, in **quibus** sunt senātōrēs praeclārī.... (28:8)

Here the relative pronoun is masculine plural because of its antecedent **amīcōs quōsdam,** and it is ablative because of its use with the preposition in its own clause.

> ...ad mercātōrem quendam **cuius** taberna nōn procul abest.... (28:10)

Here the relative pronoun is masculine singular because of its antecedent **mercātōrem quendam,** and it is genitive to indicate possession in its own clause (*whose* shop).

Exercise 28c

Here are sentences with relative clauses. Read aloud and translate.
Then explain the gender, number, and case of each relative pronoun:

1. Sextus est puer strēnuus **quī** saepe in agrīs et in hortō currit.
2. Dāvus omnēs servōs in āream **quae** est prope vīllam venīre iubet.
3. Aurēlia et Cornēlia spectābant rūsticōs **quī** in agrīs labōrābant.
4. Marcus pede vexābat Cornēliam **quae** dormīre volēbat.
5. "Lectīcāriī, **quōs** vōbīs condūxī, vōs domum ferent," inquit Titus.
6. "Hic est arcus," inquit Titus, "**quem**—"
7. Sextus iam cōgitābat dē omnibus rēbus **quās** Titus heri nārrāverat.
8. Bovēs lapidēs quadrātōs in plaustrō trahēbant ad novum aedificium **quod** Caesar cōnficit.
9. Sunt multī hominēs scelestī **quī** bona cīvium arripiunt.

Exercise 28d

In the following sentences first decide the gender, number, and case required
to make a Latin pronoun correspond to the English pronoun in italics. Then
locate the correct form of the Latin pronoun on the chart on page 4. Read
the sentence aloud with the Latin pronoun and translate:

1. Aurēliae crīnēs, *(which)* duae ancillae cūrābant, pulchrī erant.
2. Syra, *(whose)* manus tremēbat, speculum nōn bene tenēbat.
3. Ancillae, *(whose)* neglegentia Aurēliam vexāverat, ignāvae erant.
4. Mox in cubiculum iniit Cornēlia, *(whom)* Aurēlia vocāverat.
5. Servus, *(to whom)* Aurēlia pecūniam dederat, porcum ēmit.

pulcher, pulchra, pulchrum, *beautiful, pretty*

**The hairstyles of both men and women varied greatly over time. Men's beards went in and out
of fashion. Compare the cameo of Emperor Julian and his wife with the bronze busts of some
earlier Romans.**

Bronze heads, Louvre, Paris, France; sardonyx cameo, British Museum, London, England

HAIRSTYLES OF ROMAN GIRLS AND WOMEN

Roman girls and women let their hair grow long. Girls tied it in a bun at the back of the head or wound and knotted it in tresses on the top of the head. Straight hairpins of ivory, silver, or gold were used to hold the hair in place. Woollen fillets (**vittae**) were woven into the tresses as a sign of chastity. Mirrors of polished metal, not glass, were used, and slaves were specially trained to be expert hairdressers (**ōrnātrīcēs**). During some periods and especially at the imperial court and on special occasions some women went to great lengths to arrange their hair in different levels on the top of the head and to supplement their own hair with false hair. Bleaches and dyes were used, as well as

Relief sculpture of a hairdresser, circa A.D. 50
Bas relief, Landesmuseum, Hesse, Germany

A nineteenth century artist's rendition of one hairdo a Roman girl could have worn

Oil on canvas, "A Roman Boat Race" by Sir Edward John Poynter, The Maas Gallery, London, England

lotions to make the hair softer. Styles varied greatly. The poet Ovid recommended that each woman should choose the style that best suited her, and he describes some of them as follows:

> An oval face prefers a parting upon the head left unadorned. Round faces want a small knot left on top of the head, so that the ears show. Let one girl's locks hang down on either shoulder. Let another braid her hair. It is becoming to this one to let her waving locks lie loose; let that one have her tight-drawn tresses closely confined; this one is pleased with an adornment of tortoise-shell; let that one bear folds that resemble waves. I cannot enumerate all the fashions that there are; each day adds more adornments.

—Ovid, *Art of Love* III.137–152

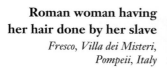

**Roman woman having
her hair done by her slave**
*Fresco, Villa dei Misteri,
Pompeii, Italy*

The poet Martial describes how a petulant woman named Lalage punished the slave who was dressing her hair because of one curl that went astray:

> A single curl of the whole concoction of hair had strayed, badly fixed in place with an insecure pin. This crime, which she noticed, Lalage avenged with her mirror and Plecusa fell wounded because of these cruel locks of hair. Stop, now, Lalage, to arrange your dire locks and let no maid touch your ill-tempered head.
>
> —Martial, *Epigrams* II.66.1–4

GOING TO THE MARKET

Cornēlia summā celeritāte sē parāvit. Brevī tempore māter et fīlia ā servīs per urbem ferēbantur. In viīs erat ingēns multitūdō hominum. Concursābant enim servī, mīlitēs, virī, puerī, mulierēs. Onera ingentia ā servīs portābantur, nam interdiū nihil intrā urbem vehiculō portātur.

Omnia quae videt Cornēlia eam dēlectant. Nunc cōnspicit poētam versūs recitantem, 5 nunc mendīcōs pecūniam petentēs, nunc lectīcam ēlegantissimam quae ab octō servīs portātur. In eā recumbit homō obēsus quī librum legit.

Subitō Cornēlia duōs servōs per viam festīnantēs cōnspicit, quōrum alter porcum parvulum portat. Eō ipsō tempore ē manibus effugit porcus. "Cavēte!" exclāmant adstantēs, sed frūstrā. Homō quīdam, quī per viam celeriter currit, porcum vītāre nōn 10 potest. Ad terram cadit. Paulisper in lutō iacet gemēns. Deinde īrā commōtus servum petit ā quō porcus aufūgit. Est rixa.

Fīnem rixae nōn vīdit Cornēlia quod servī iam sellās in aliam viam tulerant. Tandem advēnērunt ad eam tabernam quam petēbant. Dē sellīs dēscendērunt. Tum Aurēlia, "Vīdistīne," inquit, "illam lectīcam in quā recumbēbat homō obēsus? Ūnus ē lībertīs 15 Caesaris ipsīus—Sed quid accidit? Fūmum videō et flammās."

1	**summā celeritāte**, *with the greatest speed, as fast as possible*	6	**mendīcus, -ī**, m., *beggar*
	ā servīs ferēbantur, *were being carried by slaves*		**ēlegantissimus, -a, -um**, *most elegant*
2	**concursō, -āre, -āvī -ātus**, *to run to and fro, run about*	10	**adstantēs, adstantium**, m. pl., *bystanders*
4	**portātur**, *is (being) carried*	12	**rixa, -ae**, f., *quarrel*
5	**dēlectō, -āre, -āvī, -ātus**, *to delight, amuse*	13	**fīnis, fīnis**, gen. pl., **fīnium**, m., *end*
		15	**lībertus, -ī**, m., *freedman*
		16	**ipsīus**, gen. sing. of **ipse, ipsa, ipsum**
			fūmus, -ī, m., *smoke*

7 **recumbō, recumbere, recubuī**, *to recline, lie down*
12 **aufugiō, aufugere, aufūgī**, *to run away, escape*

Exercise 29a
Respondē Latīnē:

1. Quōmodo Cornēlia sē parāvit?
2. Quid in viīs vidēbant?
3. Cūr onera ā servīs portābantur?
4. Quid faciēbat poēta?
5. Quī festīnābant per viam?

6. Quid portābat alter servōrum?
7. Quis ad terram cadit?
8. Cūr Cornēlia fīnem rixae nōn vīdit?
9. Quō advēnērunt Aurēlia et Cornēlia?
10. Quid ibi vīdit Aurēlia?

The Center of Ancient Rome

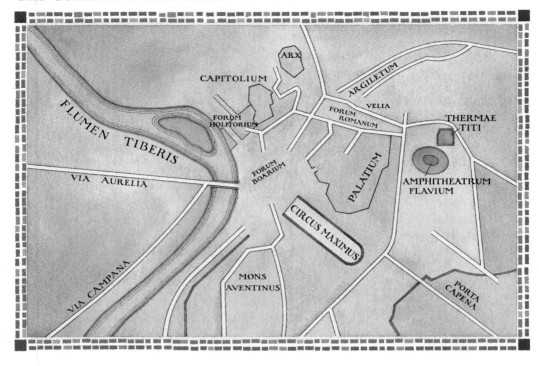

▬▬▬▬▬

Malum est cōnsilium quod mūtārī nōn potest. *It's a bad plan that can't be changed.* (Publilius Syrus 403)

Hominēs id quod volunt crēdunt. *Men believe what they want to.* (Julius Caesar)

Quī vult dare parva nōn dēbet magna rogāre. *He who wishes to give little shouldn't ask for much.*

▬▬▬▬▬

Exercise 29b

In the story on page 11, locate eight relative pronouns and explain why the particular gender, number, and case are used. Note that **quīdam, quod,** and **quid** in this passage are not relative pronouns (see below).

Exercise 29c

Read aloud and translate:

1. Servī, quī cistās portābant, hūc illūc concursābant. Cistae, quās servī portābant, plēnae erant vestium.
2. Ancillae, quae Aurēliae crīnēs cūrābant, dominam timēbant. Aurēlia, quae multīs rēbus sollicita erat, ancillās neglegentēs abīre iussit.
3. Servus, ā quō onus portābātur, gemēbat. Onus enim, quod portābat, ingēns erat.

4. Homō obēsus, cuius lectīca erat ēlegantissima, librum legēbat.
5. Porcī, quōs servī portābant, grunniēbant. Adstantēs, quī eōs audiēbant, rīdēbant.

vestis, vestis, gen. pl., **vestium,** f., *clothing, garment*

Exercise 29d
Give the Latin for the relative pronoun (in parentheses) and then read the sentence aloud and translate it:

1. Homō, (*who*) per viam currēbat, ad terram cecidit.
2. Ancilla, (*who*) crīnēs neglegenter pectēbat, Aurēliam vexābat.
3. Homō obēsus, (*whom*) servī portābant, librum legēbat.
4. Aurēlia, (*whom*) ancillae vexābant, speculum ēripuit.
5. Duo servī, (*whom*) Cornēlia cōnspexit, per viam festīnābant.
6. Brevī tempore māter et fīlia in sellās, (*which*) servī tulerant, ascendērunt.
7. Puella, (*to whom*) librum dedī, erat Cornēlia.
8. Servus, (*whose*) dominus erat īrātus, statim aufūgit.

ēripiō, ēripere, ēripuī, ēreptus, *to snatch (from)*

BUILDING THE MEANING

Many important Latin words begin with the letters *qu-*. Here are some examples:

1. relative pronouns, which you have studied extensively in Chapters 28 and 29:

> Omnia **quae** videt Cornēlia eam dēlectant. (29:5)
> *All the things **that** Cornēlia sees please her.*

2. the indefinite adjective **quīdam,** *a certain;* pl., *some.*

> Homō **quīdam,**... (29:10)
> *A certain man,...*

3. the interrogative pronouns **Quis...?** *Who?* **Quid...?** *What...?*

> Sed **quid** accidit? (29:16)
> *But **what** is happening?*

4. the causal conjunction **quod,** *because.**

> ...**quod** servī iam sellās in aliam viam tulerant. (29:13)
> *...**because** the slaves had carried the sedan chairs into another street.*

*Note that **quod** may also be a relative pronoun. When it is, it is preceded by a neuter singular antecedent, e.g., **cisium, quod appropinquābat,**...

5. the exclamatory adverb **Quam…!** *How…!*

> **"Quam** neglegentēs estis!" (28:4)
> *"How careless you are!"*

You have seen all of these words a number of times in the readings. There is another important **qu-** word that you will meet, the *interrogative adjective:*

> **Quī** vir est ille?
> *What man is that?*

> **Quae** fēmina est illa?
> *What woman is that?*

> **Quem** virum vīdistī?
> *What man did you see?*

> **Cui** fēminae illud dedistī?
> *To which woman did you give that?*

The interrogative adjective modifies a noun and introduces a question. It has exactly the same forms as the relative pronoun.

FORMS
Indefinite Adjectives

The forms of the indefinite adjective **quīdam,** *a certain;* pl., *some,* are the same as those of the relative pronoun plus the letters *-dam,* except for the letters in boldface:

Number Case	Masc.	Fem.	Neut.
Singular			
Nominative	quīdam	quaedam	quoddam
Genitive	cuiusdam	cuiusdam	cuiusdam
Dative	cuidam	cuidam	cuidam
Accusative	que**n**dam	qua**n**dam	quoddam
Ablative	quōdam	quādam	quōdam
Plural			
Nominative	quīdam	quaedam	quaedam
Genitive	quō**run**dam	quā**run**dam	quō**run**dam
Dative	quibusdam	quibusdam	quibusdam
Accusative	quōsdam	quāsdam	quaedam
Ablative	quibusdam	quibusdam	quibusdam

Interrogative Pronouns

In the singular the interrogative pronoun has identical forms in the masculine and feminine; in the plural it is the same as the relative pronoun (see page 4). We give only the singular forms here:

	Singular		
	Masc.	Fem.	Neut.
Nominative	quis	quis	quid
Genitive	cuius	cuius	cuius
Dative	cui	cui	cui
Accusative	quem	quem	quid
Ablative	quō	quō	quō

Learn the forms in the charts above thoroughly.

Exercise 29e

Read aloud and translate. Identify relative pronouns, **quod** causal, **quam** exclamatory, indefinite adjectives, interrogative adjectives, and interrogative pronouns:

1. Aurīgae, quōrum equī sunt celerrimī, nōn semper vincent.
2. Cui mercātōrī Aurēlia pecūniam dabit?
3. Mercātōrī, quī glīrēs vēndit, Aurēlia pecūniam dabit.
4. Quam ingēns est Circus! Quis tantum aedificium umquam vīdit?
5. Hī amīcī, quibuscum ad amphitheātrum crās ībimus, fēriātī erunt.
6. Ancillae quaedam crīnēs Aurēliae cūrābant.
7. Aurēlia īrāta erat quod ancillae neglegenter crīnēs cūrābant.
8. Cīvēs, quōrum clāmōrēs audīvimus, aurīgās spectābant.
9. Quam obēsus est homō quī in lectīcā librum legit!
10. Hanc urbem, in quā habitāmus, valdē amāmus.

    celerrimus, -a, -um, *fastest, very fast*

Exercise 29f

Using stories 28 and 29 as guides, give the Latin for:

1. The bedroom, in which the slave-women were taking care of the hair of their mistress, was not large.
2. Syra, whose hand was trembling, was annoying her mistress.
3. No one was able to catch the pig that escaped from the hands of the slave.
4. The fat man, whose litter was most elegant, was reading a book.
5. Aurelia, to whom the merchant sold dormice, was carrying much money.

TOWN HOUSE AND APARTMENT

The town house (**domus**) of a wealthy Roman was self-contained and usually built on one level with few, if any, windows on its outside walls. It faced inwards and most of its light came from the opening in the roof of the main hall (**ātrium**) and from the open-colonnaded garden (**peristȳlium**). Grouped around these open areas were the purpose-built rooms of the house: bedrooms (**cubicula**), study (**tablīnum**), kitchen area (**culīna**), and dining room (**trīclīnium**). Decoration and furniture in the **domus** were as splendid as its owner's pocket allowed and in some cases a second story was added. The domus-style house can be identified in towns throughout the Roman world.

A wealthy Roman would normally possess, in addition to his town house (**domus**), at least one country house (**vīlla rūstica** or **vīlla urbāna**). Cicero had several, where he could get away from the city din and summer heat, but even a **domus** provided considerable privacy and seclusion.

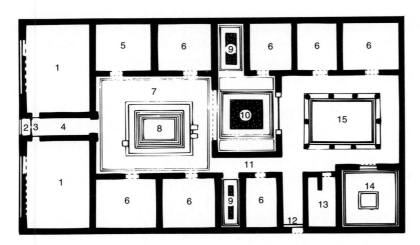

Plan of a domus

1. **tabernae** (shops)
2. **vestibulum** (entrance outside **iānua**)
3. **iānua** (double door)
4. **faucēs** (entrance passage)
5. **cella** (room for doorkeeper)
6. **cubicula** (bedrooms)
7. **ātrium** (hall)
8. **compluvium/impluvium** (roof opening and tank)
9. **āla** (alcove)
10. **tablīnum** (study)
11. **andrōn** (passage)
12. **postīcum** (servants' entrance)
13. **culīna** (kitchen)
14. **trīclīnium** (dining room)
15. **peristȳlium** (garden)

Rooms at the front or the side of a town house (**domus**) often housed shops, in which the owner of the house could conduct his business or which could be rented out. There were bakeries, butcher shops, barber shops, shoe shops, goldsmith shops, textile shops, and fast-food shops where you could get hot and cold food and drink of various sorts. There were also shops for many other kinds of activities such as washing clothes and tanning leather and for many other kinds of merchandise such as olive oil, wine, and knives. Merchants did not restrict themselves to their shops but tended to take over the street in front as well. Martial complained that there were only footpaths left in the middle of the street, that barbers endangered pedestrians with their razors as they shaved their clients, and that the grimy owners of cook-shops took over the whole street. He was happy when the emperor Domitian handed down a ruling requiring shop keepers to limit their activities to their shops. Now, Martial felt, the old Rome had been restored, which previously had become one **magna taberna,** one *huge shop* or shopping mall!

Where building space was at a premium, as in a city like Rome or a commercial town like Ostia, houses tended to grow upwards to accommodate the majority of the inhabitants. These apartment-type houses were called **īnsulae.** Sometimes they stood four or five stories high, and restrictions were introduced as early as the time of the Emperor Augustus to prevent their height exceeding 70 feet or approximately 20 meters.

Brick and concrete were commonly used in their construction, and they often had large windows and doorways enhancing their external appearance. The same rooms in the building tended to serve various functions, and there was a uniformity about the plan of each apartment in the building. Wooden shutters or canvas screens kept out the elements. Running water was rarely available above ground level, so heating and cooking often proved a hazard. Ground floor accommodation in the **īnsulae** was usually the most desirable.

While **īnsulae** could be very attractive and were often built around large central courts, some were less presentable. Often single rooms were let and conditions were cramped. Excessive reliance on wood and plaster construction led to the risk of fire or collapse, and after the fire of A.D. 64 the Emperor Nero introduced tighter control of building materials in the **īnsulae.**

On the ground floor of the **īnsula** in which Seneca, a Roman philosopher and writer, had his apartment there was a small public bath (**balneum**), and he describes some of the noises that disturbed him: the great splash made by the swimmer who likes to dive in as noisily as he can; the slapping sounds as people are being rubbed down; the noises of the man who likes to hear his own voice in the bath; the shouts of the pastrycook and the sausage-maker trying to sell their wares. Martial tells us of a schoolmaster who began shouting at his pupils in the early morning and kept his neighbors from sleeping.

ADDITIONAL READING:
The Romans Speak for Themselves: Book II: "Buildings for Different Ranks of Society," pages 1–11.

FORMS
Prefixes: Compound Verbs II

Some prefixes may undergo a change (often for ease of pronunciation) when they are added to verbs that begin with certain consonants:

1. Prefixes **ad-, con-, dis-, ex-, in-,** and **sub-** may change the final consonant of the prefix to the consonant that follows it. This process is called *assimilation*:

afferō (ad- + ferō)	**differō** (dis- + ferō)
attulī (ad- + tulī)	**effugiō** (ex- + fugiō)
allātus (ad- + lātus)	**immittō** (in- + mittō)
commoveō (con- + moveō)	**succurrō** (sub- + currō)

Note that **in-** and **con-** become **im-** and **com-** before *b* or *p*:

importō (in- + portō)	**compōnō** (con- + pōnō)

2. Prefix **ab-** becomes **au-** in front of verbs beginning with *f*:

aufugiō (ab- + fugiō)	**auferō** (ab- + ferō)

Exercise 29g
Read aloud and translate:

1. Geta effugere nōn potest.
2. Caupō Cornēliam et mātrem ad cubiculum addūxit.
3. Servī cistās in raedam impōnunt.
4. Servī onera ingentia ad vīllam apportābant.
5. Cibum ē vīllā aufert.
6. Aurēlia in cubiculum Marcī subitō irrumpit.
7. Cornēlia librum ē manibus Sextī celeriter abstulit et in hortum aufūgit.
8. Duo canēs ad Cornēliōs subitō accurrunt.
9. Viātōrēs multās fābulās dē caupōnibus scelestīs ad omnēs partēs Italiae differunt.
10. "Nōnne ēsurītis?" inquit caupō. "Mēnsās statim appōnam."

mēnsa, -ae, f., *table*   **rumpō, rumpere, rūpī, ruptus,** *to burst*

3. Sometimes the verb undergoes a change when a prefix is added:

facere, *to do*   **perficere,** *to do thoroughly, accomplish*
tenēre, *to hold*   **continēre,** *to hold together, contain*
rapere, *to snatch*   **ēripere,** *to snatch from, rescue*
capere, *to take*   **accipere,** *to take to oneself, receive*
iacere, *to throw*   **conicere,** *to throw* (emphatic)
claudere, *to shut*   **inclūdere,** *to shut in*

4. Note that some verbs change conjugation when a prefix is added:

sedeō, sedēre, *to sit*   **cōnsīdō, cōnsīdere,** *to sit down*
dō, dare, *to give*   **reddō, reddere,** *to give back*

Exercise 29h

Read aloud and translate. Then tell what the uncompounded verb would be:

1. Servī raedam reficiēbant.
2. Sextus ad terram dēcidit.
3. Subitō Sextus librum arripuit et retinuit.
4. Domina ancillās ā cubiculō īrāta exclūdit.
5. Herculēs multōs labōrēs perfēcit.
6. Servī cistam repetent quod Cornēlia aliam tunicam addere vult.
7. Cornēlius pecūniam caupōnī trādit.
8. Flāvia epistulam ā Cornēliā accipiet.
9. Illī praedōnēs pecūniam surripuērunt.
10. Caupō Cornēliōs cum rīsū excēpit.

FIRE!

Cōnspexerat Aurēlia ingentem īnsulam ē quā ēmittēbātur magna vīs fūmī ac flammārum. Cornēlia iam ad id aedificium summā celeritāte currēbat, cum Aurēlia eī clāmāvit, "Cavē, Cornēlia! Eī incendiō appropinquāre est perīculōsum."

Mox fūmus omnia obscūrābat. Cornēlia aedificium ipsum vix vidēre poterat. Multī hominēs hūc illūc concursābant. Ab incolīs omnia simul aguntur; īnfantēs ex aedificiō ā 5 mātribus efferuntur; īnfirmī ē iānuīs trahuntur; bona ē fenestrīs ēiciuntur; in viā pōnuntur cistae, lectī, ōrnāmenta.

Cornēlia spectāculum tam miserābile numquam anteā vīderat. Lacrimābant mulierēs et līberōs parvōs tenēbant; lacrimābant līberī quī parentēs suōs quaerēbant; clāmābant parentēs quī līberōs suōs petēbant. 10

Via erat plēna eōrum quī ad spectāculum vēnerant. Aliī ex adstantibus aquam portābant; aliī in īnsulam intrābant et auxilium incolīs miserīs ferēbant. Multī tamen nihil faciēbant. "Nōs certē nihil facere possumus," inquiunt. "In hāc urbe solent esse incendia quae exstinguere nōn possumus. Neque hoc aedificium neque hōs incolās servāre possumus. Ecce! In tertiō tabulātō huius īnsulae est māter cum duōbus līberīs. Hī 15 miserī flammīs paene opprimuntur. Sī incolae sē servāre nōn possunt, quid nōs facere possumus?"

(continued)

1 **īnsula, -ae,** f., *island, apartment building*	**fenestra, -ae,** f., *window*
vīs, acc., **vim,** abl., **vī,** f., *force, amount*	7 **ōrnāmenta, -ōrum,** n. pl., *furnishings*
ac, conj., *and*	8 **tam,** adv., *so*
3 **incendium, -ī,** n., *fire*	9 **parvus, -a, -um,** *small*
5 **incola, -ae,** m./f., *inhabitant, tenant*	15 **tabulātum, -ī,** n., *story, floor*
omnia...aguntur, *everything is being done*	16 **paene,** adv., *almost*
6 **īnfirmus, -a, -um,** *weak, shaky, frail*	**opprimuntur,** (they) *are being overwhelmed*

6 **ēiciō, ēicere, ēiēcī, ēiectus,** *to throw out*
9 **quaerō, quaerere, quaesīvī, quaesītus,** *to seek, look for, ask (for)*
16 **opprimō, opprimere, oppressī, oppressus,** *to overwhelm*

Exercise 30a
Respondē Latīnē:

1. Quae ex īnsulā ēmittēbantur?
2. Cui appropinquāre est perīculōsum?
3. Quid agunt incolae?
4. Quid faciēbant līberī?
5. Quid faciēbant parentēs?
6. Quī incolās adiūvērunt?

Subitō exclāmāvit ūnus ex adstantibus, "Cavēte, omnēs! Nisi statim aufugiētis, vōs omnēs opprimēminī aut lapidibus aut flammīs."

Tum Cornēlia, "Ēheu, māter!" inquit. "Ego valdē commoveor cum hōs tam miserōs 20 līberōs videō. Quis eīs auxilium feret? Quōmodo effugient? Quid eīs accidet?"

Cui respondit Aurēlia, "Id nesciō. Sine dubiō iam mortuī sunt. Sed cūr tū ita commovēris? Nōs nihil hīc facere possumus. Nisi statim fugiēmus, nōs ipsae vix servābimur. Satis tamen hodiē vīdistī. Age! Ad Forum ībimus ac glīrēs emēmus."

Illō ipsō tempore parietēs īnsulae magnō fragōre cecidērunt. Nihil manēbat nisi 25 lapidēs ac fūmus.

19	**opprimēminī,** *you will be crushed, overwhelmed*	23	**commovēris,** *you are upset*
20	**commoveor,** *I am upset*	24	**servābimur,** *we will be saved*
22	**dubium, -ī,** n., *doubt*		**pariēs, parietis,** m., *wall (of a house or room)*

20 **commoveō, commovēre, commōvī, commōtus,** *to move, upset*

Respondē Latīnē:

1. Cūr Cornēlia "Ēheu, māter!" inquit?
2. Quid Aurēlia facere vult?
3. Quōmodo parietēs īnsulae cecidērunt?

Flamma fūmō est proxima. *Flame follows smoke.* (Plautus, *Curculio* I.i.53)
Ubi fūmus, ibi ignis. *Where there's smoke, there's fire.*
Adversus incendia excubiās nocturnās vigilēsque commentus est. *Against the dangers of fires, Augustus conceived of the idea of night guards and watchmen.* (Suetonius, *Life of Augustus* 30)

The danger of fire had prompted Rome's first emperor, Augustus, in A.D. 6 to set up a fire brigade, armed with buckets, axes, and pumps. The effectiveness of this brigade was limited, however, and fire remained a constant threat in Rome. The great fire in A.D. 64 during the reign of Nero devastated half of the city, and a fire raged in the city for three days in A.D. 80, the time of our story, during the reign of Titus.

Life in the city could be dangerous:

> We live in a city largely propped up by slender poles; for this is how the inspector stops the houses falling down and, plastering over old cracks, he bids us sleep secure with disaster hanging over us. We should live where there are no fires, no alarms in the night. By the time the smoke has reached you who are still sleeping on the third floor, Ucalegon on the ground floor is already calling for water and removing his bits and pieces of furniture. For if there is an alarm on the ground floor, the last to burn will be the one protected from the rain only by the tiles where the gentle pigeons lay their eggs.

Juvenal, *Satires* III.193–202

BUILDING THE MEANING
The Vivid or Historic Present

In the story at the beginning of this chapter, the verbs in lines 5–7 switch to the present tense although they describe past events. The effect of this is to make the reader feel personally involved in Cornelia's experience.

This use of the present tense is called the *vivid* or *historic present*, and it adds vividness (as in this story) and, where the story requires it, speed and excitement. Written English normally uses a past tense to describe such actions.

Notice that in the next paragraph, where the narrative resumes, the writer returns to the past tense.

Look back in story 29 and notice how there, too, in the second and third paragraphs the writer switches to the vivid or historic present.

FORMS
Verbs: Active and Passive Voice

Compare the following sentences:

Incolae omnia **agunt.**
*The tenants **are doing** everything.*

Ab incolīs omnia **aguntur.**
*Everything **is being done** by the tenants.*

Mātrēs īnfantēs **efferunt.**
*The mothers **carry out** the babies.*

Īnfantēs ā mātribus **efferuntur.**
*The babies **are carried out** by the mothers.*

Servī onera **portābant.**
*Slaves **were carrying** the loads.*

Onera ā servīs **portābantur.**
*The loads **were being carried** by slaves.*

Flammae vōs **oppriment.**
*The flames **will overwhelm** you.*

Vōs flammīs **opprimēminī.**
*You **will be overwhelmed** by the flames.*

The verbs in the left-hand column are in the *active voice*; in the right-hand column the verbs are in the *passive voice*.

In the active voice the subject performs the action of the verb. In the passive voice the subject receives the action of the verb.

	Singular		Plural
1	míttor, *I am (being) sent*	1	míttimur, *we are (being) sent*
2	mítteris, *you are (being) sent*	2	mittíminī, *you are (being) sent*
3	míttitur, *he, she, it is (being) sent*	3	mittúntur, *they are (being) sent*

The following table gives the forms and meanings of the present passive of **mittere:**
The personal endings above (in bold italics) should be learned thoroughly; they are used on all the passive forms that follow.

The following tables give the forms of the present, imperfect, and future passive of each conjugation. Be sure to learn these forms thoroughly.

Present Passive

		1st Conjugation	2nd Conjugation	3rd Conjugation		4th Conjugation
Singular	1	pórto*r*	móveo*r*	mítto*r*	iácio*r*	aúdio*r*
	2	portá*ris*	mové*ris*	mítte*ris*	iáce*ris*	audí*ris*
	3	portá*tur*	mové*tur*	mítti*tur*	iáci*tur*	audí*tur*
Plural	1	portá*mur*	mové*mur*	mítti*mur*	iáci*mur*	audí*mur*
	2	portá*minī*	mové*minī*	mittí*minī*	iací*minī*	audí*minī*
	3	portá*ntur*	mové*ntur*	mittú*ntur*	iaciú*ntur*	audiú*ntur*

Imperfect Passive

		1st Conjugation	2nd Conjugation	3rd Conjugation		4th Conjugation
Singular	1	portā*bar*	movē*bar*	mittē*bar*	iaciē*bar*	audiē*bar*
	2	portā*bāris*	movē*bāris*	mittē*bāris*	iaciē*bāris*	audiē*bāris*
	3	portā*bātur*	movē*bātur*	mittē*bātur*	iaciē*bātur*	audiē*bātur*
Plural	1	portā*bāmur*	movē*bāmur*	mittē*bāmur*	iaciē*bāmur*	audiē*bāmur*
	2	portā*bāminī*	movē*bāminī*	mittē*bāminī*	iaciē*bāminī*	audiē*bāminī*
	3	portā*bántur*	movē*bántur*	mittē*bántur*	iaciē*bántur*	audiē*bántur*

Future Passive

		1st Conjugation	2nd Conjugation	3rd Conjugation		4th Conjugation
Singular	1	portā*bor*	movē*bor*	mítt*ar*	iáci*ar*	aúdi*ar*
	2	portā*beris*	movē*beris*	mitt*éris*	iaci*éris*	audi*éris*
	3	portā*bitur*	movē*bitur*	mitt*étur*	iaci*étur*	audi*étur*
Plural	1	portā*bimur*	movē*bimur*	mitt*émur*	iaci*émur*	audi*émur*
	2	portā*bíminī*	movē*bíminī*	mitt*éminī*	iaci*éminī*	audi*éminī*
	3	portā*búntur*	movē*búntur*	mitt*éntur*	iaci*éntur*	audi*éntur*

N.B.: The irregular verbs **esse, posse, velle,** and **nōlle** do not have passive forms. The passive forms of **ferre** are as follows:

		Present	Imperfect	Future
Singular	1	féro*r*	ferē*bar*	fér*ar*
	2	fér*ris*	ferē*bāris*	fer*éris*
	3	fér*tur*	ferē*bātur*	fer*étur*
Plural	1	féri*mur*	ferē*bāmur*	fer*émur*
	2	ferí*minī*	ferē*bāminī*	fer*éminī*
	3	ferú*ntur*	ferē*bántur*	fer*éntur*

Compare the passive forms of **ferre** to the passive forms of **mittere**.

Exercise 30b
Write out in sequence and translate the seven sentences in story 30 that contain passive verbs.

Exercise 30c
Read aloud and translate:

1. Adstantēs auxilium ferēbant; auxilium ab adstantibus ferēbātur.
2. Parentēs nōs ex hōc aedificiō efferunt; nōs ā parentibus ex hōc aedificiō efferimur.
3. Amīcī incolās servābunt; incolae ab amīcīs servābuntur.
4. Flammae tē opprimunt; tū flammīs opprimeris.
5. Lapidēs tē oppriment; tū lapidibus opprimēris.
6. Incolae ōrnāmenta ē fenestrīs ēiciēbant; ōrnāmenta ē fenestrīs ab incolīs ēiciēbantur.
7. Hī līberī miserī mē commovent; ego ab hīs miserīs līberīs commoveor.
8. Ā parentibus servāminī; ab adstantibus servābāminī; ā mātribus servābiminī.
9. Numquam audiar; vix audior; tandem audiēbar.
10. Illō spectāculō commovēbāris; tālibus spectāculīs semper commovēris; crās memoriā commovēberis.
11. Adstantēs removēbuntur; iānuae aperientur; līberī excitantur; nihil agēbātur; fūmus ēmittitur; aqua portābitur.

Exercise 30d
Change each verb from active to passive voice, keeping the same tense, person, and number; translate both verbs:

1. commoveō
2. ēicit
3. quaerēbam
4. fers
5. dūcis
6. trahēs
7. spectāmus
8. custōdiēbant
9. servābis

Exercise 30e
Using story 30 and the charts of passive verb forms as guides, give the Latin for:

1. Everything was being done by the inhabitants at the same time.
2. Their goods were being thrown out of the windows.
3. Water was being brought to the apartment house.
4. The miserable children will be overwhelmed by the flames.
5. Cornelia is very moved when she sees the miserable children.

Trahimur omnēs studiō laudis. *We are all attracted by the desire for praise.* (Cicero, *Pro Archia poeta* XI.26)

ADDITIONAL READING:
The Romans Speak for Themselves: Book II: "The Vigiles," pages 13–21.

DEADLY STRUGGLES WITHIN THE ROMAN REPUBLIC

When Tiberius Sempronius Gracchus, a tribune of the people, was clubbed to death by a mob of rioters in 133 B.C., Rome witnessed the first of a long series of violent events that marked the conflict between the old guard who ruled the Roman Senate and ambitious individuals who sought to advance their positions in the senatorial aristocracy by courting popular favor through reforms that benefitted different groups within the **populus Rōmānus.**

During the second century B.C., the Roman upper class acquired wealth that many invested in large-scale farming. As their profits grew, they added smaller farms to their holdings. Slaves replaced peasants as the workforce on these large estates. The peasants were driven into the cities where, faced with homelessness and hopeless poverty, they grew desperate and dangerous. Popular reformers, **populārēs,** gathered political strength, especially by seeking to provide displaced farmers and poor urban citizens with land and programs designed to help them. The established leaders, the **optimātēs,** who controlled the Senate, feared and opposed these rival aristocrats, who were trying to gain power at their expense through institutions outside of the Senate. The struggles between **populārēs** and **optimātēs** were marked by much blood and violence. The terms **populārēs** and **optimātēs** did not refer to political parties. They were labels like "leftist" or "right-winger," which were applied to individual aristocrats who tried to gain or retain power in either nontraditional or traditional ways.

THE GRACCHI

The Gracchi brothers became two famous **populārēs**. They were trying to reverse the decline of their family's prestige in the Senate after their father's death. Tiberius Gracchus, as tribune, disregarded the custom of presenting pending legislation to the Senate for review and obtained passage in the popular assembly of a bill distributing portions of public lands to landless peasants. His opponents in the Senate tried to block his plan by refusing to allocate money to put it in operation.

At this same time King Attalus III of Pergamum, a kingdom in Asia Minor, died and in his will bequeathed his kingdom to Rome. At Tiberius' instigation, the popular assembly passed another law that ignored the Senate's traditional control of financial matters and provided that the king's wealth be used to finance the distribution of land to the landless. Then, Tiberius boldly stood for re-election for an unprecedented second consecutive term as tribune so that he could oversee the distribution of lands. To rid themselves of this popular tribune who was undermining their wealth and power in the Senate, his opponents organized a mob that murdered him and 300 of his followers on the Capitoline Hill.

Ten years later Gaius Sempronius Gracchus, Tiberius' younger brother and an eloquent orator, was elected tribune in 123 B.C. Backed by strong popular favor, he expanded his brother's program of land allotments and instituted a program to supply grain at subsidized prices to the poor citizens in Rome. He also engineered a change in the courts that weakened the grip that those who controlled the Senate maintained on the Roman court system: juries were drawn from the class of wealthy non-senators, the equestrian order (**equitēs**), rather than from the Senate. Next, Gaius Gracchus proposed the radical concept of extending Roman citizenship to other Italian cities. Those new citizens would then have become powerful supporters of Gaius in Roman politics. Violent street clashes between supporters of Gaius and mobs incited by his opponents gave his enemies within the Senate an opportunity to declare martial law to keep the peace. One of the consuls surrounded him with a contingent of archers, and he committed suicide with the help of his slave.

GAIUS MARIUS

Gaius Marius, elected consul in 107 B.C., was the next important leader to follow a **populāris** path. A rich equestrian from Arpinum, Marius was a "new man" (**novus homō**), one of the very few Romans who succeeded in senatorial politics without the usual qualification of birth into one of the families of senatorial nobility. His base of power was the military and discontented elements in the populace. He had recruited his legions from the citizenry at large by promising his soldiers pensions of land allotments and a share in the

Marius triumphs over the Cimbri
Oil on canvas by Saverio Altamura, Museo e Gallerie Nazionali di Capodimonte, Naples, Italy

Marius amid the ruins of Carthage

*Oil on canvas by John Vanderlyn,
Albany Institute of History and Art,
Albany, New York*

spoils of war. Leading this new kind of army into Africa, Marius was victorious by 105 B.C. over Rome's enemy in North Africa, King Jugurtha.

Next, Marius and his volunteer professional army beat back the Cimbri and Teutones, Germanic tribes threatening Italy's northern borders. But when Marius returned victorious to Rome, many in both the Senate and the popular assembly balked at providing his soldiers the choice lands in Gaul and the western provinces that they had been promised. Marius' soldiers resorted to armed intimidation to get their land grants.

Over the next several years, violent unrest rocked all of Italy, and in Rome bloody power struggles continued between various aristocrats. In 87 B.C. Marius and his **populārēs** seized Rome and conducted a reign of terror against their political enemies, murdering or exiling them and confiscating their property. That reign ended with Marius' death early in his seventh consulship in 86 B.C.

LUCIUS CORNELIUS SULLA

Lucius Cornelius Sulla had become Marius' greatest rival after serving as one of his officers in the war against Jugurtha. He obtained the support of leading **optimātēs** and was elected a consul for 88 B.C. In that year, King Mithridates of Pontus, a land on the south shore of the Black Sea, seized territories under Roman control in Greece and Asia Minor and massacred thousands of Italians and Romans living in those lands. Sulla's supporters in the Senate obtained for him command of the war to punish Mithridates. Marius, however, used popular tribunes to get the command away from Sulla. Sulla unexpectedly captured Rome with his army, drove Marius into exile, killed many of his supporters, and regained the command against Mithridates. While he was gone, Marius returned with an army of his veterans, seized Rome, and was elected to his seventh consulship, during which he died.

Sulla, on his victorious return to Rome, trounced the Marian forces still holding sway there and instituted his own government by terror, as he eliminated his political enemies by a process called proscription. Routinely Sulla posted in the Forum lists of names of his opponents and also of some wealthy equestrians, whose estates might increase the bonus he had promised his troops. Romans who had been thus proscribed were outlaws: a cash reward was paid the murderers who brought in the heads of the proscribed, and Sulla took possession of their property. The Senate granted Sulla the title "dictator for stabilizing the constitution." In exchange, Sulla's reforms did away with the tribunes' power to introduce legislation and thus returned power to his supporters, who had traditionally controlled the Senate. Once he had eliminated his opponents and set in place policies that he believed would assure that **optimātēs** who had supported him would retain firm control of the government, Sulla retired from his dictatorship. He died the next year, 78 B.C., at his villa in Campania.

GNAEUS POMPEIUS

Gnaeus Pompeius (Pompey the Great) had begun his rise to favor and power by lending Sulla the support of his private army of clients for the seizure of Rome in 83 B.C. and then by suppressing Marian forces in Sicily and Africa. For these actions, Sulla reluctantly honored Pompeius with the **cognōmen** "The Great" (**Magnus**). In 77 B.C. the Senate sent Pompey to Spain to put down a rebellion of Marians there. On his triumphant return from that expedition, Pompey's army arrived in Italy in time to cut off any escape for the last of the 70,000 rebellious slaves in the army of the Thracian gladiator Spartacus. For three years (73–71 B.C.), Spartacus had terrorized the wealthy Italian landowners as the leader of a spectacular slave uprising. Pompey's timely arrival ensured the Roman army's victory over Spartacus. Pompey claimed the honor of victory at the expense of Marcus Licinius Crassus, who had done most of the work in defeating Spartacus' uprising. Despite their mutual jealousy, they cooperated on their re-entry to Rome in order to be elected consuls in the face of optimate opposition to their ambitions in the Senate. The co-consuls agreed to support a law rescinding Sulla's removal of the tribune's right to initiate legislation.

In 67 B.C., a tribune proposed a law authorizing Pompey to command a fleet and to suppress the pirates who were at that time disrupting trade in the Mediterranean Sea, a feat he completed in three months. In the following year, a praetor, Marcus Tullius Cicero, the successful orator and an ardent supporter of Pompey, spoke strongly in favor of another tribune's proposal. That one granted Pompey extraordinary powers for tightening Roman control in Asia Minor and meeting the renewed threat of Mithridates. From 66 to 62 B.C. Pompey's military campaigns succeeded in defeating Mithridates once and for all and consolidated Roman domination of the East so that it provided a solid frontier for Rome's empire.

PSEUDOLUS

Quīnta hōra est. Marcus et Sextus per ātrium ambulant, cum subitō ē culīnā cachinnus maximus audītur. Statim in culīnam puerī intrant, ubi Syrum et aliōs servōs vident.

Sextus, "Cūr vōs omnēs rīdētis?" inquit. "Iocumne audīvistis?"

Cui Syrus, "Iocō optimō dēlectāmur, domine. Est in culīnā servus quīdam cui nōmen 5 est Pseudolus. Nōn servus sed mercātor esse vidētur. Heri māne in urbem ad laniī tabernam dēscendit, nam carnem emere volēbat. 'Quantī,' inquit Pseudolus, 'est illa perna?' Ubi pretium audītur, laniō respondet, 'Ego numquam dabō tantum pretium. Praedō quidem mihi vidēris, nōn lanius. Nēmō nisi scelestus tantum petit. Ad aliam tabernam ībō neque umquam—' 10

"'Procāx es, Pseudole,' interpellat lanius. 'Per iocum sine dubiō hoc dīcis. In hāc viā nēmō carnem meliōrem habet, ut bene scīs. Hoc pretium nōn est magnum. Sī autem multum emēs, pretium fortasse minuētur. Dominus tuus, ut audīvī, crās cēnam amīcīs suīs dabit. Nōnne porcum emēs?'

"Cui Pseudolus, 'Quem porcum mihi vēndere vīs? Ille est pinguis. Da mihi illum!' 15

(continued)

2 **cachinnus, -ī**, m., *laughter*	9 **quidem**, adv., *indeed*
5 **optimus, -a, -um**, *best, very good,* *excellent*	10 **umquam**, adv., *ever*
6 **lanius, -ī**, m., *butcher*	11 **procāx, procācis**, *insolent*; as slang, *pushy*
7 **carō, carnis**, f., *meat*	12 **autem**, conj., *however, but*
Quantī...? *How much...?*	13 **multus, -a, -um**, *much*
8 **perna, -ae**, f., *ham*	15 **pinguis, -is, -e**, *fat*
pretium, -ī, n., *price*	

13 **minuō, minuere, minuī, minūtus**, *to lessen, reduce, decrease*

Exercise 31a
Respondē Latīnē:

1. Quota hōra est?
2. Ā quibus cachinnus audītur?
3. Quid servōs dēlectat?
4. Cūr Pseudolus ad tabernam laniī dēscendit?
5. Quālis homō lanius vidētur esse?
6. Quid Pseudolus faciet?
7. Estne pretium pernae magnum?
8. Minuēturne pretium?
9. Quālem porcum Pseudolus emere vult?

"'Ille porcus heri in meīs agrīs pascēbātur, meā manū cūrābātur. Nūllum porcum meliōrem in hāc urbe emēs. Senātōrī Rōmānō illum vēndere volō. Itaque tibi decem dēnāriīs eum vēndam.'

"'Decem dēnāriīs? Immō quīnque!'

"'Octō!' 20

"'Octō, sī ille lepus quoque additus erit grātīs. Sī nōn, nihil emam et ad aliam tabernam ībō.'

"'Nōn sine causā tū vocāris Pseudolus. Vōs servī, nōn nōs laniī, rēctē praedōnēs vocāminī.'

"Multum et diū clāmat lanius, sed Pseudolus nihil respondet. Tandem lanius octō 25 dēnāriōs invītus accipit; porcum et leporem Pseudolō trādit. Iam Pseudolus noster rediit et tōtam fābulam nōbīs nārrāvit. In animō habet leporem amīcō vēndere et pecūniam sibi retinēre."

"Minimē vērō!" clāmāvit Aurēlia, quae ā Forō redierat et omnia audīverat. "Syre, da mihi leporem! Pseudolus ad vīllam rūsticam mittētur. Vōs quoque puniēminī omnēs." 30

18	**dēnārius, -ī,** m., *denarius (silver coin)*		**grātīs,** adv., *free, for nothing*
19	**immō,** adv., *rather, on the contrary*	23	**rēctē,** adv., *rightly, properly*
21	**lepus, leporis,** m., *hare*	29	**vērō,** adv., *truly, really, indeed*
	additus erit, *(it) will have been added, is added*		

16 **pāscō, pāscere, pāvī, pāstus,** *to feed, pasture*
21 **addō, addere, addidī, additus,** *to add*
26 **accipiō, accipere, accēpī, acceptus,** *to receive, get*

Respondē Latīnē:

1. Ubi porcus pascēbātur?
2. Ā quō porcus cūrābātur?
3. Quid faciet Pseudolus sī lepus grātīs nōn additus erit?
4. Quid Pseudolus in animō habet facere?
5. Quis omnia audīverat?

A Roman butcher shop
Stone frieze, 2nd century B.C., Musée de la Civilisation, Paris, France

Exercise 31b

Take parts, read aloud, and translate:

In trīclīniō: Pseudolus, Syrus, aliī servī

SYRUS: Eho! Domina sine dubiō īrāta est hodiē. Ad vīllam mittēris, Pseudole. Ēheu! Nōs quoque puniēmur omnēs.

PSEUDOLUS: Ego nōn commoveor. Sī ad vīllam mittar, multōs leporēs ipse in agrīs capere poterō. 5

SYRUS: Minimē vērō! In vīllā enim servī semper custōdiuntur neque errāre possunt. Id nescīre vidēris.

PSEUDOLUS: Sine dubiō vōs puniēminī sī nōn statim hōs lectōs movēbitis. Fortasse domina mē ad vīllam mittī iubēbit. Estō! Hīc labōrāre nōlō. Vōs lectōs movēte! Ego fābulam vōbīs nārrābō. 10

SYRUS: Tacē, Pseudole! Fābulīs tuīs saepe delectāmur, sed sī cachinnus audiētur—

PSEUDOLUS: Nōlīte timēre! Domina fortasse mē reprehendit sed Cornēlius mē ad vīllam mittī nōlet. Hīc certē mē retinērī volet. Saepe enim dominus mē ad Forum mittit ubi aliquid parvō pretiō emī vult.

1 **trīclīnium, -ī,** n., *dining room*	**retinērī,** *to be held back, kept*
13 **mittī,** *to be sent*	14 **emī,** *to be bought*

12 **reprehendō, reprehendere, reprehendī, reprehēnsus,** *to blame, scold*

FORMS
Verbs: Present Passive Infinitives

Compare these sentences:

1. Aurēlia Pseudolum ad vīllam **mittere** volet.
   *Aurelia will want **to send** Pseudolus to the country house.*

2. Aurēlia Pseudolum ad vīllam ***mittī*** iubēbit.
   *Aurelia will order Pseudolus **to be sent** to the country house.*

In sentence 1, **mittere** is the present *active* infinitive; in sentence 2, **mittī** is the present *passive* infinitive. The table below shows the present active and passive infinitives of each conjugation:

1st Conjugation	2nd Conjugation	3rd Conjugation		4th Conjugation
port*āre*, to carry	mov*ēre*, to move	mítt*ere*, to send	iác*ere*, to throw	aud*īre*, to hear
port*ārī*, to be carried	mov*ērī*, to be moved	mítt*ī*, to be sent	iác*ī*, to be thrown	aud*īrī*, to be heard

Exercise 31c

Select, read aloud, and translate:

1. Incolae magna incendia (exstinguī, exstinguere, exstinguit) nōn possunt.
2. Incolae miserī lapidibus et flammīs (opprimere, opprimī, opprimunt) nōlunt.
3. Interdiū nihil intrā urbem vehiculō (portās, portārī, portātur) licet.
4. Cornēliī nūllum vehiculum intrā urbem (vidērī, vident, vidēre) poterant.
5. Syrus cachinnum ā dominā (audīvit, audīre, audīrī) nōn vult.

BUILDING THE MEANING
The Ablative Case (Consolidation)

In Chapter 12, the following uses of the ablative case were formally presented:

1. Ablative of Time When:

    Illō ipsō tempore parietēs īnsulae cecidērunt. (30:25)
    At that very moment the walls of the apartment building fell.

2. Ablative of Time within Which:

    Brevī tempore māter et fīlia ā servīs per urbem ferēbantur. (29:1–2)
    In a short time the mother and her daughter were being carried through the city by slaves.

3. Ablative of Instrument or Means (with active verbs):

    Cornēlia Flāviam **complexū** tenet. (9:20)
    Cornelia holds Flavia in an embrace.

4. Ablative of Manner:

    Parietēs īnsulae **magnō (cum) fragōre** cecidērunt. (30:25)
    The walls of the apartment building fell with a great crash.

In Chapter 24, the following use of the ablative case was formally presented:

5. Ablative of Cause:

    Tuā culpā raeda est in fossā. (14:7)
    Because of your fault the carriage is in the ditch.
    It's your fault that the carriage is in the ditch.

In recent chapters you have seen the following uses of the ablative case:

6. Ablative of Price:

    Itaque tibi **decem dēnāriīs** eum vēndam. (31:17–18)
    Therefore I will sell it to you for ten denarii.

7. Ablative of Personal Agent with Passive Verbs:

> Māter et fīlia **ā servīs** per urbem ferēbantur. (29:1–2)
> *The mother and her daughter were being carried through the city **by slaves**.*

> **Ab incolīs** omnia simul aguntur. (30:5)
> *Everything is being done at the same time **by the tenants**.*

Note that when the action of the passive verb is carried out by a person (*personal agent*) the preposition **ā** or **ab** is used with the ablative case.

N.B. The ablative of instrument or means is used with both active verbs (see 3 above) and passive verbs (see 8 below).

8. Ablative of Instrument or Means (with passive verbs):

> Interdiū nihil intrā urbem **vehiculō** portātur. (29:3–4)
> *During the day nothing is carried **by/in a vehicle** within the city.*

> **Iocō optimō** dēlectāmur. (31:5)   *We are amused **by an excellent joke**.*

Note that when the action of the passive verb is carried out by a thing (*instrument* or *means*) a preposition is not used with the ablative case.

Exercise 31d

Select the appropriate verb, read aloud, and translate:

1. (a) Puerōs Rōmānōs patrēs saepe _____.
   (b) Puerī Rōmānī ā patribus _____.
   (verberant/verberāmus/verberantur)

2. (a) Uxōrēs Rōmānae ā virīs semper _____.
   (b) Uxōrēs virī Rōmānī semper _____.
   (amābant/amābantur/amātis)

3. (a) Hic liber ā mē tibi _____.
   (b) Hunc librum tibi _____.
   (dabitur/dabit/dabō)

4. (a) Omnēs convīvae cibō magnopere _____.
   (b) Omnēs convīvās cibus magnopere _____.
   (dēlectant/dēlectat/dēlectantur)

5. (a) Mercātor ipse manū porcum _____.
   (b) Porcus manū mercātōris _____.
   (cūrābās/cūrābātur/cūrābat)

6. (a) Lepus ā mercātōre grātīs _____.
   (b) Mercātor leporem grātīs _____.
   (addētur/addent/addet)

7. (a) Domina Pseudolum ad vīllam _____.
   (b) Pseudolus ad vīllam ā dominā _____.
   (mittētur/mittet/mittent)

8. (a) Flammae incolās miserōs _____.
   (b) Incolae miserī flammīs _____.
   (opprimēbantur/opprimēbant/opprimēbātis)

9. (a) Vehicula onera ingentia _____.
   (b) Onera ingentia vehiculīs _____.
   (portantur/portant/portārī)

10. (a) Cornēlia incendiō _____.
    (b) Incendium Cornēliam _____.
    (commōvētur/commōvēre/commōvet)

convīva, -ae, m., *guest (at a banquet)*   **magnopere,** adv., *greatly*

Exercise 31e

In Exercise 31d, locate the sentences that contain:

1. ablative of personal agent
2. ablative of means or instrument or cause

- - - - -

Laudātur ab hīs, culpātur ab illīs. *He's praised by these and blamed by those.* (Horace)
Avārus animus nūllō satiātur lucrō. *A greedy mind is satisfied with no (amount of)*
gain. (Publilius Syrus 55)

- - - - -

FORMS
Demonstrative Adjectives and Pronouns

In Chapter 26 the demonstrative adjectives and pronouns **hic** *this* and **ille** *that* were formally presented. Review them, using the charts at the back of this book. In Chapter 27 the forms of **is, ea, id** were formally presented as a pronoun meaning *he, she,* and *it.* Review the forms of this pronoun, using the chart at the back of this book. The forms of **is, ea, id** may also function as adjectives meaning *this* or *that* according to the context, e.g., <u>eō</u> **ipsō tempore,** *at* <u>*that*</u> *very moment.*

You have met two other words that may function as either demonstrative adjectives or pronouns:

ipse, ipsa, ipsum, intensive, *himself, herself, itself, themselves, very*

īdem, eadem, idem, *the same*

The forms of these demonstrative adjectives and pronouns are as follows. They should be learned thoroughly:

Number Case	Masc.	Fem.	Neut.
Singular			
Nominative	ipse	ipsa	ipsum
Genitive	ipsīus	ipsīus	ipsīus
Dative	ipsī	ipsī	ipsī
Accusative	ipsum	ipsam	ipsum
Ablative	ipsō	ipsā	ipsō
Plural			
Nominative	ipsī	ipsae	ipsa
Genitive	ipsōrum	ipsārum	ipsōrum
Dative	ipsīs	ipsīs	ipsīs
Accusative	ipsōs	ipsās	ipsa
Ablative	ipsīs	ipsīs	ipsīs

Compare the forms of **ipse, ipsa, ipsum** above with those of **ille, illa, illud.**

The forms of **īdem, eadem, idem** are the same as those of **is, ea, id** plus the letters *-dem*, except for the letters in boldface:

Number Case	Masc.	Fem.	Neut.
Singular			
Nominative	**ī**dem	eadem	idem
Genitive	eiusdem	eiusdem	eiusdem
Dative	eīdem	eīdem	eīdem
Accusative	eu**n**dem	ea**n**dem	idem
Ablative	eōdem	eādem	eōdem
Plural			
Nominative	eīdem	eaedem	eadem
Genitive	eōru**n**dem	eāru**n**dem	eōru**n**dem
Dative	eīsdem	eīsdem	eīsdem
Accusative	eōsdem	eāsdem	eadem
Ablative	eīsdem	eīsdem	eīsdem

Exercise 31f

IN VIĀ SACRĀ

A great man in Rome would normally have men of lower rank (**clientēs**) who looked upon him as their patron (**patrōnus**) and attended him on public occasions. Clients who came along unbidden with their master to a **cēna** were referred to scornfully as **umbrae**, *shadows*. In this conversation, the brothers Vibidius and Servilius discuss how to get Gaius to invite them to his dinner party as members of Messalla's retinue.

Take parts, read aloud, and translate:

VIBIDIUS: Ecce, mī frāter! Vidēsne hanc domum? Est ea dē quā tibi saepe dīxī. Ibi enim multae et optimae cēnae dantur. Eae cēnae sunt per tōtam urbem celebrēs. Hodiē, ut dīcunt omnēs, dominus huius domūs multōs convīvās ad cēnam accipiet. Optima cēna ab illō dabitur. Ab omnibus multum vīnum bibētur et multae fābulae nārrābuntur. Ego et tū invītābimur? Mox sciē- 5
mus. Ecce enim appropinquat dominus ipse, Gaius Cornēlius, quī ā quattuor servīs in lectīcā maximā portātur.

SERVĪLIUS: At nōs eī dominō nōn nōtī sumus. Quōmodo ab eō ad cēnam invītābimur?

VIBIDIUS: Sine dubiō is ad Forum portābitur et extrā Cūriam dēpōnētur. Tum in Cūriam intrābit sōlus. Eōdem tempore quō ē lectīcā dēscendet, nōs eī oc- 10
currēmus et dīcēmus, "Nōnne tū es Gaius Cornēlius, amīcus nostrī patrōnī Messallae, cuius clientēs fidēlissimī sumus? Numquam sine nōbīs ad cēnam venit Messalla."

SERVĪLIUS: Tum Gaius nōs invītābit ad cēnam?

VIBIDIUS: Fortasse. 15

SERVĪLIUS: Fortasse? Minimē vērō! Nōs vocābit umbrās, nōn clientēs Messallae.

3 **celeber, celebris, celebre,** *famous*
8 **nōtus, -a, -um,** *known*
12 **fidēlissimus, -a, -um,** *most faithful*

5 **bibō, bibere, bibī,** *to drink*

Exercise 31g

In the story in Exercise 31f above, locate and translate all sentences that contain examples of the demonstrative adjectives and pronouns **hic, haec, hoc; ille, illa, illud; is, ea, id; ipse, ipsa, ipsum;** and **īdem, eadem, idem**. State whether the word is being used as an adjective or a pronoun, and if it is used as an adjective tell what word it modifies.

Exercise 31h

Using story 31 as a guide, give the Latin for:

1. Very loud laughter was heard from the kitchen by the children.
2. The slaves were amused by a very good joke.
3. If Pseudolus buys/will buy a lot, the price will be reduced by the butcher.
4. You slaves are rightly called robbers.
5. That pig and this hare are handed over to Pseudolus.

CHAPTER 32

DINNER PREPARATIONS

The most substantial meal of the day was the dinner (**cēna**), eaten in the late afternoon, while it was still daylight; the richer classes, who could afford lamps or torches, sometimes began later or prolonged the dinner farther into the evening.

Earlier in the day the Romans ate little; in the early morning they took only a drink of water or wine and a piece of bread; this was called **iēntāculum**, and was similar to the "continental" rolls and coffee of the present day. The midday meal (**prandium**) would also be cold, possibly something left over from the previous day's **cēna**; this also was merely a snack.

In the early days of Rome, the dinner was eaten in the **ātrium,** but as manners became more sophisticated, a special room was set aside as a dining room. From the second century B.C., the adoption of the Greek custom of reclining at meals demanded a special arrangement of couches and tables that was called in Greek *triklinion* (tri-klin-ion, "three-couch-arrangement"), a word borrowed into Latin as **trīclīnium**. In this arrangement three couches (Latin **lectī**) were set around a table or several small tables, and the name **trīclīnium** came to be used for the dining room itself. At the time of our story, the male diners reclined. The wives who attended the dinner party would sit and not recline. Slaves cut up the food before serving so that the diners could eat with one hand. Though the Romans had spoons and knives, food was generally conveyed to the mouth by the fingers. Napkins (**mappae**) were sometimes provided by the host; guests often brought their own napkins and carried away with them any food they did not eat from their own portions.

Preparations for a banquet

Fragment of mosaic pavement from Carthage, Louvre, Paris, France

Abhinc trēs diēs amīcī quīdam ā Gaiō Cornēliō ad cēnam invītātī erant. Quā dē causā Aurēlia in Forō glīrēs ēmerat. Porcus quoque ā Pseudolō ēmptus erat. Iam diēs cēnae aderat. Māne servī in Forum missī sunt et ibi comparāvērunt holera, pānem, pullōs. Ōva quoque et māla et multa alia comparāta sunt, nam cum senātor Rōmānus amīcōs ad cēnam invītāvit, cēna optima parārī dēbet. 5

Iam hōra cēnae appropinquābat. Dum in culīnā cibus coquēbātur, ancillae trīclīnium parābant. Mēnsa ā servīs in medium trīclīnium iam allāta erat; trēs lectī circum mēnsam positī erant.

Trīclīnium Cornēliī erat pulcherrimum atque ōrnātissimum. In parietibus erant pictūrae pulcherrimae. In aliā pictūrā canis Cerberus ē rēgnō Plūtōnis extrahēbātur, in 10 aliā Mercurius ad Charōnem mortuōs addūcēbat, in aliā Orpheus ad īnferōs dēscendēbat.

Cornēlius servōs festīnāre iubēbat, nam iam erat nōna hōra. Aurēlia, semper sollicita, ancillās vehementer incitābat. Subitō ancilla quaedam, quae Aurēliam magnopere timēbat, hūc illūc festīnāns ūnum ē candēlābrīs cāsū ēvertit. Candēlābrum in lectum dēiectum est; statim effūsum est oleum in strāta; haec celeriter ignem cēpērunt. Aurēlia 15 īrāta ancillam neglegentem reprehendēbat, sed Cornēlius celeriter palliō ignem exstīnxit.

"Bonō animō es!" inquit Cornēlius. "Ecce! Ignis iam exstīnctus est!" Tum aliae ancillae ab illō vocātae sunt: "Syra! Phrygia! Strāta alia ferte! Necesse est omnia statim reficere, nam convīvae mox aderunt." Omnia Cornēliī iussa facta sunt. (continued)

1 **invītātī erant,** *(they) had been invited*
quā dē causā, *for this reason*
3 **comparō, -āre, -āvī, -ātus,** *to buy,*
obtain, get ready
holus, holeris, n., *vegetable*
pānis, pānis, gen. pl., **pānium,** m.,
bread
4 **pullus, -ī,** m., *chicken*
ōvum, -ī, n., *egg*
mālum, -ī, n., *apple*
7 **allāta erat,** *(it) had been brought in*
circum, prep. + acc., *around*
9 **pulcherrimus, -a, -um,** *most/very*
beautiful

10 **rēgnum, -ī,** n., *kingdom*
11 **īnferī, -ōrum,** m. pl., *the underworld*
14 **candēlābrum, -ī,** n., *candelabrum,*
lamp-stand
cāsū, *by chance, accidentally*
15 **oleum -ī,** n., *oil*
strātum, -ī, n., *sheet, covering*
ignis, ignis, gen. pl., **ignium,**
m., *fire*
16 **pallium, -ī,** n., *cloak*
17 **Bonō animō es!/este!** *Be of good*
mind! Cheer up!
19 **iussa, -ōrum,** n. pl., *commands, orders*

6 **coquō, coquere, coxī, coctus,** *to cook*
7 **afferō, afferre, attulī, allātus,** irreg., *to bring, bring to, bring in*
14 **ēvertō, ēvertere, ēvertī, ēversus,** *to overturn, upset*
15 **dēiciō, dēicere, dēiēcī, dēiectus,** *to throw down;* pass., *to fall*
effundō, effundere, effūdī, effūsus, *to pour out;* pass., *to spill*

Exercise 32a Respondē Latīnē:

1. Quī ad cēnam invītātī erant?
2. Quid servī in Forō comparāvērunt?
3. Quid ancillae faciēbant?
4. Quae pictūrae in parietibus trīclīniī erant?
5. Quid Aurēlia faciēbat?
6. Quid fēcit ancilla quaedam?
7. Quō īnstrūmentō Cornēlius ignem exstīnxit?

Adveniēbant convīvae, in quibus erant complūrēs clientēs quī ad cēnam invītātī erant. 20
Convīvae mappās sēcum ferēbant, nam cum cēna cōnfecta erit, in mappīs cibum auferre
eīs licēbit. Paulisper in ātriō stābant, Cornēlium exspectantēs. Tandem ā Cornēliō ipsō
cōmiter salūtātī sunt.

Aberat nēmō nisi Titus Cornēlius, patruus Marcī. Paulisper eum exspectābant
omnēs; sed tandem, quamquam ille nōndum advēnerat, convīvae in trīclīnium ductī sunt. 25
Soleae dēpositae ā servīs ablātae sunt. Omnēs in lectīs accubuērunt et cēnam
exspectābant.

20 **complūrēs, -ēs, -a,** *several*
21 **cōnfecta erit,** *(it) is/will have been*
   finished

23 **cōmiter,** adv., *courteously, graciously, in*
   a friendly way
26 **solea, -ae,** f., *sandal*

   21 **auferō, auferre, abstulī, ablātus,** irreg., *to carry away, take away*
   26 **accumbō, accumbere, accubuī, accubitūrus,** *to recline (at table)*

Respondē Latīnē:

1. Quid convīvae sēcum ferēbant?
2. Cūr convīvae in ātriō stābant?
3. Quid tandem Cornēlius fēcit?

4. Quis aberat?
5. Quō convīvae ductī sunt?

FORMS
Verbs: Perfect, Pluperfect, and Future Perfect Passive

Look at these sentences with verbs in the passive voice:

Perfect Passive:

   Trīclīnium **parātum est.**

   Amīcī **invītātī sunt.**

*The dining room **was prepared/has been
prepared.***
*Friends **were invited/have been invited.***

Pluperfect Passive:

   Porcus **ēmptus erat.**
   Trēs lectī **positī erant.**

*A pig **had been bought.***
*Three couches **had been placed.***

Future Perfect Passive:

   Cēna **cōnfecta erit.**
   Māla **comparāta erunt.**

*Dinner **will have been finished.***
*Apples **will have been bought.***

It is obvious from these examples that the *passive* forms of the *perfect*, *pluperfect*, and *future perfect* tenses are very different from their corresponding active forms. Here are passive forms of these tenses for **portāre**:

			Perfect Passive		Pluperfect Passive		Future Perfect Passive	
Singular	1	portátus, -a	sum	portátus, -a	éram	portátus, -a	érō
	2	portátus, -a	es	portátus, -a	érās	portátus, -a	éris
	3	portátus, -a, -um	est	portátus, -a, -um	érat	portátus, -a, -um	érit
Plural	1	portátī, -ae	súmus	portátī, -ae	erámus	portátī, -ae	érimus
	2	portátī, -ae	éstis	portátī, -ae	erátis	portátī, -ae	éritis
	3	portátī, -ae, -a	sunt	portátī, -ae, -a	érant	portátī, -ae, -a	érunt

Be sure to learn these forms thoroughly.

NOTES

1. Verbs of all four conjugations and the irregular verb **ferre** follow the same patterns in the perfect, pluperfect, and future perfect passive. They all use forms of the verb **esse** plus the *perfect passive participle*, which you learned in Chapter 20 and which is the fourth principal part of a transitive verb, e.g., **portō, portāre, portāvī, portātus**.

    a. To form the *perfect passive*, use the *present* tense of **esse**, e.g., **portātus** *sum*, **portātus** *es*.

    b. To form the *pluperfect passive*, use the *imperfect* tense of **esse**, e.g., **portātus** *eram*, **portātus** *erās*.

    c. To form the *future perfect passive*, use the *future* tense of **esse**, e.g., **portātus** *erō*, **portātus** *eris*.

2. The perfect passive participle in these verb forms agrees with the subject in gender and number and will always be nominative in case:

Puer laudāt*us* est.	*The boy was/has been praised.*
Māter laudāt*a* est.	*The mother was/has been praised.*
Aedificium laudāt*um* est.	*The building was/has been praised.*
Puerī laudāt*ī* sunt.	*The boys were/have been praised.*
Mātrēs laudāt*ae* sunt.	*The mothers were/have been praised.*
Aedificia laudāt*a* sunt.	*The buildings were/have been praised.*

Exercise 32b

Read aloud and translate:

1. Servus, nōmine Pseudolus, in Forum missus est.
2. Glīrēs ab Aurēliā ēmptī erant.
3. Cum trīclīnium parātum erit, convīvae intrābunt.
4. Servī iocō optimō dēlectātī sunt.
5. Ē culīnā magnus cachinnus audītus erat.
6. Cum lepus ab Aurēliā inventus erit, Pseudolus pūniētur.
7. "Tū, Pseudole," inquit Aurēlia, "leporem emere nōn iussus es."
8. "Ego illō spectāculō miserābilī," inquit Cornēlia, "valdē commōta sum."
9. Octō dēnāriī ā laniō acceptī sunt.
10. "Cum ā Cornēliō salūtātī erimus," inquit ūnus ē convīvīs, "servī eius nōs ad trīclīnium addūcent."

Exercise 32c

Select, read aloud, and translate:

1. _____ ā mātre vocāta erat.
   Ancilla/Līberī/Eucleidēs
2. _____ ex īnsulā ēmissae sunt.
   Fūmus/Ōrnāmenta/Flammae
3. _____ in mēnsā positus erat.
   Pānis/Glīrēs/Mappa
4. _____ ā laniō minūtum est.
   Dēnāriī/Pretium/Porcus
5. _____ in Forō comparātī erant.
   Ōva/Glīrēs/Porcus
6. _____ ā servō allāta erunt.
   Māla/Mappa/Mulier
7. _____ in hāc tabernā ēmpta est.
   Carō/Holera/Lepus
8. _____ ā līberīs petītae sunt.
   Adstantēs/Auxilium/Mātrēs

Exercise 32d

Change each verb from active to passive voice, keeping the same tense, person, and number; translate both verbs. You may use masculine, feminine, or (if appropriate) neuter endings on the perfect passive participles:

1. dūxit
2. portāvistī
3. posuerat
4. oppressimus
5. commōvī
6. accēperit
7. mīserāmus
8. audīverātis
9. tulērunt

Mythological scenes dealing with the underworld, such as those adorning the walls of the Cornelii dining room, have remained popular subjects of art through the ages to this day. Pictured: Charon the Ferryman, who brought souls to the underworld for a fee.

Oil on canvas, "Psyche and Charon" by John Roddam Spencer-Stanhope, Roy Miles Gallery, London

Exercise 32e

Using story 32 and the chart on page 43 as guides, give the Latin for:

1. Vegetables had been bought in the Forum by the slaves.
2. The food was cooked in the kitchen.
3. The table has been brought by the slaves into the middle of the dining room.
4. Cerberus had been dragged from the kingdom of Pluto.
5. When the dinner is finished/will have been finished, the guests will carry food away in napkins.

Ālea iacta est. *The die has been cast.* **Said by Julius Caesar at the Rubicon River. (Suetonius, *Caesar* 32)**

Word Study VIII

4th Declension Nouns

Many 4th declension nouns are formed from the stem of the fourth principal part of verbs. For example, **adventus, -ūs,** m., *arrival*, is made from the stem of **adventūrus**, the fourth principal part of **adveniō**. English words are often derived from this kind of 4th declension noun by dropping the *-us* ending e.g., *advent*, "an arrival."

Exercise 1

Give the Latin 4th declension noun (nom. sing., gen. sing., and gender) that may be formed from the fourth principal part of each of the following verbs, and give the meaning of the noun:

1. prōcēdere	3. habēre	5. audīre	7. colere
2. trānsīre	4. agere	6. exīre	8. trahere

Exercise 2

Give the English words derived by dropping the *-us* ending from each 4th declension noun formed in Exercise 1 above, and give the meaning of each English word.

Exercise 3

Give the Latin verb to which each of these nouns is related, and give the meanings of both verb and noun:

1. **rīsus, -ūs,** m.	4. **gemitus, -ūs,** m.	7. **cōnspectus, -ūs,** m.
2. **lātrātus, -ūs,** m.	5. **cursus, -ūs,** m.	8. **aditus, -ūs,** m.
3. **reditus, -ūs,** m.	6. **discessus, -ūs,** m.	9. **cāsus, -ūs,** m.

More Compound Verbs

The following exercise on compound verbs uses the principles of word formation discussed in Chapter 27, Word Study VII, and Chapter 29.

Exercise 4

After each Latin verb is a group of English words that are derived from compounds of that simple verb. Give the present active infinitive of the compound Latin verb from which each English word is derived, and give the meanings of both the compound Latin verb and the English word:

mittō, mittere, mīsī, missus

1. commit
2. submit
3. remit
4. transmit
5. admit
6. emit
7. permit
8. promise

iaciō, iacere, iēcī, iactus

1. project
2. reject
3. subject
4. eject
5. inject
6. interject
7. conjecture
8. trajectory

faciō, facere, fēcī, factus

1. effect
2. affect
3. defect
4. perfect
5. infect
6. confection
7. suffice
8. affection

trahō, trahere, trāxī, tractus

1. abstract
2. attract
3. contract
4. detract
5. distract
6. extract
7. retract
8. subtract

CHAPTER

33

AT DINNER

Cornēlius ancillīs signum dat. Prīmum aqua ab ancillīs portātur et convīvae manūs lāvant. Dum hoc faciunt, omnibus convīvīs mulsum datur. Deinde fercula ē culīnā efferuntur, in quibus est gustātiō—ōva et olīvae nigrae, asparagus et bōlētī liquāmine aspersī. Intereā ā convīvīs multae fābulae nārrantur, multa dē rēbus urbānīs dīcuntur: alius dē incendiīs nārrat, alius dē pestilentiā in urbe, alius dē amphitheātrō, aedificiō 5 ingentī quod mox dēdicābitur. Aliquid novī audīre omnēs dēlectat. Dum convīvae haec et multa alia nārrant, gustātiō editur, mulsum bibitur.

Tum servī gustātiōnem auferunt; deinde ab eīsdem servīs magnum ferculum in trīclīnium fertur, in mediā mēnsā pōnitur. In eō est porcus ingēns et circum porcum glīrēs quōs Aurēlia ēmerat. Ab aliīs servīs pōcula convīvārum vīnō optimō complentur. 10 Dum convīvae haec spectant extrā trīclīnium magnus tumultus audītur. Subitō in trīclīnium magnō cum strepitū irrumpit Titus Cornēlius.

Mussant convīvae, "Cūr Titus noster sērō venīre solet neque sē umquam excūsat?"

At Titus, ad locum suum lentē ambulāns, "Salvēte, amīcī omnēs!" inquit. "Salvē, mī frāter! Amīcō cuidam in popīnā occurrī." 15

(continued)

2 **mulsum, -ī, n.,** *wine sweetened with honey*
3 **gustātiō, gustātiōnis, f.,** *hors d'oeuvre, first course*
  niger, nigra, nigrum, *black*
  bōlētus, -ī, m., *mushroom*
  liquāmen, liquāminis, n., *garum (a sauce made from fish, used to season food)*
4 **aspersus, -a, -um,** *sprinkled*
  rēs urbānae, rērum urbānārum, f. pl., *affairs of the city/town*
5 **pestilentia, -ae, f.,** *plague*
8 **ferculum, -ī, n.,** *dish, tray*
10 **pōculum, -ī, n.,** *cup, goblet*
14 **locus, -ī, m.,** *place*
15 **popīna, -ae, f.,** *eating-house, bar*

7 **edō, esse, ēdī, ēsus,** irreg., *to eat*
10 **compleō, complēre, complēvī, complētus,** *to fill*
12 **irrumpō, irrumpere, irrūpī, irruptus,** *to burst in*

Exercise 33a
Respondē Latīnē:

1. Quid prīmum ad convīvās portātur?
2. Quid prīmum ē culīnā effertur?
3. Quibus dē rēbus nārrant convīvae?
4. Quās rēs edunt convīvae dum mulsum bibunt?
5. Quid in mediā mēnsā pōnitur post gustātiōnem?
6. Quōmodo intrat Titus in trīclīnium?
7. Cūr Titus sērō vēnit?

Gaius, quamquam īrātissimus erat, nihil tamen dīxit quod hōc tempore frātrem reprehendere nōlēbat. Statim signum servīs dedit. Tum aliī ex eīs porcum scindēbant, aliī carnem ad convīvās portābant. Nōn omnibus dē porcō datum est: clientibus quidem data sunt pullōrum frusta.

Gaius servō, "Puer," inquit, "da frātrī meō quoque frusta pullī! Nōlī eī dē 20 porcō dare!"

Nunc omnēs cibum atque vīnum habēbant. Omnēs cēnam laudābant. Etiam clientēs, quamquam frusta modo habēbant, ūnā cum cēterīs clāmābant, "Euge! Gaius Cornēlius cēnam optimam dare solet. Nēmō meliōrem coquum habet. Nōnne coquum ipsum laudāre dēbēmus?" 25

Itaque coquus vocātus ab omnibus laudātus est.

Tandem fercula ā servīs ablāta sunt. Simul Gaius servōs iussit secundās mēnsās in trīclīnium portāre. Servī, quamquam dēfessī erant, hūc illūc currēbant. Ūvae, māla, pira in trīclīnium portāta sunt. Passum quoque in mēnsā positum omnibus est datum.

16 **īrātissimus, -a, -um,** *most/very angry*
18 **dē porcō datum est,** *some pork was given*
19 **frustum, -ī,** n., *scrap*
23 **ūnā,** adv., *together*
    cēterī, -ae, -a, *the rest, the others*
    Euge! *Hurray!*

24 **coquus, -ī,** m., *cook*
27 **secundae mēnsae, -ārum,** f. pl., *second course, dessert*
28 **ūva, -ae,** f., *grape, bunch of grapes*
    pirum, -ī, n., *pear*
29 **passum, -ī,** n., *raisin-wine*

17 **scindō, scindere, scidī, scissus,** *to cut, split, carve*

Respondē Latīnē:

1. Cūr Gaius nihil dīxit?
2. Quibus convīvīs data sunt frusta pullōrum?
3. Quae Titō data sunt?
4. Cūr coquus vocātus est?
5. Quās rēs convīvae postrēmō edunt?

BUILDING THE MEANING
Perfect Passive Participles I

Look at the following sentence:

Coquus **vocātus** ab omnibus laudātus est. (33:26)

In Chapter 32 you learned that perfect passive participles are used with forms of **esse** to produce the passive voice of the perfect, pluperfect, and future perfect tenses, e.g., **laudātus est.**

A different use of the perfect passive participle is shown at the beginning of the sentence above. Here the participle **vocātus** modifies a noun and indicates an action that took place before the action of the main verb: the cook was first summoned and then praised. The sentence can be translated in various ways. The most literal translation is:

*The cook, **having been summoned**, was praised by everyone.*

Any of the following translations might make better English:

After being summoned, the cook was praised by everyone.
When summoned, the cook was praised by everyone.
When the cook had been summoned, he was praised by everyone.
The cook was summoned and praised by everyone.

Similarly, the following sentence can be translated in a variety of ways:

Aurēlia neglegentiā eārum **vexāta** speculum ēripuit.
***Having been annoyed** by their carelessness, Aurelia snatched away the mirror.*
(literal translation)
Annoyed by their carelessness, Aurelia snatched away the mirror.
Because/Since Aurelia was annoyed by their carelessness, she snatched away the mirror.
Aurelia, who was annoyed by their carelessness, snatched away the mirror.

Note from the translations offered above that perfect passive participles can often be translated into English as relative clauses or as clauses introduced by conjunctions such as *when*, *after*, *because*, *since*, or *although*.

The perfect passive participle is a verbal adjective that has the endings of an adjective of the 1st and 2nd declensions (like **magnus, -a, -um**). Therefore, it must agree in gender, case, and number with the noun or pronoun it modifies:

<u>Soleae</u> **dēpositae** ā servīs ablātae sunt. (32:26)
<u>*The sandals*</u> ***having been set down*** *were carried away by the slaves.*
The sandals, which had been set down, were carried away by the slaves.

Exercise 33b
Give two translations for each of the following sentences: one in which the perfect passive participle is translated literally and the other in which it is translated using a relative clause or a clause introduced by *when, after, because, since,* or *although*:

1. Convīvae ad cēnam invītātī ā Cornēliō ipsō cōmiter salūtātī sunt.
2. Ancillae festīnāre iussae aquam ad convīvās lentē portāvērunt.
3. Convīvae in trīclīnium ductī in lectīs accubuērunt.
4. Magnum ferculum ā servīs ē culīnā lātum in mediā mēnsā positum est.
5. Servī ā Gaiō iussī frusta pullī frātrī eius dedērunt.
6. Porcus ā servīs scissus ad mēnsam portātus est.
7. Ūvae in trīclīnium portātae omnibus convīvīs datae sunt.
8. Cēna optima ā Cornēliō data ab omnibus laudāta est.
9. Coquus ab omnibus laudātus laetus erat.
10. Titus in trīclīnium ductus, "Salvē, mī frāter!" inquit.

Exercise 33c

During the course of Cornelius' dinner party, the guests would have exchanged news or gossip and entertained one another with stories. The Romans enjoyed stories of magic like the following, an adaptation of a tale told by Niceros, a guest at Trimalchio's dinner party in Petronius' *Satyricon*.

Read aloud and translate:

Ubi adhūc servus eram, in urbe Brundisiō habitābāmus. Illō tempore Melissam amābam, ancillam pulcherrimam quae in vīllā rūsticā habitābat. Forte dominus meus ad urbem proximam abierat; ego igitur Melissam vīsitāre cōnstituī, sōlus tamen īre nōluī. Erat autem mihi amīcus quīdam, quī mēcum īre poterat. Mīles erat, homō fortis et temerārius.   5

Mediā nocte discessimus. Lūna lūcēbat tamquam merīdiē. Vēnimus ad sepulcra prope viam sita. Mīles meus inter sepulcra iit; ego cōnsēdī et stēlās numerābam. Deinde rem mīram vīdī: omnia vestīmenta ab amīcō meō exūta in terrā prope viam dēposita sunt. Dī immortālēs! Nōn per iocum dīcō! Ille subitō lupus factus est! Ego stābam tamquam mortuus. Lupus tamen ululāvit et in   10
silvam fūgit.

Prīmum perterritus eram. Anima mihi in nāsō erat! Deinde ad stēlās prōcessī quod vestīmenta eius īnspicere volēbam. Vestīmenta dēposita tamen lapidea facta erant. Paulisper ibi stābam immōbilis. Gladium tamen strīnxī et umbrās cecīdī dōnec ad vīllam rūsticam pervēnī. Melissa mea ad portam vīllae mihi occurrit.   15
"Dolēmus," inquit, "quod nōn prius vēnistī; auxiliō tuō caruimus. Lupus enim vīllam intrāvit et omnia pecora tamquam lanius necābat. Nec tamen dērīsit. Servus enim noster eum gladiō vulnerāvit."

Ubi haec audīvī, perterritus eram. Neque dormīre neque in vīllā manēre potuī, sed summā celeritāte aufūgī. Postquam vēnī in illum locum in quō   20
vestīmenta lapidea facta erant, invēnī nihil nisi sanguinem. Ubi domum pervēnī, iacēbat mīles meus in lectō tamquam bōs; ā medicō cūrābātur. Tum scīvī mīlitem esse versipellem! Neque posteā potuī aut cum illō pānem esse aut illum amīcum meum vocāre.

2 **forte**, adv., *by chance*
3 **proximus, -a, -um**, *nearby*
6 **lūna, -ae**, f., *moon*
 tamquam, conj., *just as if*
 merīdiē, adv., *at noon*
7 **situs, -a, -um**, *located, situated*
 inter, prep. + acc., *between, among*
 stēla, -ae, f., *tombstone*
8 **numerō, -āre, -āvī, -ātus**, *to count*
 vestīmentum, -ī, n., *clothing;* pl.,
 clothes
9 **Dī immortālēs!** *Immortal gods! Good
 heavens!*
10 **ululō, -āre, -āvī, -ātus**, *to howl*
12 **anima, -ae**, f., *soul, "heart"*
 nāsus, -ī, m., *nose*

13 **lapideus, -a, -um**, *of stone, stony*
14 **umbra, -ae**, f., *shadow, shade
 (of the dead)*
 cecīdī, *I slashed at*
15 **dōnec**, conj., *until*
16 **prius**, adv., *earlier*
17 **pecus, pecoris**, n., *livestock, sheep
 and cattle*
18 **vulnerō, -āre, -āvī, -ātus**, *to wound*
21 **sanguis, sanguinis**, m., *blood*
22 **medicus, -ī**, m., *doctor*
23 **versipellis, versipellis**, gen. pl.,
 versipellium (**vertō**, *to
 change* + **pellis**, *skin*), m., *werewolf*
 posteā, adv., *afterward*

8 **exuō, exuere, exuī, exūtus**, *to take off*
12 **prōcēdō, prōcēdere, prōcessī, prōcessūrus**, *to go forward*
16 **careō, carēre, caruī, caritūrus** + abl., *to need, lack*
17 **dērīdeō, dērīdēre, dērīsī, dērīsus**, *to laugh at, get the last laugh*

**Roman
tableware**

RECIPES AND MENUS

The following are recipes from a Roman cookbook of the fourth century A.D. by Apicius.

STUFFED DORMICE

Stuff the dormice with minced pork, the minced meat of whole dormice, pounded with pepper, pine-kernels, asafetida (a kind of garlic), and fish sauce.* Sew up, place on tile, put in oven, or cook, stuffed, in a small oven.

SALT FISH WITHOUT FISH

Cook liver, grind and add pepper and fish sauce or salt. Add oil. Use rabbit, kid, lamb, or chicken liver; shape into a fish in a small mold, if liked. Sprinkle virgin oil over it.

HOMEMADE SWEETS

1. Stone dates, stuff with nuts, pine-kernels, or ground pepper. Roll in salt, fry in cooked honey, and serve.
2. Remove the crust from wheaten loaf, break up in largish morsels. Steep in milk, fry in oil, pour honey over, and serve.

*A staple of Roman cooking, fish sauce (**liquāmen** or **garum**) was made from a mash of finely chopped fish, which had been placed in the sun to ferment.

While menus must have varied very much between rich and poor people, and even between the day-to-day fare and the banquet for a special occasion, all Latin references to the **cēna** suggest that a basic menu was as follows:

1. **gustātiō** (hors d'oeuvre): egg dishes, eaten with **mulsum** (wine sweetened with honey)
2. **cēna** (the main course or courses): fish, game, poultry, pork, with wine
3. **secundae mēnsae** (dessert): usually fruit, with wine

Clientēs were sometimes invited to fill up spare places, but they were not given as good food and wine as the more important guests. Here a "client" expresses his indignation at this treatment:

If you are asked to dinner by the great man, this is his way of paying you in full for all your services. So if after a couple of months he takes it into his head to invite you, his overlooked client (he can't leave that third place on the lowest couch unoccupied!), you're meant to feel your dearest prayer has been answered.

Oh dear me! what a meal! You are given wine that fresh-clipped wool wouldn't soak up. The great man himself drinks a brand bottled in the days when consuls wore their hair long.

The cup your host is holding is studded with beryl. No one trusts you with gold, or if you are given a precious cup, there's a slave watching you, and all the gems on it have been counted.

Even the water is different for clients; and it will be given you by the bony hand of a fellow you'd rather not meet at midnight among the tombstones of the Via Latina.

All the big houses are full of insolent slaves these days. Another one will grumble as he hands you a morsel of bread you can hardly break, or lumps of dough gone moldy. For your host meanwhile there is kept a tender loaf, snow-white and made from the choicest flour.

You see that huge lobster he's getting now! You'll get a tiny little crab with half an egg around it.

He is served a lamprey. For you—an eel, first cousin to a water-serpent; or maybe a pike that's made its way to Rome up the sewers.

Before the host a huge goose's liver is placed, and a boar piping hot, then truffles. All you can do is sit and watch.

Before the guests will be set some dubious toadstools; before the host a fine mushroom.

Is it the expense he grudges? Not a bit! What he wants is to see you squirm. There's nothing on earth so funny as a disappointed belly!

—Juvenal, *Satires V* (extracts)

In Petronius' novel, the *Satyricon*, we are given a glimpse of an elaborate **cēna** given by the wealthy and ostentatious Gaius Trimalchio. The following excerpt illustrates the lengths to which a host might go in order to impress and entertain his dinner guests. A huge roast pig is brought into the dining room, and Trimalchio, eyeing it critically, suddenly becomes angry:

"What? Hasn't this pig been gutted? I swear it has not. Call the cook in here!" The poor cook came and stood by the table and said that he had forgotten to gut it. "What? Forgotten?" shouted Trimalchio. "Off with his shirt!" In a moment the cook was stripped and stood sadly between two torturers. Then everyone began to beg him off, saying: "These things will happen; do let him go; if he does it again none of us will say a word for him." But Trimalchio's face softened into smiles. "Well," he said, "if your memory is so bad, clean him here in front of us." The cook put on his shirt, seized a knife, and carved the pig's belly in various places with a shaking hand. At once the slits widened under the pressure from within, and sausages and black puddings tumbled out. At this the slaves burst into spontaneous applause and shouted, "God bless Gaius!

—Petronius, *Satyricon* 49–50 (abridged)

REVIEW VII: CHAPTERS 28–33

Exercise VIIa: Relative Pronouns
Give the Latin for the relative pronoun in italics, and then read the sentence aloud and translate it:

1. Aurēlia, (*whose*) crīnēs Phrygia neglegenter pectēbat, vexāta erat.
2. Līberī, (*whose*) clāmōrēs ab Aurēliā et Cornēliā audiēbantur, flammīs oppressī sunt.
3. Sextus, (*to whom*) Syrus iocum Pseudolī nārrāvit, dēlectābātur.
4. Servī, (*whom*) Aurēlia in urbem mīserat, holera, pānem, pullōs ēmērunt.
5. Magnus tumultus, (*which*) Titus extrā trīclīnium fēcit, ā convīvīs audītus est.
6. Coquus vocātus ā convīvīs (*who*) cēnāverant laudātus est.
7. Pseudolus, ā (*whom*) porcus ēmptus est, mercātor esse vidēbātur.
8. Cēnae (*which*) Cornēlius dare solet optimae sunt.
9. Convīvae, (*whom*) Cornēlius invītāverat, iam domum intrābant.
10. Iocus, (*by which*) servī dēlectābantur, ā Pseudolō nārrātus est.

Exercise VIIb: *is, ea, id*
Supply the correct form of **is**, **ea**, **id** to substitute as a pronoun for the italicized word(s), read aloud, and translate:

1. Audīvistīne *iocum* Pseudolī? _____ nōn audīvī.
2. *Pseudolīne* iocum audīvistī? _____ iocum nōn audīvī.
3. Vīdistisne *flammās* in tertiō tabulātō īnsulae? _____ vīdimus.
4. Trāditne lanius porcum et leporem *Pseudolō*? _____ trādit.
5. Quid post cēnam *convīvīs* licēbit? _____ cibum auferre licēbit.
6. In ferculō erant *olīvae nigrae*. _____ ā convīvīs eduntur.

Exercise VIIc: *hic, haec, hoc*
Supply the correct form of **hic**, **haec**, **hoc**, read aloud, and translate:

1. Aurēlia glīrēs in (*this*) tabernā ēmit.
2. Aurēlia et Cornēlia flammās in tertiō tabulātō (*of this*) īnsulae vīdērunt.
3. Pseudolus octō dēnāriōs (*to this*) laniō dedit.
4. (*This*) magnum ferculum porcum ingentem et multōs glīrēs habet.
5. Ab (*these*) servīs holera, pānis, pullī feruntur.

Exercise VIId: Other Adjectives
In the sentences in Exercise VIIc, supply the correct forms of the following where you previously supplied forms of **hic**, **haec**, **hoc**; then read each new sentence aloud, and translate it:

1. quīdam, quaedam, quoddam
2. ipse, ipsa, ipsum
3. īdem, eadem, idem

Exercise VIIe: Passive Forms of Verbs

Give the requested forms of the following verbs in the present, imperfect, future, perfect, pluperfect, and future perfect. Give all forms in the passive voice:

	Present	Imperfect	Future	Perfect	Pluperfect	Future Perfect
1. ferō *(3rd sing.)*	_____	_____	_____	_____	_____	_____
2. commoveō *(1st pl.)*	_____	_____	_____	_____	_____	_____
3. scindō *(infinitive)*	_____					
4. capiō *(2nd sing.)*	_____	_____	_____	_____	_____	_____
5. audiō *(2nd pl.)*	_____	_____	_____	_____	_____	_____
6. commoveō *(infinitive)*	_____					
7. incitō *(1st sing.)*	_____	_____	_____	_____	_____	_____
8. addō *(2nd sing.)*	_____	_____	_____	_____	_____	_____
9. inveniō *(infinitive)*	_____					
10. accipiō *(3rd pl.)*	_____	_____	_____	_____	_____	_____
11. dēmōnstrō *(infinitive)*	_____					
12. dēbeō *(3rd sing.)*	_____	_____	_____	_____	_____	_____

Exercise VIIf: Passive Forms of Verbs

Read aloud and translate:

1. Complūrēs clientēs ā Cornēliō ad cēnam invītātī erant.
2. Soleae ā servīs ablātae sunt.
3. Olīvae et asparagus ab omnibus edēbantur.
4. Coquus ab omnibus convīvīs laudātur.
5. Vīnum allātum omnibus datum est.
6. Illī bōlētī, sī liquāmine aspersī erunt, omnēs convīvās dēlectābunt.
7. Coquus inductus ab omnibus laudātus est.

Exercise VIIg: Passive Forms of Verbs

Complete the following sentences according to the cues provided:

1. Trēs porcī ā Pseudolō _____ _____. (had been bought)
2. Magnum incendium ā praedōnibus _____ _____. (was made)
3. Multae epistulae ā Flāviā _____ _____. (will have been sent)
4. Complūrēs convīvae ā Cornēliō _____ _____. (were invited)
5. Ancilla ab Aurēliā numquam _____ _____. (was praised)
6. Porcus _____ nōn poterat. (to be caught)
7. Coquus _____ vult. (to be praised)

Exercise VIIh: Ablative of Instrument or Means and Ablative of Personal Agent
Identify the phrases that would require the preposition **ā** or **ab**:

1. The first course was carried in by the slaves.
2. Pseudolus was not frightened by Aurelia.
3. The building was overwhelmed by a huge fire.
4. All the guests were delighted by the story.
5. The pig had been raised by the butcher.

Exercise VIIi: Prefixes
Add the given prefixes to the following verbs, and make any necessary changes in the prefix and the verb. Translate the resulting form:

	Compound Verb	Translation
1. re + facimus	_____	_____
2. ex + fūgistī	_____	_____
3. ab + ferēbat	_____	_____
4. in + mīserō	_____	_____
5. ad + capiēbam	_____	_____
6. ad + currēbant	_____	_____
7. con + tenēbās	_____	_____
8. ab + fugiunt	_____	_____
9. ad + tulimus	_____	_____
10. re + ībimus	_____	_____

Orpheus
Roman mosaic, Blanzy,
Musée Municipal, Laon,
France

Exercise VIIj: Reading Comprehension

Read the following passage and answer the questions below with full sentences in Latin:

ORPHEUS AND EURYDICE

Multae fābulae nārrantur dē Orpheō quī ā Mūsīs doctus erat citharā lūdere. In pictūrā in trīclīniō Cornēliī sitā Orpheus ad īnferōs dēscendit. Cūr? Dēscendit quod uxor eius Eurydicē morte abrepta iam sub terrā ā Plūtōne tenēbātur. Dolōre oppressus Orpheus cōnstituit Plūtōnī appropinquāre et uxōrem ab eō petere.

Iānua rēgnī Plūtōnis ā Cerberō, cane ferōcī quī tria habēbat capita, cus-   5
tōdiēbātur. Orpheus, quod semper ēsuriēbat Cerberus, frusta cibī ad eum coniēcit et, dum cibus arripitur ā Cerberō, in rēgnum intrāvit. Per umbrās ībat Orpheus; uxōrem diū et dīligenter quaerēbat. Tandem Plūtō dolōre eius commōtus, "Licet tibi," inquit, "uxōrem tuam redūcere, sed hāc condiciōne: Eurydicē exībit ad lūcem tē sequēns; tū vetāris eam respicere. Sī tū respiciēs, ea   10
retrahētur neque umquam iterum ad vīvōs remittētur."

Mox Eurydicē ex umbrīs dūcēbātur. Tum Orpheum sequēns ad lūcem lentē ascendēbat. Orpheus, quamquam uxōrem vidēre valdē dēsīderābat, ascendēbat neque respexit. Iam ad lūcem paene adveniēbant cum Orpheus amōre oppressus est. Respexit. Eurydicē revocāta ad Plūtōnem retracta est neque ad lūcem   15
umquam reddita est.

1 **cithara, -ae,** f., *lyre*	9 **condiciō, condiciōnis,** f., *condition,*
citharā lūdere, *to play (on) the lyre*	*stipulation*
3 **dolor, dolōris,** m., *grief*	11 **vīvus, -a, -um,** *living*
5 **ferōx, ferōcis,** *fierce*	14 **amor, amōris,** m., *love*

   3 **abripiō, abripere, abripuī, abreptus,** *to snatch away*
  10 **respiciō, respicere, respexī, respectus,** *to look back (at)*

1. By whom was Orpheus taught to play the lyre?
2. What had happened to Eurydice?
3. Where was Pluto holding Eurydice?
4. Why did Orpheus decide to approach Pluto?
5. Who was guarding the kingdom of Pluto?
6. What was Cerberus doing when Orpheus entered the kingdom of Pluto?
7. Was Pluto moved by Orpheus' grief?
8. What was Orpheus forbidden to do?
9. What will happen to Eurydice if Orpheus looks back at her?
10. What overwhelmed Orpheus?

Exercise VIIk: Translation

Translate the following groups of words taken from the story in Exercise VIIj:

1. ā Mūsīs doctus erat (1)
2. uxor eius Eurydicē morte abrepta (3)
3. dolōre oppressus (3–4)
4. Plūtō dolōre eius commōtus (8–9)
5. Eurydicē ex umbrīs dūcēbātur (12)
6. Orpheus amōre oppressus est (14–15)
7. Eurydicē revocāta (15)
8. retracta est (15)
9. reddita est (16)

THE COMMISSATIO

The Roman **cēna** was a major occasion in the daily routine. During the meal wine was drunk, usually mixed with water in the drinking-cup (**pōculum**) to suit the drinker's taste, for undiluted wine (**merum**) was thick and sweet.

Sometimes the dessert course (**secundae mēnsae**) was followed by a drinking party (**commissātiō**) for the male guests who were usually supplied with garlands (**corōnae**) to wear on their heads or around their necks. Originally these were worn not merely for ornament but in the belief that their perfume lessened the effect of the wine. Thus garlands were made with flowers (**flōrēs**), especially roses and violets, and also with herbs, such as parsley (**apium**), and with ivy (**hedera**). Later, and especially in winter, garlands were made with other materials such as copper foil or colored silks. Perfumes (**unguenta**) were also liberally provided at the **commissātiō**. These were applied to the hair and face and even mixed with the wine!

At the **commissātiō** a "master of the drinking" (**arbiter bibendī**) was appointed to determine the strength of wine to be drunk. He was often selected by throwing knucklebones (**tālī**) from a cylindrical box (**fritillus**). The **tālī** were oblong, rounded at the two ends, having four sides with the values l, 3, 4, and 6 respectively. The highest throw was called **Venus**, when the four **tālī** came up all different; the lowest throw was **canis**—four "ones." Another poor throw was **sēniō**—a combination containing sixes.

The **arbiter bibendī** decided the number of measures (**cyathī**) of water to be added to the wine in the bowl. He might also determine the number and order of the toasts: the formula for the toast was **bene** followed by the dative case, as in a play by Plautus:

> Bene mihi, bene vōbīs, bene amīcae meae.
> *Health to me, to you, and to my girlfriend.*

**Dice and counting pieces
used by Romans in games**
*Musée Alesia,
Alise-Sainte-Reine, France*

ADDITIONAL READING:
The Romans Speak for Themselves: Book II: "The Commissatio," pages 23–31.

Cornelius' dinner party continues with a **commissātiō**:

Plūs vīnī est allātum, et omnibus convīvīs corōnae flōrum datae sunt. Aliī corōnās rosārum, aliī hederae corōnās induērunt. Gaius apiō modo sē corōnāvit, sed Titus et rosās et unguenta poposcit, nam in popīnā prope Forum multum vīnum iam biberat.

Ūnus ē convīvīs, cui nōmen erat Messalla, clāmāvit, "Quis creābitur arbiter bibendī?"

"Nōn tū certē, Messalla," inquit alter. "Aliī vīnum sine aquā bibunt, sed tū aquam 5 sine vīnō bibis."

Cui Messalla, "Cūr nōn Gaius ipse? Quis enim est prūdentior quam Gaius? Ille enim aquam et vīnum prūdenter miscēbit, neque sinet convīvās nimis vīnī bibere."

"Minimē!" interpellat Titus magnā vōce. "Hōc modō creāre arbitrum nōn licet. Fer tālōs! Nōn nisi tālīs rēctē creātur arbiter bibendī." 10

Paulisper tacēbant omnēs. Tum Gaius, "Estō! Fer tālōs! Necesse est omnia rēctē facere."

Statim igitur tālī cum fritillō allātī in mēnsā positī sunt. Ā Gaiō prīmō iactī sunt tālī. "Est sēniō!" ab omnibus clāmātum est. Deinde ūnus ē convīvīs tālōs mīsit. "Canis!" omnēs cum rīsū clāmāvērunt. Identidem tālī missī sunt, sed nēmō Venerem iēcit. 15

Tandem Titus tālōs arripit et in fritillō magnā cum cūrā pōnit. "Meum Herculem," inquit, "invocō." Tum fritillum vehementer movet. Omnēs Titum attentē spectant. Subitō mittuntur tālī.

"Est Venus!" exclāmat Titus. "Vīcī! Vīcī! Herculēs mihi favet! Nunc tempus est bibendī. Iubeō duās partēs aquae et trēs partēs vīnī." Prīmum tamen merum arripit et 20 pōculum suum complet. "Bene tibi, Gaī!" clāmat et pōculum statim haurit. "Bene tibi, Messalla!" clāmat et iterum pōculum haurit. Subitō collāpsus est.

"Non bene tibi, Tite!" inquit Gaius. "Ēheu! Nimis vīnī iam hausistī." Servī Titum vīnō oppressum auferunt. Titus erat bibendī arbiter pessimus omnium.

1	**plūs vīnī,** *more wine*	9	**modus, -ī,** m., *way, method*
4	**creō, -āre, -āvī, -ātus,** *to appoint*	16	**cūra, -ae,** f., *care*
7	**prūdentior,** *wiser*	17	**invocō, -āre, -āvī, -ātus,** *to invoke,*
	quam, adv., *than*		*call upon*
8	**prūdenter,** adv., *wisely, sensibly*	22	**collāpsus est,** *he collapsed*
	nimis, adv., *too much*	24	**pessimus, -a, -um,** *worst*

3 **poscō, poscere, poposcī,** *to demand, ask for*
8 **misceō, miscēre, miscuī, mixtus,** *to mix*
   sinō, sinere, sīvī, situs, *to allow*
21 **hauriō, haurīre, hausī, haustus,** *to drain*

Exercise 34a
Respondē Latīnē:

1. Quālēs corōnās convīvae induērunt?
2. Quid Titus in popīnā fēcerat?
3. Cūr est Gaius prūdentior quam aliī convīvae?
4. Quid Titus poscit?
5. Quis prīmum tālōs iēcit?
6. Quid Titus arripit?
7. Quem Titus invocat?
8. Quantum vīnī Titus hausit?

Building The Meaning
Adjectives: Positive, Comparative, and Superlative Degrees

Look at these sentences:

Positive:
Gaius est **laetus**.   *Gaius is **happy**.*

Comparative:
Messalla est **laetior** quam Gaius.   *Messalla is **happier** than Gaius.*

Superlative:
Titus est **laetissimus** omnium.   *Titus is **happiest** of all.*

Adjectives have *positive, comparative,* and *superlative degrees.* In the sentences above you can recognize the comparative by the letters **-ior** and the superlative by the letters **-issimus**.

The comparative can have several meanings; for example, **prūdentior** can mean *wiser, rather wise,* or *too wise.* In the first sense it is often followed by **quam**, *than*:

Nēmō est **prūdentior** <u>quam</u> Gaius.
*No one is **wiser** <u>than</u> Gaius.*

The superlative can also have several meanings; for example, **prūdentissimus** can mean *wisest* or *very wise.* In the first sense it is often used with a partitive genitive:

Gaius est **prūdentissimus** <u>omnium</u>.
*Gaius is **the wisest** <u>of all</u>.*

The ancient custom of drinking wine was connected to the religious mystery cult of Dionysus, the god of the vine, the grape, and of vegetation in general. Pictured is a detail from a Roman fresco depicting followers of Dionysus.
Fresco, Villa dei Misteri, Pompeii, Italy

Exercise 34b

Locate comparative or superlative forms in the following stories or exercises and translate the sentences in which they occur. Try some of the alternative translations given above:

1. 29:5–7
2. 31f:11–12
3. 33:24
4. 34:7

FORMS
Adjectives: Positive, Comparative, and Superlative

1. Study these further examples of positive, comparative, and superlative adjectives:

Positive	Comparative	Superlative
1st and 2nd declension adjectives:		
molest*us*, *-a*, *–um*	molest*ior*, molest*ius*	molest*issimus*, *-a*, *–um*
3rd declension adjectives:		
brev*is*, *-is*, *-e*, *short*	brev*ior*, brev*ius*	brev*issimus*, *-a*, *–um*
fēlīx, fēlīc*is*, *lucky*	fēlīc*ior*, fēlīc*ius*	fēlīc*issimus*, *-a*, *–um*
prūdēns, prūdent*is*, *wise*	prūdent*ior*, prūdent*ius*	prūdent*issimus*, *-a*, *–um*

2. Note what happens with adjectives that end in *-er:*

1st and 2nd declension adjectives ending in -er:		
miser, miser*a*, miser*um*	miser*ior*, miser*ius*	miser*rimus*, *-a*, *–um*
pulcher, pulchr*a*, pulchr*um*	pulchr*ior*, pulchr*ius*	pulcher*rimus*, *-a*, *–um*
3rd declension adjectives ending in -er:		
celer, celer*is*, celer*e*, *swift*	celer*ior*, celer*ius*	celer*rimus*, *-a*, *–um*
ācer, ācr*is*, ācr*e*, *keen*	ācr*ior*, ācr*ius*	ācer*rimus*, *-a*, *–um*

3. Most 3rd declension adjectives that end in *-lis* form their comparatives and superlatives regularly:

fidēl*is*, *-is*, *-e*, *faithful*	fidēl*ior*, fidēl*ius*	fidēl*issimus*, *-a*, *–um*

Exceptions: six 3rd declension adjectives that end in *-lis* form their superlatives irregularly, as does **facilis**:

facil*is*, *-is*, *-e*, *easy*	facil*ior*, facil*ius*	facil*limus*, *-a*, *–um*

The other adjectives are **difficilis**, *difficult*; **similis**, *similar*; **dissimilis**, *dissimilar*, **gracilis**, *slender*; and **humilis**, *humble*.

4. Note that you can usually recognize the superlative by the endings *-issimus*, *-rimus*, or *-limus*.

Exercise 34c

Form the comparatives and superlatives of the following 1st and 2nd
declension adjectives (meanings are given for adjectives you have not yet had):

1. longus, -a, -um
2. asper, aspera, asperum, *rough*
3. īrātus, -a, -um
4. scelestus, -a, -um
5. aeger, aegra, aegrum, *sick*

Exercise 34d

Form the comparatives and superlatives of the following 3rd declension
adjectives (meanings are given for adjectives you have not yet had):

1. ēlegāns, ēlegantis
2. pinguis, -is, -e
3. celeber, celebris, celebre
4. difficilis, -is, -e, *difficult*
5. nōbilis, -is, -e, *noble*

Irregular Comparative and Superlative Adjectives

Some very common adjectives are irregular in the comparative and superlative:

Positive	Comparative	Superlative
bonus, -a, -um, *good*	melior, melius, *better*	optimus, -a, -um, *best*
malus, -a, -um, *bad*	peior, peius, *worse*	pessimus, -a, -um, *worst*
magnus, -a, -um, *big*	maior, maius, *bigger*	maximus, -a, -um, *biggest*
parvus, -a, -um, *small*	minor, minus, *smaller*	minimus, -a, -um, *smallest*
multus, -a, -um, *much*	plūs,* *more*	plūrimus, -a, -um, *most, very much*
multī, -ae, -a, *many*	plūrēs, plūra, *more*	plūrimī, -ae, -a, *most, very many*

*Note that **plūs** is not an adjective but a neuter substantive, usually found with a partitive
genitive, e.g., Titus **plūs vīnī** bibit. *Titus drank **more (of the) wine**.*

Exercise 34e

Complete the comparison of the following adjectives by giving the missing items:

Positive	Comparative	Superlative
longus	_____	longissimus
_____	stultior	stultissimus
	melior	_____
multus	_____	_____
_____	_____	maximus
_____	ingentior	ingentissimus
_____	peior	_____
_____	pulchrior	pulcherrimus
	minor	_____

Adjectives: Case Endings of Comparatives and Superlatives

All superlatives have the same endings as the 1st and 2nd declension adjective **magn*us***, **magn*a***, **magn*um***, e.g., **laetissim*us***, **laetissim*a***, **laetissim*um***.

The comparatives have endings like those of 3rd declension nouns. Here are the forms of the comparative. Note in particular the neuter nominative and accusative singular form: **laet*ius***:

Number Case	Masc.	Fem.	Neut.
Singular			
Nominative	laetior	laetior	laetius
Genitive	laetiōr*is*	laetiōr*is*	laetiōr*is*
Dative	laetiōr*ī*	laetiōr*ī*	laetiōr*ī*
Accusative	laetiōr*em*	laetiōr*em*	laetius
Ablative	laetiōr*e*	laetiōr*e*	laetiōr*e*
Plural			
Nominative	laetiōr*ēs*	laetiōr*ēs*	laetiōr*a*
Genitive	laetiōr*um*	laetiōr*um*	laetiōr*um*
Dative	laetiōr*ibus*	laetiōr*ibus*	laetiōr*ibus*
Accusative	laetiōr*ēs*	laetiōr*ēs*	laetiōr*a*
Ablative	laetiōr*ibus*	laetiōr*ibus*	laetiōr*ibus*

Compare these forms with those of 3rd declension nouns and adjectives. Note the differences from the endings of 3rd declension adjectives.

NOTE:

When given in vocabulary lists, comparatives will be listed as follows: **melior, melior, melius**, gen., **meliōris**, *better*.

Exercise 34f

Change the italicized adjectives to the comparative and then to the superlative. Translate the new sentences. Try some of the alternative translations given above:

1. Gaius, quamquam *īrātus* erat, frātrem nōn reprehendit.
2. Aurēlia, quod erat *sollicita*, ancillās festīnāre iubēbat.
3. Puerī ā Cornēliō vīsī ad cubiculum *parvum* rediērunt.
4. Senātor pecūniam servīs *ignāvīs* nōn dederat.
5. Omnēs convīvae in lectīs *magnīs* accubuērunt.
6. Cēna ā coquō *bonō* parāta ab ancillīs efferēbātur.
7. Ancillae quae hūc illūc currēbant vīnum ad convīvās *fēlīcēs* portāvērunt.
8. Aliī convīvae corōnās rosārum *pulchrārum* induērunt.
9. Plaustrum *novum* ā Cornēliō ēmptum ad vīllam rūsticam missum est.
10. Pater puerī *molestī* mussāvit, "Numquam puerum peiōrem vīdī!"

Exercise 34g

Using story 34 and the presentation of comparative and superlative adjectives as guides, give the Latin for:

1. Titus had already drunk too much wine.
2. No one had drunk more wine.
3. No one is wiser than Gaius, for he always mixes water and wine wisely.
4. Titus was the luckiest when he threw the knucklebones.
5. Titus was very miserable when he collapsed.

Exercise 34h

Take parts, read aloud, and translate:

REFLECTIONS AFTER DINNER

Postquam convīvae discessērunt, nē tum quidem cubitum iērunt Cornēlius et
Aurēlia, nam multa dē convīviō inter sē dīcēbant.

AURĒLIA:	Placuitne tibi cēna, Gaī?
CORNĒLIUS:	Ita vērō! Tū quidem omnia optimē ēgistī. Coquus nōbīs
	cēnam parāvit optimam quae ab omnibus laudābātur. 5
	Quam ingēns erat ille porcus! Maiōrem porcum numquam
	vīdī. Glīrēs quoque suāviōrēs numquam ēdī.
AURĒLIA:	Cūr tam sērō advēnit Titus? Quid eī acciderat?
CORNĒLIUS:	Nihil! Amīcō veterī in popīnā occurrerat!
AURĒLIA:	ln popīnā? Ubi? 10
CORNĒLIUS:	Prope Forum Rōmānum.
AURĒLIA:	Omnēs popīnae sunt foedae, sed foedissimae omnium sunt
	popīnae prope Forum sitae.
CORNĒLIUS:	Ita vērō! Iam ēbrius erat cum in trīclīnium irrūpit. Omnēs
	convīvae erant īrātissimī. 15
AURĒLIA:	Fit in diēs molestior.
CORNĒLIUS:	Sed hāc nocte erat molestissimus.
AURĒLIA:	Quōmodo?
CORNĒLIUS:	Missī sunt tālī; arbiter bibendī creātus est ille; iussit duōs
	cyathōs aquae et trēs cyathōs vīnī! 20
AURĒLIA:	Paulātim igitur fīēbat magis ēbrius?
CORNĒLIUS:	Minimē! Statim factus est maximē ēbrius, nam nīl nisi
	merum bibit! "Bene tibi, Gaī!" clāmat et, "Bene tibi,
	Messalla!" tum collāpsus est vīnō oppressus. Hominem
	magis ēbrium quam Titum numquam vīdī. 25
AURĒLIA:	Quid tum accidit?
CORNĒLIUS:	Iussī servōs eum lectīcā portāre domum quam celerrimē.
AURĒLIA:	Fortasse crās fīet vir vīnō abstinentissimus!
CORNĒLIUS:	Fortasse!

1 **nē...quidem,** *not even*
2 **convīvium, -ī,** n., *feast, banquet*
3 **placeō, -ēre, -uī** + dat., *to please*
4 **optimē,** adv., *very well, excellently*
7 **suāvis, -is, -e,** *sweet, delightful*
9 **vetus, veteris,** *old*
12 **foedus, -a, -um,** *filthy, disgusting*
14 **ēbrius, -a, -um,** *drunk*
16 **in diēs,** *every day, day by day*

20 **cyathus, -ī,** m., *small ladle, measure (of wine)*
21 **paulātim,** adv., *gradually*
    magis, adv., *more*
22 **maximē,** adv., *very much, very*
    nīl, *nothing*
27 **quam celerrimē,** adv., *as quickly as possible*
28 **vīnō abstinēns,** *refraining from wine, abstemious*

    16 **fīō, fierī, factus sum,** irreg., *to become, be made, be done, happen*

Exercise 34i

Here is a famous poem by Catullus (ca. 84–54 B.C.), in which he extends a dinner invitation to his friend Fabullus. This is a piece of original Latin that you can easily read at this stage with the help of the vocabulary given below. After reading the poem consider whether the invitation to dinner is serious or facetious.

Read aloud and translate:

> Cēnābis bene, mī Fabulle, apud mē
> paucīs, sī tibi dī favent, diēbus,
> sī tēcum attuleris bonam atque magnam
> cēnam, nōn sine candidā puellā
> et vīnō et sale et omnibus cachinnīs.   5
> Haec sī, inquam, attuleris, venuste noster,
> cēnābis bene: nam tuī Catullī
> plēnus sacculus est arāneārum.
> Sed contrā accipiēs merōs amōrēs
> seu quid suāvius ēlegantiusvest: 10
> nam unguentum dabo, quod meae puellae
> dōnārunt Venerēs Cupīdinēsque,
> quod tū cum olfaciēs, deōs rogābis,
> tōtum ut tē faciant, Fabulle, nāsum.

           —Catullus 13

2 **paucī, -ae, -a,** *few*
4 **candidus, -a, -um,** *white, fair-skinned, beautiful*
5 **sal, salis,** m., *salt, wit*
6 **venuste noster,** *my charming fellow*
8 **sacculus, -ī,** m., *small bag (used for holding money)*
    arānea, -ae, f., *cobweb*
9 **contrā,** adv., *in return*
    merus, -a, -um, *pure*
10 **seu = sīve,** conj., *or if*

    quid suāvius ēlegantiusvest (= **ēlegantiusve est**), *there is anything sweeter or more elegant*
    -ve, enclitic conj., *or*
12 **dōnō, -āre, -āvī, -ātus,** *to give*
    dōnārunt = dōnāvērunt
    Venus, Veneris, f., *Venus (the goddess of love)*
    Cupīdō, Cupīdinis, m., *Cupid (the son of Venus)*
14 **ut tē faciant,** *that they make you*

CHAPTER 35

CRIME

Postquam Aurēlia cubitum iit, Cornēlius adhūc in ātriō manēbat sollicitus. Eucleidēs enim māne ierat domum frātris quī in colle Quirīnālī habitābat. Iam media nox erat neque Eucleidēs domum redierat. Quid eī acciderat?

Tandem intrāvit Eucleidēs, sanguine aspersus. Cornēlius, "Dī immortālēs! Quid tibi accidit?" clāmāvit. Eucleidēs nihil respondit; ad terram ceciderat. Statim servī ad ātrium   5 vocātī celerrimē concurrērunt. Eucleidēs in lectō positus est et vulnera eius lauta atque ligāta sunt. Diū iacēbat immōbilis. Tandem animum recuperāvit et lentē oculōs aperuit. Postquam aliquid vīnī bibit, rem tōtam explicāvit.

"Hodiē māne, dum in urbem dēscendō, poētae cuidam occurrī cui nōmen est Marcus Valerius Mārtiālis. Breviōre itinere mē dūxit ad eam īnsulam in quā habitat frāter meus.   10 Plūrima dē praedōnibus huius urbis mihi nārrāvit. Ego tamen vix eī crēdidī. Sed, ubi īnsulae iam appropinquābāmus, hominēs quōsdam in popīnam intrantēs cōnspeximus.

"'Cavē illōs!' inquit Mārtiālis. 'Illī sunt praedōnēs scelestissimī. Nocte sōlus per hās viās ambulāre nōn dēbēs.'"

(continued)

2 **collis, collis,** gen. pl., **collium,** m.,
    hill
   Quirīnālis, -is, -e, *Quirinal (referring
     to the Quirinal Hill, one of the seven
     hills of Rome)*

4 **deus, -ī,** m., *god*
6 **vulnus, vulneris,** n., *wound*
7 **ligō, -āre, -āvī, -ātus,** *to bind up*

11 **crēdō, crēdere, crēdidī, crēditus** + dat., *to trust, believe*

Exercise 35a
Respondē Latīnē:

1. Cūr Cornēlius sollicitus in ātriō manēbat?
2. Quō māne ierat Eucleidēs?
3. Quid fēcērunt servī Cornēliī, postquam Eucleidēs cecidit?
4. Quid fēcit Eucleidēs, postquam tandem animum recuperāvit?
5. Cui occurrit Eucleidēs, dum in urbem dēscendit?

"Tōtum diem apud frātrem meum mānsī. Post cēnam optimam domum redīre 15
cōnstituī. Quamquam nox erat, nihil perīculī timēbam. Sēcūrus igitur per Subūram
ambulābam cum subitō ē popīnā quādam sē praecipitāvērunt duo hominēs quī fūstēs
ferēbant. Timōre affectus, celerius ambulābam. Facile tamen mē cōnsecūtī sunt. Ab
alterō percussus sum, sed baculō mē fortissimē dēfendī. Tum ā tergō ab alterō correptus
ad terram cecidī. Mihi est adēmptum baculum, adēmpta pecūnia. Abiērunt illī rīdentēs. 20
Diū prōnus in lutō iacēbam. Tandem surrēxī et summā difficultāte domum rediī."
    Cornēlius, "Doleō quod vulnera gravia accēpistī. Stultissimus tamen fuistī."
    Cui Eucleidēs, "Ita vērō, domine! Sed iam prūdentior sum. Nōn iterum nocte sōlus
per viās urbis ambulābō."

16 **sēcūrus, -a, -um,** *carefree, unconcerned*
    Subūra, -ae, f., *Subura (a section of*
        Rome off the Forum, known for its
        night life)
17 **fūstis, fūstis,** gen. pl., **fūstium,** m.,
        club, cudgel
18 **timor, timōris,** m., *fear*
    affectus, -a, -um, *affected, overcome*

    celerius, adv., *more quickly*
    facile, adv., *easily*
    cōnsecūtī sunt, *they overtook*
19 **fortissimē,** adv., *most/very bravely*
    tergum, -ī, n., *back, rear*
21 **prōnus, -a, -um,** *face down*
    summus, -a, -um, *greatest, very great*
22 **gravis, -is, -e,** *heavy, serious*

19 **percutiō, percutere, percussī, percussus,** *to strike*
    corripiō, corripere, corripuī, correptus, *to seize, grab*
20 **adimō, adimere, adēmī, adēmptus** + dat., *to take away (from)*

Respondē Latīnē:

1. Quibus occurrit Eucleidēs, dum domum redit?
2. Quid fēcērunt praedōnēs, postquam Eucleidem cōnsecūtī sunt?
3. Quid est perīculōsissimum nocte facere?

BUILDING THE MEANING
Comparisons

Latin sentences in which a direct comparison is made may take one of two patterns:

Sextus est molestior **quam** Marcus.   *Sextus is more annoying **than** Marcus.*
Sextus est molestior **Marcō.**

In the first example, **quam** (*than*) is used with the same case on either side of it (i.e.,
molestior and **Marcus** are both nominative). In the second example, no word for "than"
is used, and **Marcō** is ablative.

Sometimes an ablative (e.g., **multō,** *much*; **paulō,** *a little*) is used with comparatives to
indicate the degree of difference. This is called the *ablative of degree of difference*:

Sextus est **multō** molestior quam   *Sextus is more annoying **by much** than*
    Marcus.   *Marcus.*
Sextus est **multō** molestior Marcō.   *Sextus is **much** more annoying than Marcus.*

Exercise 35b

Using the following lists of names and comparative adjectives, make up pairs of sentences that express comparisons according to the patterns in the discussion above:

> Marcus, Sextus, Aurēlia, Cornēlius, Cornēlia, Flāvia, Eucleidēs, Titus, Dāvus, Pseudolus
>
> minor, maior, pulchrior, īrātior, laetior, miserior, scelestior, prūdentior, stultior, dīligentior

> **dīligēns, dīligentis,** *diligent, painstaking, thorough*

Exercise 35c

Using the names and adjectives from Exercise 35b above, and changing each adjective to superlative, make one sentence for each name, according to the following examples:

> Dāvus est dīligentissimus omnium.
> Flāvia est miserrima omnium.

Exercise 35d

Read aloud and translate:

1. Hic servus est ignāvissimus omnium. Nūllum servum ignāviōrem habet Cornēlius.
2. Cornēliī coquus est optimus omnium. Nēmō meliōrem coquum habet quam Cornēlius.
3. Līberī laetissimī sunt quod crās fēriātī erunt.
4. Mārtiālis Eucleide est multō prūdentior.
5. Ego semper habeō multō minus pecūniae quam tū.
6. Marcus est maximus līberōrum, Sextus est minimus.
7. Flāvia est paulō minor Marcō, sed multō maior Cornēliā.
8. Ad amīcum epistulam longissimam mittam, ad frātrem breviōrem.
9. Dāvus est servus optimus. Sine dubiō nēmō est dīligentior.
10. Coquus plūs cibī in culīnā parābat.

▬▬ ▬▬ ▬▬ ▬▬

Exēgī monumentum aere perennius. *I have erected a monument more lasting than bronze.* (Horace, *Odes* III.30.1)
Fāmā nihil est celerius. *Nothing is swifter than rumor.* (adapted from Vergil, *Aeneid* IV.174)
Mea mihi cōnscientia plūris est quam omnium sermō. *My conscience is more to me than what the world says.* (Cicero, *Letters to Atticus* XII.28.2)

▬▬ ▬▬ ▬▬ ▬▬

Adverbs

In Chapter 13, adverbs were presented as words that expand the meaning of a sentence by modifying verbs, other adverbs, or adjectives. Sometimes adverbs are formed from adjectives, but many adverbs are not.

Exercise 35e
In story 35, locate the following adverbs that are not formed from adjectives, and tell what word each modifies:

1. 35:1, adhūc.
2. 35:2, māne.
3. 35:2, iam.
4. 35:4, tandem.
5. 35:5, statim.
6. 35:7, diū.
7. 35:9, hodiē māne.
8. 35:11, vix.
9. 35:14, nōn.
10. 35:23, iterum.

FORMS
Adverbs: Positive

1. Adverbs may be formed from adjectives of the 1st and 2nd declensions by adding *-ē* to the base of the adjective:

Adjective	**Adverb**
strēnu*us*, *-a*, *-um*	strēnu*ē*, *strenuously, hard*

    But note:

bon*us*, *-a*, *-um*	ben*e*, *well*
mal*us*, *-a*, *-um*	mal*e*, *badly*

2. Adverbs may be formed from adjectives of the 3rd declension by adding *-iter* to the base of the adjective or *-er* to bases ending in *-nt*:

brev*is*, *-is*, *-e*	brev*iter*, *briefly*
prūdēns, prūdent*is*	prūdent*er*, *wisely*

    But note:

facil*is*, *-is*, *-e*	facil*e*, *easily.*

Exercise 35f

Give the adverbs (and their meanings) that may be formed from these adjectives:

1. **ignāvus, -a, -um,** *lazy*
2. **fortis, -is, -e,** *brave*
3. **lentus, -a, -um,** *slow*
4. **neglegēns, neglegentis,** *careless*
5. **miser, misera, miserum,** *unhappy*
6. **ferōx, ferōcis,** *fierce*
7. **gravis, -is, -e,** *serious*
8. **laetus, -a, -um,** *happy*
9. **vehemēns, vehementis,** *violent*
10. **īrātus, -a, -um,** *angry*
11. **celer, celeris, celere,** *swift*
12. **pulcher, pulchra, pulchrum,** *beautiful*

Adverbs: Comparative and Superlative

Adverbs also have comparative and superlative forms.

The neuter singular comparative adjective (ending in **-ius**) is used as the comparative adverb.

The superlative adjective ends in **-us**, **-a**, **-um**; the superlative adverb ends in **-ē**. Study these examples:

laet**ē**, *happily*	laet**ius**	laet**issimē**
fēlīc**iter**, *luckily*	fēlīc**ius**	fēlīc**issimē**
celer**iter**, *quickly*	celer**ius**	celer**rimē**
prūdent**er**, *wisely*	prūdent**ius**	prūdent**issimē**

Note the following as well:

diū, *for a long time*	diūt**ius**	diūt**issimē**
saepe, *often*	saep**ius**	saep**issimē**
sērō, *late*	sēr**ius**	sēr**issimē**

Some adverbs are irregular. Compare these forms with their related adjectives:

bene, *well*	**melius,** *better*	**optimē,** *best*
male, *badly*	**peius,** *worse*	**pessimē,** *worst*
facile, *easily*	**facilius,** *more easily*	**facillimē,** *most easily*
magnopere, *greatly*	**magis,** *more*	**maximē,** *most*
paulum, *little*	**minus,** *less*	**minimē,** *least*
multum, *much*	**plūs,** *more*	**plūrimum,** *most*

Be sure to learn these forms thoroughly.

The comparative adverb, like the comparative adjective, can have several meanings; for example, **lentius** can mean *more slowly, rather slowly,* or *too slowly.* In the first sense it may be followed by a comparison using **quam** or the ablative without **quam** (cf. note on comparisons, p. 72):

> Eucleidēs lentius **quam** puerī ambulat.
> Eucleidēs lentius **puerīs** ambulat.
> *Eucleides walks more slowly **than** the boys.*

The ablative of degree of difference may be used with comparative adverbs:

> Eucleidēs **multō** lentius quam puerī ambulat.
> Eucleidēs **multō** lentius puerīs ambulat.
> *Eucleides walks **much** more slowly than the boys.*

The superlative adverb, like the superlative adjective, also has more than one meaning; for example, **lentissimē** can mean *most slowly* or *very slowly.* In the first sense it is often followed by a partitive genitive:

> Dāvus lentissimē **omnium** ambulat.
> *Davus walks most slowly **of all**.*

Exercise 35g
Study the forms in the completed columns and then fill in the other columns. Be sure you can give the meaning of every form:

Adjectives			Adverbs		
longus	longior	longissimus	longē	_____	_____
lentus	_____	_____	lentē	lentius	lentissimē
pulcher	pulchrior	pulcherrimus	pulchrē	_____	_____
fortis	fortior	fortissimus	fortiter	_____	_____
brevis	brevior	brevissimus	breviter	_____	_____
facilis	_____	_____	facile	facilius	facillimē
certus	certior	certissimus	certē	_____	_____
fidēlis	_____	_____	fidēliter	fidēlius	fidēlissimē
rēctus	_____	_____	rēctē	rēctius	rēctissimē
ferōx	ferōcior	ferōcissimus	ferōciter	_____	_____

> **longē,** adv., *far*
> **certus, -a, -um,** *certain*
> **rēctus, -a, -um,** *right, proper*

Exercise 35h

Read aloud and translate. Try some of the alternative translations suggested above:

1. Diūtius manēre mihi nōn licet. Necesse est mihi celerrimē ad urbem redīre.
2. Hic puer optimē omnium scrībit.
3. Nēmō celerius quam frāter meus currere potest.
4. Sextus paulō celerius Marcō currere potest.
5. Dē perīculīs viārum saepissimē audīvimus.
6. Per viās urbis lentē ambulāre volō.
7. Cornēlius īrātissimus erat quod frāter sērius advēnit.
8. Titus plūrimum bibit.
9. Eucleidī praedōnēs pecūniam adēmērunt atque quam celerrimē discessērunt.
10. Sextus in hortō quam diūtissimē lūdēbat.

> **quam** + a superlative adjective or adverb = *as...as possible*, e.g., **quam celerrimē**, *as quickly as possible*

Exercise 35i

Using story 35 and the presentation of adverbs as guides, give the Latin for:

1. Eucleides returned home very late.
2. He lay motionless a long time and regained his senses rather slowly.
3. Eucleides had walked through the Subura too bravely and had feared no danger.
4. When two men hurled themselves out of a bar, Eucleides ran as quickly as possible.
5. He lay in the mud a very long time.

Canis timidus vehementius lātrat quam mordet. *A timid dog barks more fiercely than he bites.* (adapted from Q. Curtius Rufus, *Exploits of Alexander* VII.4.13)
ALTIUS, CITIUS, FORTIUS *Higher, faster, stronger.* (Motto of the Olympic Games)

ADDITIONAL READING:
The Romans Speak for Themselves: Book II: "Violence in the Streets of Rome,"
pages 33–39.

CICERO, CAESAR, AND THE COLLAPSE OF THE REPUBLIC

Marcus Tullius Cicero reached the peak of his political career in 63 B.C., when he took office as one of the consuls. As an equestrian from Arpinum and a **novus homō**, he had plied his skills as an orator to fuel his rise to the top magistracy. His main opponent in the election had been the ruthless aristocrat Lucius Sergius Catilina, who conspired to assassinate Cicero as part of a plot to overthrow the government and seize power by force. In a series of actions that one can track in Cicero's four famous orations *Against Catiline (In Catilinam)*, the consul drove Catiline out of the city, publicized the details of his plot, and saw to the execution of a group of co-conspirators. Catiline attempted to continue his rebellion from his military base in Etruria. He died, however, in a battle with the Roman army in 62 B.C. Cicero thereafter earnestly advocated a "concord of orders" (**concordia ōrdinum**), the joining together of senators and equestrians to work in support of the republican constitution.

Cicero and the magistrates discovering the tomb of Archimedes
Oil on canvas by Bejamin West, Christie's, London, England

At this point in time, 62 B.C., Pompey returned from his successful campaigns in the East and, contrary to the fears of many, disbanded his army. But many Senators feared the growing power of the popular military hero and refused to approve land grants to Pompey's veterans. He formed a three-man political alliance (**factiō**) with Caesar and Crassus, whose own ambitions were being blocked by the same people. Their alliance is known as the First Triumvirate. Caesar, with the help of Pompey's armed veterans, won passage in 59 B.C. of the veterans' land bill. Caesar's reward for his key effort in this success was a five-year term as proconsular governor of the province of Cisalpine Gaul and Illyricum, which gave him the opportunity to conquer Transalpine Gaul. Crassus obtained financial concessions for wealthy equestrians who backed him.

During the first year of his proconsulship, Caesar led his legions to a rapid succession of victories. By 50 B.C., he had all of Transalpine Gaul under his legions' control and had annexed it as a new province of Rome's empire. Further, he crossed the English Channel and attacked Britain.

While Caesar was away campaigning in Gaul, the political scene in Rome grew violent as **populārēs** and **optimātēs** battled one another for power. One victim who survived physically was Cicero, but his career as a political leader and the moderate voice of the **optimātēs** was destroyed.

The death of Julia, Pompey's wife and Caesar's daughter, weakened the triumvirate in 54 B.C. In the following year, the **factiō** broke apart completely when Crassus was killed in battle against the Parthian Empire in Syria. Violence in the streets escalated as political mobs beset one another, armed factions scuffled, and mass riots erupted. In 52 B.C. the Senate authorized Pompey to quell the rioting in Rome by using his troops and then got him elected sole consul. Leading **optimātēs** in the Senate steadily pressed him to turn against the popular hero Caesar, whom Pompey increasingly viewed as his chief rival now that Crassus was dead.

In January of 49 B.C. the Senate issued a **senātūs cōnsultum ultimum** empowering Pompey to direct Caesar to disband his army. Caesar responded by leading his legions across the Rubicon River, the northern boundary of Italy, and beginning an advance toward Rome. Civil war erupted with Caesar fighting Pompey and the leading **optimātēs**, who were now backing him in the Senate.

As Caesar rapidly advanced toward Rome, Pompey and his allies fled to Greece, where Pompey could recruit and train a new army. His plan, apparently, was to be able to attack Caesar in Italy with both this eastern army and his troops stationed in Spain. Once Pompey had abandoned Italy, Caesar, with almost no opposition, became the master of Rome.

Caesar began to build a fleet so that he could go after Pompey. While his ships were being prepared, he crossed over land into Spain and quickly subdued Pompey's army there. Thus he removed the threat of being surrounded. Then he returned to Rome, secured the consulship, and set sail for Greece. After a nearly disastrous attempt to defeat Pompey in a siege at Dyrrhacchium, Caesar was forced to withdraw to Thessaly, with

Pompey in pursuit. On the plain of Pharsalus in August of 48 B.C., however, Caesar's battle-hardened legions routed Pompey's larger army. Pompey managed to escape and flee to Egypt, in hope of finding refuge there, but the agents of King Ptolemy XIII murdered him and sent his head to Caesar.

Caesar became dictator in October of the same year and followed Pompey's trail to Egypt, where he began a three-year series of campaigns that would finalize his victory as the head of the Roman state. In Alexandria, Caesar fought against King Ptolemy and deposed him. He then set Cleopatra on the throne to assure that Egypt would be friendly to Rome. From there Caesar advanced to Asia Minor and defeated Pharnaces, son of Mithridates, in a war that lasted only days. This victory, the story goes, prompted Caesar's dispatch to Rome, "I came, I saw, I conquered" (**Vēnī, vīdī, vīcī**). In 46 B.C. Caesar celebrated his Gallic, Alexandrian, Pontic, and African triumphs, all in the span of one month. Gigantic parades celebrated Caesar's achievements, displaying the rich spoils from conquered lands and famous prisoners of war and raised his popularity to new heights. The following year, Caesar went once more to Spain, where he wiped out the last of the resistance forces, which were under the command of Pompey's sons.

Territory of the Late Roman Republic

80 CHAPTER 35

Julius Caesar
Compidoglio, Rome, Italy

In 44 B.C. Caesar was the unchallenged head of the Roman state. He accepted the title "dictator for life" (**dictātor perpetuus**). As dictator Caesar continued his program of reforms. He granted Roman citizenship to people in Gallia Narbonensis and sent Romans from the city to create colonies in the provinces, thus increasing his number of clients. There was also a public works program: expanding the Forum, building the Basilica Julia and the temple of Venus Genetrix, and rebuilding the Curia. Through the so-called Julian reform, Caesar adapted an Egyptian solar calendar, which we still use today in modified form, for use in Rome.

Caesar made it increasingly clear that he intended to rule Rome himself and not to bring back the Senate-dominated republican constitution. He weakened the old guard's power in the Senate by appointing a diverse group of new senators from the equestrian order and from cities in other parts of Italy. The **optimātēs** resented Caesar's evident desire to be king, especially when they saw him put on a purple robe and sit on a golden chair. Romans had hated the title "king" (**rēx**) since the ouster of Tarquinius Superbus and could not easily accept the thought that one man might change the government of the free city-state of Rome into a monarchy, although the old form of government was ill-suited for ruling an empire. On the Ides of March, 44 B.C., a group of Roman senators, armed with daggers and led by Gaius Cassius and Marcus Brutus, assassinated Caesar under the gaze of Pompey's statue. By their plot they hoped to rescue the Republic from the threat of the would-be tyrant.

WORD STUDY IX

Adjective Suffixes *-ōsus, -idus,* and *-bilis*

When added to the base of a Latin noun, the suffix *-ōsus, -ōsa, -ōsum* creates an adjective meaning *full of…*:

> **fābula, -ae,** f., *story*
> base: **fābul-** + *-ōsus* = **fābulōsus, -a, -um,** *"full of story,"* legendary

English words derived from these adjectives commonly end in *-ous* (sometimes *-ious*, *-eous*, or *-ose*), e.g., *fabulous*, which means "astonishing" (as in legend or myth).

Exercise 1

Give the Latin adjective ending in *-ōsus* for each of the nouns below and give its English derivative. Give also the meaning of the Latin adjective and its English derivative. Is the meaning of the English derivative the same as that of the Latin adjective?

1. **numerus, -ī,** m.
2. **onus, oneris,** n.
3. **pretium, -ī,** n. (*in the derivative* t *changes to* c)
4. **glōria, -ae,** f.
5. **cūra, -ae,** f.
6. **labor, labōris,** m.
7. **tumultus, -ūs,** m. (*add* u *to base:* **tumultu-**)
8. **iocus, -ī,** m. (*derivative begins with* j *and ends in* -ose)
9. **perīculum, -ī,** n. (*derivative drops* -cu- *from* **perīculum**)
10. **verbum, -ī,** n., *word*

The addition of the suffix *-idus, -ida, -idum* to the base of the present infinitive of a Latin verb (often of the 2nd conjugation) creates a Latin adjective meaning *tending to…* or *inclined to…*:

> **timēre,** *to fear*
> infinitive base: **tim-** + *-idus* = **timidus, -a, -um,** *"tending to fear,"* afraid

Exercise 2

For each Latin verb below, give the Latin adjective ending in *-idus* and give its English derivative. Use the English derivative in a sentence that illustrates its meaning:

1. **sordēre,** *to be dirty*
2. **stupēre,** *to be astonished*
3. **placēre,** *to please, to be agreeable*
4. **vīvere,** *to be alive, to live*
5. **valēre,** *to be strong*
6. **rapere,** *to seize, to tear away*
7. **lūcēre,** *to be light, to shine*
8. **frīgēre,** *to be cold*

The suffix *-bilis, -bilis, -bile*, when added to the base of the present infinitive (sometimes the perfect passive participial stem) of a Latin verb, creates an adjective that usually means *able to be....* In adjectives formed from 1st conjugation verbs, the suffix is preceded by **-ā-**; in adjectives formed from verbs of other conjugations, the suffix is preceded by **-i-**:

> **laudāre,** *to praise*
> infinitive base: **laud- + -ā- + -bilis = laudābilis, -is, -e,** *"able to be praised,"*
>   *praiseworthy*

> **reprehendere,** *to scold*
> perfect passive participial stem: **reprehēns- + -i- + -bilis = reprehēnsibilis, -is,**
>   **-e,** *"able to be scolded,"* *blameworthy*

English words derived from these Latin adjectives generally end in *-ble*, e.g., *laudable* and *reprehensible*.

Note that whether the English word ends in *-able* or *-ible* is usually determined by the conjugation of the original Latin verb: *-able* usually comes from a Latin verb of the 1st conjugation and *-ible* from a verb of one of the other conjugations.

Exercise 3

For each of the following Latin verbs, give the adjective ending in **-bilis**, and give the English derivative and its meaning. Use the infinitive base in Nos. 1–9, and the perfect passive participial stem in No. 10.

1. audīre
2. crēdere
3. excūsāre
4. habitāre
5. legere

6. portāre
7. revocāre
8. vincere
9. vulnerāre
10. vidēre

N.B.: On some Latin adjectives (and their English derivatives), the suffix **-bilis** means *able to....* rather than *able to be....* The following verbs produce adjectives of this type:

11. dēlectāre
12. stāre
13. terrēre

Latin in the Law

One of the greatest achievements of the Romans was the spread of the rule of law throughout their empire. From its first codification in the Law of the Twelve Tables in the fifth century B.C. to its ultimate expression in the *Corpus iuris civilis* of the emperor Justinian in the sixth century A.D., Roman law formed the foundation for the development of modern legal systems. The rights of inheritance, the notion of private property, the sanctity of contracts—these and many other common legal concepts have their origins in Roman law.

It is not surprising, therefore, that Latin words and phrases are still in use in the practice of law today. Some of these Latin legal expressions have been incorporated into everyday English. For example, an *alibi* (Latin for *elsewhere*) in law is a claim that the accused was not at the scene of the crime and is therefore not guilty; in everyday language, however, the word refers to any sort of excuse.

Exercise 4

Look up the italicized expressions in an English dictionary (or a law dictionary) and explain the meaning of each of the following phrases:

1. a *prima facie* case
2. a plea of *nolo contendere*
3. to serve a *subpoena*
4. the *onus probandi* of the prosecution
5. a writ of *habeas corpus*
6. the responsibility of the school *in loco parentis*
7. the necessary *corpus delicti*
8. an *ex post facto* law
9. a *bona fide* (*mala fide*) offer
10. an offense *malum in se* (*malum prohibitum*)
11. *de facto* (*de jure*) segregation
12. testimony of an *amicus curiae*
13. caught *in flagrante delicto*
14. a claim that the accused is *non compos mentis*

Exercise 5

Give an example to illustrate each of these Latin legal maxims:

1. Ignorantia legis neminem excusat. *Ignorance of the law is no excuse.*
2. Caveat emptor. *Let the buyer beware.*
3. Res ipsa loquitur. *The matter speaks for itself.*
4. De minimis non curat lex. *The law does not concern itself with trifles.*
5. Nemo est supra leges. *No one is above the law.*
6. Publicum bonum privato est praeferendum. *Public good is to be preferred over private.*
7. Potior est conditio possidentis. *Possession is nine-tenths of the law.*
8. Qui tacet consentire videtur. *Silence is taken as consent.*
9. Qui facit per alium, facit per se. *He who acts through another acts by himself.*
10. Nemo debet bis vexari pro una et eadem causa. *No one ought to be tried twice for one and the same reason.*

CHAPTER 36

A LETTER

Cornēlia Flāviae S.D.

Hodiē Nōnīs Novembribus illam epistulam accēpī quam tū scrīpsistī Kalendīs
Novembribus. Eam iterum iterumque lēgī, quod tē maximē dēsīderō. Quam celeriter
tua epistula hūc advēnit! Quīnque modo diēbus! Heri aliam epistulam Brundisiī scrīptam
accēpit pater meus. Haec epistula ā Valeriō prīdiē Īdūs Octōbrēs scrīpta Rōmam post 5
vīgintī diēs advēnit!

Valerius, ut scīs, est adulēscēns pulcher et strēnuus quī cum patre suō diū in Bīthȳniā
morātus est. Nunc in Italiam Brundisium regressus est. Brundisiō Īdibus Novembribus
proficīscētur et Rōmam a.d. iii Kal. Dec. adveniet.

Quam libenter eum rūrsus vidēbō! Sānē tamen multō libentius tē vidēbō ubi tū 10
Rōmam veniēs! Tum tē libentissimē nōs omnēs accipiēmus!

(continued)

Note that the Romans did not start a letter with "Dear So-and-So." They put the name of
the person sending it (in the nominative case) followed by the name of the person to whom
it was sent (in the dative case), and after that the letters **S.D.** (**salūtem dīcit,** *sends greetings*)
or **S.P.D.** (**salūtem plūrimam dīcit,** *sends fondest greetings*). There was no signature at the
end, but simply the word **valē.**

2 **Nōnīs Novembribus,** *on November 5*
  Kalendīs Novembribus, *on*
    November 1
3 **-que,** enclitic conj., *and*
4 **hūc,** adv., *here, to here*
  Brundisiī, *at Brundisium*
5 **prīdiē,** adv. + acc., *on the day before*
  prīdiē Īdūs Octōbrēs, *on October 14*
6 **vīgintī,** *twenty*
7 **adulēscēns, adulēscentis,** m., *young
  man*

8 **morātus est,** *he has stayed*
  regressus est, *he has returned*
  Īdibus Novembribus, *on November 13*
9 **proficīscētur,** *he will set out*
  **a.d. iii Kal. Dec. = ante diem
    tertium Kalendās Decembrēs,** *on
    November 29*
10 **libenter,** adv., *gladly*
  rūrsus, adv., *again*
  sānē, adv., *certainly, of course*

Exercise 36a
Respondē Latīnē:

1. Quō diē Cornēlia epistulam Flāviae accēpit?
2. Quis epistulam ad patrem Cornēliae mīsit?
3. Ubi nunc est Valerius?
4. Quem Cornēlia libentissimē vidēbit?

In epistulā tuā multa rogābās dē perīculīs urbānīs. Abhinc trēs diēs in īnsulā quādam magnum incendium vīdimus. Nihil miserābilius umquam vīdī. Quamquam enim maior pars incolārum ē perīculō effūgit, māter et duo līberī quōs in tertiō tabulātō cōnspeximus effugere nōn poterant. Ēheu! Hī miserī flammīs oppressī sunt. Ubi dē illā mātre et līberīs cōgitō, valdē commoveor. 15

Heri vesperī Eucleidēs noster, ab urbe domum rediēns, duōs hominēs ē popīnā quādam exeuntēs vīdit. Quī hominēs, ubi Eucleidem cōnspexērunt, statim eum secūtī sunt. Eucleidēs effugere cōnātus est, sed frūstrā. Quō celerius currēbat ille, eō celerius currēbant hominēs. Facile eum cōnsecūtī sunt. Ō miserrimum Eucleidem! Ā praedōnibus 20 correptus ac fūstibus percussus, gravissimē vulnerātus est. Vix quidem sē domum trāxit.

Sed dē perīculīs satis! Hodiē māter pulcherrimam mihi pallam ēmit, quae mihi valdē placuit. Sed trīstis sum quod lānam semper trahō. Trīstissima autem sum quod tē nōn videō. Fortasse tū Rōmam cum patre veniēs. Nōnne tū patrī hoc persuādēbis? Tē plūrimum dēsīderō. Scrībe, sīs, quam saepissimē. Valē! 25

18 **quī hominēs,** *which/those men*
    secūtī sunt, *(they) followed*
19 **cōnātus est,** *(he) tried*

quō celerius...eō celerius..., *the faster...the faster...*
23 **trīstis, -is, -e,** *sad*
25 **sīs = sī vīs,** *if you wish, please*

24 **persuādeō, persuādēre, persuāsī, persuāsus,** *to make something* (acc.) *agreeable to someone* (dat.); *to persuade someone of something*

Respondē Latīnē:

1. Dē quibus rēbus Flāvia in epistulā rogābat?
2. Quid Cornēlia in īnsulā quādam vīdit?
3. Quid Cornēliae placuit?
4. Cūr est Cornēlia trīstis?

FORMS
Dates

In each month there were three special days from which Romans calculated all dates:

The Kalends (**Kalendae, -ārum,** f. pl.) were always on the 1st of the month.
The Nones (**Nōnae, -ārum,** f. pl.) usually fell on the 5th of the month.
The Ides (**Īdūs, Īduum,** f. pl.) usually fell on the 13th of the month.

But in March, May, July, and October, the Nones were on the 7th and the Ides were on the 15th.

Actual dates were expressed in the following ways:

1. The ablative of time when indicates that the date coincides with one of the special days:

    Kalendīs Aprīlibus, *on April 1*   **Nōnīs Februāriīs,** *on February 5*
    Īdibus Mārtiīs, *on March 15*

Compare **eō diē,** *on that day.*

2. The word **prīdiē** + *accusative* indicates the day before one of the special days:

> **prīdiē Kalendās Maiās** (lit., *on the day before May 1*), *on April 30*
> **prīdiē Īdūs Octōbrēs,** *on October 14.*

3. A phrase beginning **ante diem (a.d.)** is used to express all other dates:

> **ante diem iv Kalendās Decembrēs** (lit., *on the fourth day before December 1*), *on November 28.* (When calculating, you should include the special day and count backwards, e.g., Dec. 1, Nov. 30, Nov. 29, Nov. 28.)

> **ante diem viii Īdūs Mārtiās** (lit., *on the eighth day before the Ides of March*), *on March 8.*

Here are the Latin names for the months, expressed as adjectives:

Iānuārius, -a, -um	**Iūlius, -a, -um**
Februārius, -a, -um	**Augustus, -a, -um**
Mārtius, -a, -um	**September, Septembris, Septembre**
Aprīlis, -is, -e	**Octōber, Octōbris, Octōbre**
Maius, -a, -um	**November, Novembris, Novembre**
Iūnius, -a, -um	**December, Decembris, Decembre**

4. The Romans designated years by the names of the consuls, the chief Roman magistrates, who were elected annually. The ablative case is used: **Antoniō et Cicerōne cōnsulibus** = 63 B.C.

> **cōnsul, cōnsulis,** m., *consul*

5. They also designated years by counting from the foundation of Rome, which was set at a year corresponding to 753 B.C. These dates were expressed with the initials A.U.C. (**ab urbe conditā,** *from the foundation of the city*).

> **condō, condere, condidī, conditus,** *to found*

To convert a Roman year to our system, follow these rules:

a. If the A.U.C. date is 753 or less, subtract it from 754 and you will obtain a B.C. date.
b. If the A.U.C. date is 754 or greater, subtract 753 from it and you will obtain an A.D. date.

Examples:

> 691 A.U.C. (less than 753)
>
> $$754$$
> $$-691$$
> $$\overline{63}\ \text{B.C. (the year of Cicero's consulship)}$$

833 A.U.C. (greater than 754)

$$\begin{array}{r} 833 \\ -753 \\ \hline 80 \end{array}$$ A.D. (the year of our story)

To convert a year designated according to our system to a Roman year, follow these rules:

a. If the year is B.C., subtract it from 754.
b. If the year is A.D., add it to 753.

Examples:

$$\begin{array}{r} 754 \\ -63 \\ \hline 691 \end{array}$$ B.C. (the year of Cicero's consulship)

A.U.C.

$$\begin{array}{r} 753 \\ +80 \\ \hline 833 \end{array}$$ A.D. (the year of our story)

A.U.C.

Exercise 36b

Give English equivalents for the following dates:

1. Kalendīs Iānuāriīs
2. Kalendīs Decembribus
3. Kalendīs Iūniīs
4. Nōnīs Augustīs
5. Nōnīs Octōbribus
6. Īdibus Mārtiīs
7. Īdibus Maiīs
8. Īdibus Septembribus
9. prīdiē Kalendās Februāriās
10. prīdiē Kalendās Iūliās
11. prīdiē Nōnās Augustās
12. prīdiē Īdūs Iānuāriās
13. prīdiē Īdūs Novembrēs
14. ante diem iv Kalendās Iūniās
15. ante diem iii Nōnās Iūliās
16. a.d. vi Kal. Apr.
17. a.d. xviii Kal. Maiās
18. a.d. xii Kal. Feb.
19. a.d. vi Nōn. Mārt.
20. a.d. iv Īd. Feb.

Roman girl reading a letter

Oil on canvas, "Neaera Reading a Letter from Catullus" by Henry J. Hudson, Bradford Art Galleries and Museums, England

Exercise 36c
Give Roman equivalents for the following dates:

1. Today's date
2. Your own birthday
3. The foundation of Rome (April 21)
4. Cicero's birthday (January 3, 106 B.C.)
5. The date of the assassination of Julius Caesar (March 15, 44 B.C.)
6. Martial's birthday (March 1, A.D. 40)
7. The date of the Emperor Titus' accession to power (June 23, A.D. 79).
8. The date of the eruption of Mount Vesuvius (August 24, A.D. 79)

Exercise 36d
Using story 36 and the discussion of Roman dates above as guides, give the Latin for:

1. Cornelia received a letter on October 10 that Flavia had written on October 5.
2. On November 3 Cornelia and her mother saw a great fire.
3. On November 4 Eucleides was struck and very seriously wounded by robbers.
4. On November 5 Aurelia bought a very beautiful palla for Cornelia.
5. On November 29 Valerius will arrive at Rome.

▬ ▬ ▬

ad Kalendās Graecās, *until the Greek Kalends* (Since there were no Kalends in the Greek calendar, this phrase means the event will never happen.)

▬ ▬ ▬ ▬

BUILDING THE MEANING
Translating *quam*

You have now met several uses of **quam**. The following clues should help you choose the correct meaning:

1. In a comparison:
   clue: *comparative adjective or adverb before* **quam**—translate *than*:

   > Marcus est prūdent**ior quam** Sextus.
   > *Marcus is wiser **than** Sextus.*

2. In a phrase with a superlative:
   clue: *superlative adjective or adverb after* **quam**—translate the phrase *as...as possible*:

   > Scrībe **quam** saep**issimē**. (36:25)
   > *Write **as often as possible**.*

3. In an exclamation:
clue: *adjective or adverb after* **Quam**—translate *How...!* or *What a...!*

> **Quam molestus** puer est Sextus!
> ***What a troublesome** boy Sextus is!*

> **Quam celeriter** tua epistula hūc advēnit! (36:3–4)
> ***How quickly** your letter arrived here!*

4. In a question:
clue: *adjective or adverb after* **Quam** *and question mark at the end of the sentence*—translate *How...?*

> **Quam molestus** est Sextus? Sextus est molestior quam Marcus.
> ***How troublesome** is Sextus? Sextus is more troublesome than Marcus.*

5. In a relative clause:
clue: *singular feminine noun as antecedent of* **quam**—translate *whom, which,* or *that*:

> <u>Illam epistulam</u> accēpī **quam** tū scrīpsistī Kal. Nov. (36:2–3)
> *I have received <u>that letter</u> **that** you wrote on November 1.*

> Cornēlia dē <u>Flāviā</u> **quam** Baiīs relīquerat saepe cōgitābat.
> *Cornelia often used to think about <u>Flavia</u>, **whom** she had left behind in Baiae.*

Exercise 36e
Read aloud and translate:

1. Quam pulcher adulēscēns est Valerius! Libentissimē eum accipiēmus.
2. Nihil miserābilius quam illud incendium vīdī.
3. Mulier illa miserrima quam Cornēlia in tertiō tabulātō sitam cōnspexit ex incendiō effugere nōn poterat.
4. Nēmō erat magis ēbrius quam Titus, nam plūs vīnī quam cēterī biberat.
5. Quam pulchra est illa palla quam māter mihi ēmit! Mihi valdē placet.
6. Mīlitēs Rōmānī quī audācissimī erant semper quam fortissimē sē dēfendēbant.
7. Quamquam celerius ambulābat Eucleidēs, praedōnēs eum mox cōnsecūtī sunt.
8. Quam graviter vulnerātus est!
9. Quam celeriter praedōnēs currere possunt? Celerius quam Eucleidēs currere possunt.

audāx, audācis, *bold*

HELGE'S SPINNING

Chapter 6 told how the slave-women in the Cornelius household were spinning wool into strands of yarn at the country house in Baiae, and Cornelia in her letter to Flavia complains of constantly spinning wool at home in Rome. In fact, all women in the ancient world spun and wove, from the humblest peasant to the wife of the emperor. Helge, the Ubian woman you met in previous Frontier Life sections was no exception, having learned the craft as a child from her mother.

The region around Ara Ubiorum was noted for its sheep. The sheep, in fact, was probably one of the very first animals domesticated by man, its fleece used for weaving cloth for clothing and blankets since prehistoric times. The story that follows takes us back to the first year of Helge's marriage to Lucius.

As is done today, the sheep were sheared in the spring so they would not suffer through the summer in their heavy fleeces. Helge's father had sheared sheep, and so had

Penelope, wife of Ulysses, working at her loom
Oil on canvas, "Penelope and Her Suitors" by J.W. Waterhouse, City of Aberdeen Art Gallery and Museums Collections, Scotland

Lucius on the farm in Italy where he was raised. The shears used by both Lucius and Helge's father were identical to those used in modern times until the invention of electric clippers, and it was with a pair of these shears that, in the spring, Lucius and his companions sheared the sheep owned by Numistronius, their centurion, who had a farm near Ara Ubiorum.

Lucius began the shearing with a particularly large ram. With the help of two of his fellow legionaries, he wrestled the ram to the ground and tied its front and back feet so the animal could not run away. Grasping the shears directly above the two blades, Lucius straddled the ram and applying gentle, oblique pressure removed the entire fleece at once, flipping the heavy animal over on one side or the other as necessary. As the lanolin, the natural oil in the sheep's fleece, built up on Lucius' shears, he dipped them into a bucket of water to clean them as he worked.

After all the sheep were sheared, each fleece was spread out and cut apart, and the wool was separated into grades according to its quality. The thickest and strongest fleece came from the sheep's back, and the next thickest came from the sides. The fleece from the belly was soft and airy—just right for tunics. The worst wool came from the legs and tail, where it was apt to be encrusted with dirt. The wool was carefully placed into bags, each marked as to the quality of fleece it contained.

Helge and her friend, Helena Favonia, who also lived in the area surrounding the military camp, were now ready to convert the wool into tunics and cloaks for the legionaries. First, the wool was washed in cold water and beaten with sticks to remove dirt, leaves, and thorns and to detach fibers for easier carding. Then Helge and Helena carded the wool, a task that meant working it through the teeth of flat iron combs with their fingers over and over, separating the fibers from one another.

Finally, after washing the carded wool, this time in warm soapy water, Helge and Helena were ready to dye it. For the cloaks, the wool would be left the natural color of the sheep or dyed brown. However, the tunics had to be a red color by legion order, and it was this color that Helge prepared by filling a pot with water, scraps of iron from the legion armory, and the sour red wine (**posca**) issued to Roman legionaries. To enhance the reddish color, she added some dry stalks of a plant called madder. Letting the pot sit over the fire until just warm, Helge dumped the wool into the mixture and stirred it until it was thoroughly saturated with the dye. Lifting it out, she wrung out the wool and rinsed it in plain water. Wringing it out again, she dipped it into water that had been poured through wood ashes to fix the color. She repeated this process over and over until she had wool of just the right hue.

Helge knew the art of creating good dyes of many bright colors created by using native plants and metals. But the Romans scorned those bright colors for clothing, considering them barbarian.

The washed, correctly colored, and dry wool, placed in baskets, was now ready for spinning. A simple spindle with a circular whorl mounted on it was used throughout the ancient world. The Roman poet Catullus describes how the Fates spun the threads of destiny by twirling this very same instrument with skillful movements of their fingers:

> The right hand lightly drawing out the thread shaped it with fingers turned upwards and then with a twisting movement of the thumb turned downwards twirled the spindle balanced by the circular whorl.

So Helge spun the brick-red wool into strands of yarn.

As the yarn became longer, Helge wound it on the shaft of her spindle. She and Helena continued to spin until the baskets of wool were empty.

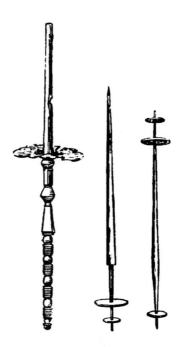

Spindles with circular whorls

CHAPTER 37

OFF TO SCHOOL

Māne in urbe fuit strepitus maximus; canēs lātrābant, servī per viās currēbant, sed neque Marcus neque Sextus sē mōvit. Adhūc in lectō iacēbat Sextus et sēcum cōgitābat: "Quis est mē miserior? Cotīdiē ante lūcem mihi necesse est ad lūdum proficīscī. Sed ad lūdum īre vereor. In lūdō numquam laudor; semper castīgor. Illōs versūs Vergiliī memoriā tenēre nōn possum. Ille grammaticus mē experītur, et cotīdiē eadem dīcit: 'Tū, 5 Sexte, nihil scīs quod semper loqueris,' vel 'Es puer pessimus,' vel 'Nisi dīligentius labōrābis, verberāberis.' Itaque domī manēre volō."

Ita cōgitābat Sextus cum Eucleidēs paedagōgus in cubiculum ingressus est. "Surgite, puerī!" inquit. "Nōlīte diūtius in lectō manēre! Est enim tempus ad lūdum proficīscī, ubi Palaemōn, grammaticus ille ērudītissimus, vōs laetus accipiet. Vōs docēbit plūrima quae 10 vōbīs erunt ūtilissima."

Nihil respondērunt puerī; invītī ē lectō surrēxērunt, vestēs induērunt, ē domō ēgressī sunt. Nōndum lūcēbat, sed cum Eucleide in viās urbis profectī sunt. Lanternam eīs praeferēbat Eucleidēs.

Subitō cōnspexit Marcus tabernam quandam. "Ecce, Eucleidēs!" clāmāvit Marcus. 15 "Vidēsne illam tabernam? Est pīstrīnum. Licetne nōbīs aliquid cibī emere?"

(continued)

3 **cotīdiē,** adv., *daily*, *every day*	6 **loqueris,** *you are talking*
lūdus, -ī, m., *school*	**vel,** conj., *or*
proficīscī, *to set out*	8 **paedagōgus, -ī,** m., *tutor*
4 **vereor,** *I am afraid*	**ingressus est,** *(he) entered*
castīgō, -āre, –āvī, –ātus, *to rebuke, reprimand*	10 **ērudītus, -a, -um,** *learned, scholarly*
Vergilius, -ī, m., *Vergil (Roman poet)*	11 **ūtilis, -is, -e,** *useful*
5 **grammaticus, -ī,** m., *secondary school teacher*	12 **ēgressī sunt,** *(they) went out*
	13 **profectī sunt,** *(they) set out*
experītur, *(he) tests*	16 **pīstrīnum, -ī,** n., *bakery*

14 **praeferō, praeferre, praetulī, praelātus,** irreg., *to carry X* (acc.) *in front of Y* (dat.)

Exercise 37a
Respondē Latīnē:
1. Cūr miser est Sextus?
2. Quandō necesse est ad lūdum proficīscī?
3. Cūr Sextus in lūdō semper castīgātur?
4. Quālis grammaticus (ut dīcit Eucleidēs) est Palaemōn?
5. Quid Palaemōn puerōs docēbit?
6. Cūr necesse erat Eucleidī lanternam puerīs praeferre?

"Estō," respondit Eucleidēs. "Nōn sērō est. Etiamsī nōs aliquid cibī edēmus, tamen ad tempus ad lūdum perveniēmus."

Puerī igitur scriblītās emunt, Eucleidēs pānem et paulum vīnī. Dum iēntāculum dēvorant, Marcus et Sextus inter sē loquuntur. Tandem iterum profectī mox lūdō 20 appropinquābant.

17 **etiamsī,** conj., *even if*
18 **ad tempus,** *on time*
19 **scriblīta, -ae,** f., *tart or pastry with cheese filling*

paulum, -ī, n., *a small amount, a little*
iēntāculum, -ī, n., *breakfast*
20 **loquuntur,** *(they) talk*

Respondē Latīnē:

1. Ubi Eucleidēs et puerī iēntāculum emunt?   2. Quid emunt puerī? Quid Eucleidēs?

FORMS
Deponent Verbs

Look at these sentences:

Eucleidēs effugere **cōnātus est.**	*Eucleides **tried** to escape.*
Praedōnēs eum **cōnsecūtī sunt.**	*The robbers **overtook** him.*
Sed ad lūdum īre **vereor.**	*But **I am afraid** to go to school.*
Semper **loqueris.**	***You are** always **talking**.*
Grammaticus mē **experītur.**	*The teacher **tests** me.*
Brundisiō **proficīscētur.**	***He will set out** from Brundisium.*
Tempus est **proficīscī.**	*It is time **to set out**.*

In each of the above examples, the Latin verb in boldface has a *passive* ending but its meaning is *active*. Verbs that behave in this way are called *deponent verbs*.

NOTES:

1. Deponent verbs occur in all four conjugations and are conjugated the same as *passive* forms of regular verbs. Deponents are *translated* with *active* meanings:

Regular Verb: Passive	**Deponent Verb**
Laudātur. *He is praised.*	**Cōnātur.** *He tries.*
Laudārī potest. *He is able to be praised.*	**Cōnārī** potest. *He is able to try.*

2. Deponent verbs have only *three* principal parts:

    1st: 1st person singular, present tense: **cōnor,** *I try, I am trying, I do try*
    2nd: present infinitive: **cōnārī,** *to try, to be trying*
    3rd: 1st person singular, perfect tense: **cōnātus sum,** *I tried, I have tried*

	Present	Infinitive	Perfect	Meaning
1st Conj.	cónor	cōnā́rī	cōnā́tus sum	*to try*
2nd Conj.	véreor	verḗrī	véritus sum	*to be afraid*
3rd Conj.	lóquor	lóquī	locútus sum	*to speak*
(*-iō*)	regrédior	régredī	regréssus sum	*to go back*
4th Conj.	expérior	experī́rī	expértus sum	*to test*

3. The *perfect participle* of a deponent verb, although passive in form, is translated *actively*:

> Puerī in viās urbis **ēgressī** mox lūdō appropinquābant.
> *The boys, **having gone out** into the streets of the city, soon were approaching the school.*

Here is a chart showing sample forms of deponent verbs. Note that the singular imperatives have forms identical to the present active infinitive of non-deponent verbs. In the future and imperfect tenses only the singular forms are shown. In the perfect, pluperfect, and future perfect tenses only the 1st person singular forms are shown.

			1st Conjugation	2nd Conjugation	3rd Conjugation		4th Conjugation
Present Infinitive			cōnā́rī	verḗrī	lóquī	régredī	experī́rī
Imperative			cōnā́re	verḗre	lóquere	regrédere	experī́re
			cōnā́minī	verḗminī	loquíminī	regredíminī	experī́minī
Present	Singular	1	cónor	véreor	lóquor	regrédior	expérior
		2	cōnā́ris	verḗris	lóqueris	regréderis	experíris
		3	cōnā́tur	verḗtur	lóquitur	regréditur	experítur
	Plural	1	cōnā́mur	verḗmur	lóquimur	regrédimur	experímur
		2	cōnā́minī	verḗminī	loquíminī	regredíminī	experíminī
		3	cōnā́ntur	verḗntur	loquúntur	regrediúntur	experiúntur
Imperfect	Singular	1	cōnā́bar	verḗbar	loquḗbar	regrediḗbar	experiḗbar
		2	cōnābā́ris	verēbā́ris	loquēbā́ris	regrediēbā́ris	experiēbā́ris
		3	cōnābā́tur	verēbā́tur	loquēbā́tur	rebrediēbā́tur	experiēbā́tur
Future	Singular	1	cōnā́bor	verḗbor	lóquar	regrédiar	expériar
		2	cōnā́beris	verḗberis	loquḗris	regrediḗris	experiḗris
		3	cōnā́bitur	verḗbitur	loquḗtur	regrediḗtur	experiḗtur
Perfect		1	cōnā́tus sum	véritus sum	locútus sum	regréssus sum	expértus sum
Pluperfect		1	cōnā́tus éram	véritus éram	locútus éram	regréssus éram	expértus éram
Future Perfect		1	cōnā́tus erō	véritus érō	locútus érō	regréssus érō	expértus érō

You have met forms of the following deponent verbs so far (listed by conjugation):

    1st: **cōnor, cōnā́rī, cōnā́tus sum,** *to try* (36:19)
            moror, morā́rī, morā́tus sum, *to delay, remain, stay* (36:8)
    2nd: **vereor, verḗrī, veritus sum,** *to be afraid, fear* (37:4)

3rd: **collābor, collābī, collāpsus sum,** *to collapse* (34:22)
          cōnsequor, cōnsequī, cōnsecūtus sum, *to catch up to, overtake* (35:18)
          loquor, loquī, locūtus sum, *to speak, talk* (37:6)
          proficīscor, proficīscī, profectus sum, *to set out, leave* (36:9)
          sequor, sequī, secūtus sum, *to follow* (36:18)

(*-iō*)   **ēgredior, ēgredī, ēgressus sum,** *to go out, leave* (37:12)
          ingredior, ingredī, ingressus sum, *to go in, enter* (37:8)
          regredior, regredī, regressus sum, *to go back, return* (36:8)

4th: **experior, experīrī, expertus sum,** *to test, try* (37:5)

Exercise 37b

Here are some forms of deponent verbs. Translate them into English:

1. proficīscuntur
2. experientur
3. secūtī erāmus
4. morātae sunt
5. verēbimur
6. ēgrederis
7. profectī eritis
8. sequere
9. collābī
10. cōnsequēbātur

Exercise 37c

Refer to the principal parts of the verbs listed above and say the following in Latin:

1. We have tried.
2. You (*sing.*) enter.
3. They had set out.
4. Speak, boys!
5. I will test.
6. She was following.
7. You (*pl.*) collapsed.
8. Don't be afraid, Sextus!
9. They will have returned.
10. We were delaying.
11. He has gone out.
12. I will try to overtake you.

Exercise 37d

Read aloud and translate:

1. Quid puellae facere cōnantur? Puellae pallam facere cōnantur. Quid tū facere cōnāris? Ego labōrāre cōnor. Quid vōs facere cōnāminī? Nōs dormīre cōnāmur.
2. Quandō nōs vīsitāre cōnāberis? Ego mox vōs vīsitāre cōnābor. Amīcī meī quoque vōs vīsitāre cōnābuntur. Nōs omnēs eōdem diē vōs vīsitāre cōnābimur.
3. Quis loquitur? Ego nōn loquēbar. Nōs cum magistrō loquēbāmur.
4. Quō puerī proficīscuntur? Rōmam proficīscuntur. Nōs cum eīs proficīscēmur. Nōnne vōs quoque proficīscī vultis?
5. Quandō puerī ē lūdō ēgredientur? Puerī ē lūdō ēgredientur sextā hōrā. Ēgrediēturne cum puerīs magister? Minimē vērō! Magister in lūdō morābitur.
6. Quandō tū proficīscēris? Ubi māter domum regressa erit, ego proficīscar. Puer prīmā lūce proficīscētur. Servī nunc proficīscī nōn possunt. Mox sequentur.

7. Paulisper in urbe morātī sumus. Cūr morātī estis? Ego morātus sum quod patrem vidēre volēbam. Amīcī meī morātī sunt quod aedificia urbis vidēre volēbant.
8. Prīmā lūce servī Cornēliī in viās ēgressī sunt. Illōs praedōnēs scelestōs sequī cōnātī sunt sed eōs cōnsequī nōn potuērunt.
9. Nōlī in lectō diūtius morārī, Sexte. Cōnāre illōs versūs Vergiliī memoriā tenēre. Fortasse ā grammaticō hodiē laudāberis sī nōn nimis loquēris.
10. Cornēlius convīvīs, "Intrāte, amīcī!" inquit. "Ingrediminī domum meam! Vōs libentissimē excipiō." Convīvae quam celerrimē ingressī inter sē magnō cum strepitū in ātriō colloquēbantur.

sextus, -a, -um, *sixth*   **magister, magistrī,** m., *schoolmaster*

Exercise 37e

In each sentence below, replace the verb in italics with the appropriate form of the deponent verb in parentheses, keeping the same tense, person, and number; then translate the new sentence:

1. Valerius Brundisiō Īdibus Novembribus *discessit*. (proficīscor)
2. Ā grammaticō laudātī sumus quod versūs memoriā tenēre *potuerāmus*. (cōnor)
3. Tabellārius ex urbe quam celerrimē *exībit*. (ēgredior)
4. Māter et Cornēlia in illā tabernā diūtissimē *manēbant*. (moror)
5. "Hīc *sedē*, Marce," inquit Eucleidēs. (moror) "Nōlī mē *vexāre*!" (sequor)
6. Eucleidēs per urbis viās nocte ambulāre *nōn vult*. (vereor)
7. "Ego prīmus," inquit Marcus, "in lūdum *intrāvī*." (ingredior)

Exercise 37f

Using story 37 and the information on deponent verbs as guides, give the Latin for the following. Use deponent verbs whenever possible:

1. Marcus and Sextus were staying in their beds.
2. Marcus and Sextus set out for school before dawn every day.
3. Why are you afraid to go to school, Sextus?
4. The teacher will test Sextus.
5. Sextus always talks in school, never works diligently, and is often beaten by the teacher.

Forsan miserōs meliōra sequentur. *For those in misery perhaps better things will follow.* (Vergil, *Aeneid* XII.153)
Multī fāmam, cōnscientiam paucī verentur. *Many fear their reputation, few their conscience.* (Pliny, *Letters* III.20)
Vir sapit quī pauca loquitur. *It is a wise man who speaks little.* (Anonymous)

ROMAN EDUCATION I

THE EARLIEST YEARS: EDUCATION IN THE HOME

Little is known about the early training of Roman boys and girls, but certainly the home played the most important part. During the first seven years education was chiefly in the hands of the mother:

> In the good old days, every citizen's son was brought up, not in the chamber of some hired nurse, but in his mother's lap. Thus we are told Cornelia, the mother of the Gracchi, directed their upbringing. The same was true of Aurelia, the mother of Caesar, and of Atia, the mother of Augustus.
>
> —Tacitus, *Dialogue* 28

This was not the time of formal instruction; it was the influence of the home on the child that was the greatest at this stage:

> In ancient times it was the established custom that Romans should learn from their elders not only by watching but also by listening. The father of each one served as his teacher.
>
> —Pliny, *Letters* VIII.14

The home was always considered the natural place for early training, and the practice of sending children to school away from their home town, although it increased in later years, was looked upon with suspicion by some:

> Surely it is a matter of great importance that your children should study here rather than anywhere else. Where can they live more happily than in their native town, or be more strictly brought up than under their parents' eye, or be educated at less expense than at home? What an easy matter it would be to hire teachers and add to their salaries the money you now spend on lodgings, traveling, and all you have to purchase away from home.
>
> —Pliny, *Letters* IV.13

Roman classroom scene

THE PRIMARY SCHOOL

At the age of seven, if their fathers could afford it, children were sent to school—the **lūdus litterārius**—to be taught their "letters" by a schoolmaster, generally called **litterā-tor** or **magister lūdī**. (Note that the Romans used the same word **lūdus** for both *play* and *school*.) The teacher's pay was small, for teaching was not considered very highly as a profession. The curriculum at this stage was limited to three subjects—reading, writing, and arithmetic.

Education at home, however, was not unusual, for there was no state education. It was usually in the hands of a tutor—most often a Greek slave or freedman.

Occasionally, we read of fathers who themselves looked after the education of their sons. This was true of Cato and Aemilius Paulus, but note their different ideas and ideals:

> As soon as Cato's son began to learn with understanding, his father took him in charge and taught him to read, although he had a very good slave, called Chilo, who was a schoolteacher and was already teaching many boys. But Cato did not think it right, as he himself says, that his son should be scolded by a slave or pulled by the ear when slow to learn, nor that such an important thing as education should be left to a slave. He himself therefore taught him reading, law, and gymnastics and also gave him instruction in how to throw a javelin, to fight in armor, to ride and box, to endure both heat and cold, and to swim.
>
> —Plutarch, *Cato the Elder* 20

Aemilius Paulus himself looked after the education of his children. He brought them up in the old-fashioned Roman way as he himself had been brought up, but he was even more enthusiastic about Greek education. For this reason their teachers of grammar, logic, and rhetoric, their teachers of sculpture and drawing, those in charge of their dogs and horses, and those who taught them how to hunt, were all Greeks.

—Plutarch, *Aemilius Paulus* 6

In schools, discipline was generally very strict. Martial, speaking of one schoolmaster as "a person hated by both girls and boys," continues:

The crested cocks have not yet broken the silence of the night, but you are making a noise by roaring savagely and thrashing your pupils.

—Martial, *Epigrams* IX.68

Many Romans followed the Greek custom of sending their children to school accompanied by a slave (**paedagōgus**) to look after their conduct, manners, and morals:

It is the job of the **paedagōgus** to make the boy learn what his teacher has taught him by encouraging and shouting at him, by fetching out the strap, and by using the cane. He makes him do his work by driving every lesson into his head.

—Libanius, *Orations* 58.8

REVIEW VIII: CHAPTERS 34–37

Exercise VIIIa: Comparative and Superlative of Adjectives and Adverbs

Supply in the blanks comparative and superlative adjectives or adverbs corresponding to the positive forms in the original statements. Read aloud and translate:

1. Messalla coquum *bonum* habet. Titus coquum _____ habet quam Messalla. Cornēlius coquum _____ omnium habet.
2. Messalla tālōs *dīligenter* iacit. Cornēlius tālōs _____ iacit Messallā. Titus tālōs _____ omnium iacit.
3. Eucleidēs ad lūdum *lentē* proficīscitur. Marcus ad lūdum _____ proficīscitur quam Eucleides. Sextus ad lūdum _____ omnium proficīscitur.
4. Marcus *bene* scrībit. Eucleidēs _____ Marcō scrībit. Grammaticus _____ omnium scrībit.
5. Messalla ē poculō *pulchrō* bibit. Titus ē poculō _____ bibit quam Messalla. Cornēlius ē poculō omnium _____ bibit.
6. Coquus Messallae cēnam *celeriter* parat. Coquus Titī cēnam _____ parat quam coquus Messallae. Coquus Cornēliī cenam _____ omnium parat.
7. Eucleidēs ē lectō *sērō* surgit. Marcus ē lectō _____ surgit quam Eucleidēs. Sextus ē lectō _____ omnium surgit.
8. Messalla *multum* vīnī bibit. Cornēlius _____ vīnī bibit Messallā. Titus omnium _____ vīnī bibit.
9. Cornēlius *magnā* vōce clāmat. Messalla _____ vōce clāmat quam Cornēlius. Titus omnium _____ vōce clāmat.
10. Praedōnēs tabernārium *ferōciter* verberāvērunt. Praedōnēs lanium _____ verberāvērunt quam tabernārium. Praedōnēs Eucleidem _____ omnium verberāvērunt.

Exercise VIIIb: Forms of Deponent Verbs

Give the requested forms of the following deponent verbs:

	Present	Imperfect	Future	Perfect	Pluperfect	Future Perfect
1. sequor *(3rd sing.)*	____	____	____	____	____	____
2. loquor *(1st pl.)*	____	____	____	____	____	____
3. vereor *(3rd pl.)*	____	____	____	____	____	____
4. cōnor *(1st sing.)*	____	____	____	____	____	____
5. collābor *(2nd sing.)*	____	____	____	____	____	____
6. regredior *(3rd pl.)*	____	____	____	____	____	____
7. moror *(2nd pl.)*	____	____	____	____	____	____
8. experior *(3rd sing.)*	____	____	____	____	____	____

Exercise VIIIc: Imperatives of Deponent Verbs

Give the singular and plural imperatives of the following deponent verbs:

	Singular	Plural
1. cōnor	_____	_____
2. loquor	_____	_____
3. regredior	_____	_____
4. experior	_____	_____
5. vereor	_____	_____

Exercise VIIId: Active Forms of Non-deponent Verbs

Give the requested forms of the following verbs in the active voice:

	Present	Imperfect	Future	Perfect	Pluperfect	Future Perfect
1. vincō *(2nd sing.)*	____	____	____	____	____	____
2. compleō *(1st sing.)*	____	____	____	____	____	____
3. hauriō *(2nd pl.)*	____	____	____	____	____	____
4. excitō *(1st pl.)*	____	____	____	____	____	____
5. percutiō *(3rd pl.)*	____	____	____	____	____	____
6. crēdō *(3rd sing.)*	____	____	____	____	____	____

Exercise VIIIe: Passive Forms of Non-deponent Verbs

Repeat Exercise VIIId, but give the requested forms of the verbs in the passive voice.

Exercise VIIIf: Imperatives of Non-deponent Verbs

Give the singular and plural active imperatives of the verbs in Exercise VIIId.

Exercise VIIIg: Reading Comprehension

Read the following passage and answer the questions below with full sentences in Latin:

THE TROJAN HORSE

Graecī, quī iam decem annōs Troiam obsidēbant, domum regredī valdē cupiēbant. Mussābant igitur, "Quōmodo Troiānī vincentur? Cōnsilium novum et melius capiēmus. Equum ligneum aedificābimus quem extrā mūrōs urbis relinquēmus. In eō pōnentur fortissimī ē mīlitibus nostrīs. Deinde ad īnsulam vīcīnam ipsī proficīscēmur et nōs ibi cēlābimus. Fortasse equus in urbem ā 5 Troiānīs trahētur."

Postquam Graecī abiērunt, laetissimī ex urbe ēgressī sunt Troiānī. Equum ligneum spectant. "Quid est hoc?" rogant. "Cūr equus tantus ē lignō factus est? Cūr Graecī hunc equum relīquērunt?"

Aliī, "Cavēte Graecōs!" inquiunt. "Nōlīte eīs crēdere." Aliī, "Gaudēte!" 10
inquiunt. "Equus, sī intrā mūrōs ductus erit, urbem nostram custōdiet et
dēfendet."

Itaque maximō gaudiō equum intrā mūrōs trahere cōnstituērunt. Nox erat.
Troiānī somnō vīnōque oppressī per tōtam urbem dormiēbant. Ecce! Dē equō
dēscendērunt Graecī. Intereā cēterī ex īnsulā regrediēbantur et urbem quam 15
celerrimē petēbant. Eī quī in equō cēlātī erant portās Graecīs aperuērunt. Magnō
cum strepitū irrūpērunt. Undique clāmor et tumultus, undique incendia et
caedēs. Mātrēs sollicitae cum līberīs per viās currēbant; flammae omnia dēlēbant.
Urbs tandem capta est.

1	**annus, -ī,** m., *year*	18	**caedēs, caedis,** gen. pl., **caedium,** f.,
2	**cōnsilium capere,** *to form a plan*		*slaughter*
3	**ligneus, -a, -um,** *wooden*		

   1 **obsideō, obsidēre, obsēdī, obsessus,** *to besiege*
   2 **cupiō, cupere, cupīvī, cupītus,** *to desire, want*
 18 **dēleō, dēlēre, dēlēvī, dēlētus,** *to destroy*

1. For how many years had the Greeks been besieging Troy?
2. What kind of plan did the Greeks want to adopt?
3. What did they build?
4. Where did they put it?
5. Where did the other Greeks hide?
6. What did the Trojans do after the Greeks left?
7. What were the Trojans saying who did not trust the Greeks?
8. When did the Trojans drag the horse within the walls?
9. Why didn't the Trojans see the Greeks when they descended from the horse?
10. What were the other Greeks doing at this very time?
11. Who opened the gates to the Greeks?

Exercise VIIIh: Discriminating between Deponent Verbs and Passive Forms of Regular Verbs

The verbs below are taken from the story in Exercise VIIIg. Say whether the verb is a deponent verb or a passive form of a regular verb. Then give a translation of the verb that would fit the context in the story.

1. regredī (1)
2. vincentur (2)
3. pōnentur (4)
4. proficīscēmur (5)
5. trahētur (6)
6. ēgressī sunt (7)
7. factus est (8)
8. regrediēbantur (15)
9. cēlātī erant (16)
10. capta est (19)

THE LESSONS BEGIN

Omnēs puerī in lūdum vix ingressī erant cum grammaticus ita coepit: "Abhinc trēs mēnsēs prīmus liber Aenēidis ā vōbīs lēctus est. Quis ē vōbīs dē Aenēā mihi nārrāre potest?"

Cui ūnus ē discipulīs respondit: "Urbs Troia ā Graecīs decem annōs obsidēbātur, sed tandem capta et incēnsa est. Effūgit ē ruīnīs illīus urbis Aenēās, et ūnā cum patre filiōque 5 suō et complūribus amīcīs ex Asiā nāvigāvit, nam terram petēbat quae Hesperia vocāta est. Postquam multa terrā marīque passus est, ad Siciliam vix vēnit. Atque ubi ē Siciliā profectus est, maxima tempestās nāvēs complūrēs dēlēvit. Aenēās ipse, ad Āfricam tempestāte āctus, cum septem modo nāvibus ad urbem quandam advēnit ubi ā rēgīnā Dīdōne cōmiter acceptus ad convīvium invītātus est."

(continued) 10

1 **coepit,** (*he*) *began*
2 **mēnsis, mēnsis,** m., *month*
   Aenēis, Aenēidis, f., *the* Aeneid
      (*an epic poem by Vergil*)
   Aenēās, Aenēae, m., *Aeneas (son of Venus and Anchises and legendary ancestor of the Romans)*
4 **discipulus, -ī,** m., *pupil*
   annus, -ī, m., *year*

5 **ruīna, -ae,** f., *collapse, ruin*
6 **nāvigō, -āre, -āvī, -ātus,** *to sail*
   terra, -ae, f., *earth, ground, land*
7 **mare, maris,** abl. sing., **marī,** gen. pl., **marium,** n., *sea*
8 **tempestās, tempestātis,** f., *storm*
   nāvis, nāvis, gen. pl., **nāvium,** f., *ship*
9 **rēgīna, -ae,** f., *queen*
10 **Dīdō, Dīdōnis,** f., *Dido (queen of Carthage)*

4 **obsideō, obsidēre, obsēdī, obsessus,** *to besiege*
5 **incendō, incendere, incendī, incēnsus,** *to burn, set on fire*
7 **patior, patī, passus sum,** *to suffer, endure*
8 **dēleō, dēlēre, dēlēvī, dēlētus,** *to destroy*

Exercise 38a
Respondē Latīnē:

1. Quī urbem Troiam obsidēbant?
2. Quis ē ruīnīs urbis effūgit?
3. Quibuscum ex Asiā nāvigāvit?
4. Quam terram petēbat Aenēās?
5. Quid passus est?
6. Quō īnstrūmentō nāvēs complūrēs dēlētae sunt?
7. Quot nāvēs ad terram advēnērunt?
8. Ā quō Aenēās in Āfricā acceptus est?

THE LESSONS BEGIN **109**

Tum grammaticus, "Rēs optimē nārrāta est. Sed quid in convīviō factum est?"

Cui alter discipulus, "Rēgīna plūrima rogābat dē urbe Troiā, dē rēbus Troiānīs, dē perīculīs itineris. Tandem omnēs convīvae tacuērunt et Aenēās multa et mīra nārrāre coepit."

Hoc respōnsum grammaticō maximē placuit; quī, "Nunc," inquit, "nōs ipsī audiēmus 15
ea quae ab Aenēā nārrāta sunt. Nunc legēmus aliquōs versūs ē secundō librō Aenēidis.
Age, Marce! Mihi recitā illōs versūs!"

Marcus igitur ita recitāre coepit:

> Conticuēre omnēs intentīque ōra tenēbant.
> Inde torō pater Aenēās sīc orsus ab altō: 20
> "Īnfandum, rēgīna, iubēs renovāre dolōrem."
> *They all fell silent and were eager to listen.*
> *Then from his lofty couch Father Aeneas thus began:*
> *"Unspeakable, O Queen, is the grief you bid me revive."*

16 **aliquī, -ae, -a,** *some*

Optimum est patī quod ēmendāre nōn possīs. *It is best to endure what you cannot change.* (Seneca, *Moral Epistles* CVII.9)

Caelum, nōn animum, mūtant, quī trāns mare currunt. *Those who run off across the sea change their climate but not their mind.* (Horace, *Epistles* I.II.27)

Like Dido in the *Aeneid* or Ariadne in earlier myth, a woman might help a hero only to be abandoned. *"Ariadne in Naxos," oil on canvas, Evelyn de Morgan, The de Morgan Foundation, London*

FORMS
Numbers in Latin

	Cardinal	Ordinal
I	ūnus, -a, -um, *one*	prīmus, -a, -um, *first*
II	duo, -ae, -o, *two*	secundus, -a, -um, *second*
III	trēs, trēs, tria, *three*	tertius, -a, -um, *third*
IV	quattuor, *four*	quārtus, -a, -um
V	quīnque, *five*	quīntus, -a, -um
VI	sex, *six*	sextus, -a, -um
VII	septem, *seven*	septimus, -a, -um
VIII	octō, *eight*	octāvus, -a, -um
IX	novem, *nine*	nōnus, -a, -um
X	decem, *ten*	decimus, -a, -um
XI	ūndecim, *eleven*	ūndecimus, -a, -um
XII	duodecim, *twelve*	duodecimus, -a, -um
XIII	tredecim, *thirteen*	tertius decimus, -a, -um
XIV	quattuordecim, *fourteen*	quārtus decimus, -a, -um
XV	quīndecim, *fifteen*	quīntus decimus, -a, -um
XVI	sēdecim, *sixteen*	sextus decimus, -a, -um
XVII	septendecim, *seventeen*	septimus decimus, -a, -um
XVIII	duodēvīgintī, *eighteen*	duodēvīcēsimus, -a, -um
XIX	ūndēvīgintī, *nineteen*	ūndēvīcēsimus, -a, -um
XX	vīgintī, *twenty*	vīcēsimus, -a, -um
L	quīnquāgintā, *fifty*	quīnquāgēsimus, -a, -um
C	centum, *a hundred*	centēsimus, -a, -um
D	quīngentī, -ae, -a, *five hundred*	quīngentēsimus, -a, -um
M	mīlle, *a thousand*	mīllēsimus, -a, -um

N.B. The cardinal numbers from **quattuor** to **centum** do not change their form to indicate case and gender.

The question word **Quot...?** requires an answer from the *cardinal* column:

Quot līberōs habēbat lībertus? Septem habēbat.
How many children did the freedman have? He had seven.

The word **Quotus...?** requires an answer from the *ordinal* column:

Quota hōra est? Est nōna hōra.
What time is it? It is the ninth hour.

Exercise 38b

Read aloud and translate:

1. Puerī novem hōrās dormīvērunt. Tempus est eōs excitāre.
2. Convīvae sex hōrās morābantur. Cēna Cornēliī erat optima.
3. Ulixēs multa terrā marīque passus domum decimō annō pervēnit.
4. Quot librī Aenēidis sunt? Duodecim sunt librī Aenēidis.
5. Quota hōra est? Est sexta hōra.
6. Quotus mēnsis annī est Aprīlis? Aprīlis mēnsis annī est quārtus.
7. Ōlim Mārtius mēnsis erat prīmus annī, et septimus vocātus est mēnsis September, octāvus mēnsis October, nōnus mēnsis November, decimus mēnsis December. Nunc mēnsis Iānuārius est prīmus annī.
8. Quot sorōrēs habēbat Dīdō? Ūnam sorōrem Annam nōmine habēbat Dīdō.
9. Marcus ā grammaticō rogātus aliquōs versūs ē secundō librō Aenēidis bene recitāvit.
10. Aenēās, ut in sextō Aenēidis librō legimus, in Plūtōnis rēgnum dēscendit.

Ulixēs, Ulixis, m., *Ulysses, Odysseus (Greek hero of the Trojan War)*

Exercise 38c

Give equivalents for the following in Arabic numerals:

1. XXX
2. XXIV
3. XVII
4. XIX
5. LX
6. CV
7. DXC
8. MDCCLXXVI
9. XLIV
10. CLIX.

Exercise 38d

Give the Latin for each of the following questions (each of your questions should expect a numerical answer), and then give an appropriate answer:

1. What hour is it?
2. What month is it?
3. How many months are there in a year?
4. How many brothers and how many sisters do you have?
5. How many books have you read today?

ROMAN EDUCATION II

THE SECONDARY SCHOOL: THE GRAMMATICUS

After five years at a **lūdus litterārius**, children were sent to a **grammaticus**, a grammarian. Secondary education was more restricted, for only the wealthy could send their children to these schools. Here they studied both Latin and Greek literature. In addition, the **grammaticus** would teach mathematics, natural science, astronomy, philosophy, and music, but only in so far as these subjects were relevant to understanding the works of Greek and Latin literature that were read in the schools.

Students had to learn to read aloud books in which there was no punctuation or even spaces between words, and to recite them. They also had to be able to answer very detailed questions on every word of the books they were reading. A favorite author, from the end of the first century B.C. onwards, was Publius Vergilius Maro, whom we call Vergil. He had written a great poem called the *Aeneid* (because its hero was Aeneas) about the origins of the Romans.

We can get some idea of what a lesson in the school of a **grammaticus** might have been like from a grammarian called Priscian who lived in the sixth century A.D. Here is part of a series of questions and answers that he gives on the first line of the second book of Vergil's *Aeneid*.

Conticuēre omnēs intentīque ōra tenēbant.

"Partēs ōrātiōnis quot sunt?"	*"How many parts of speech are there?"*
"Sex."	*"Six."*
"Quot nōmina?"	*"How many nouns?"*
"Duo. *Omnēs* et *ōra*."	*"Two.* **omnēs** *and* **ōra**.*"*
"Quot verba?"	*"How many verbs?"*
"Duo. *Conticuēre* et *tenēbant*."	*"Two.* **conticuēre** *and* **tenēbant**.*"*
"Quid aliud habet?"	*"What else does it have?"*
"Participium *intentī* et coniūnctiōnem *-que*."	*"A participle* **intentī** *and a conjunction* **-que**.*"*
"*Conticuēre* —quae pars ōrātiōnis est?"	*"What part of speech is* **conticuēre**?*"*
"Verbum."	*"A verb."*
"Quāle?"	*"What tense?"*
"Perfectum"	*"The perfect."*
"Quōmodo dictum?"	*"How is it described?"*
"Indicātīvō coniugātiōnis secundae."	*"Indicative, of the second conjugation."*
"Cuius significātiōnis?"	*"What voice is it?"*
"Actīvae."	*"Active."*
"Dīc passīvum."	*"Tell me the passive."*

And so it goes on for many more questions, each word being treated in the same way.

HIGHER EDUCATION

After assuming the **toga virīlis** at age sixteen, a boy was ready for the most advanced stage of Roman education—that of the teacher of rhetoric (**rhētor**). From the **rhētor** he learned the art of public speaking, a necessary qualification for anyone aspiring to high office in law or politics.

A few favored youths completed their education by further study of rhetoric and philosophy at Athens or some other foreign city.

ATTITUDES TO EDUCATION

Horace's father, though a freedman of moderate means, did not consider it too great a sacrifice to give his son the best possible education. Horace recalls his father's efforts with pride and gratitude:

> My father refused to send me to Flavius' (the local) school where the big sons of the local gentry went, with school-bag and writing-tablets over their left shoulders, bringing their school fees of eight **asses*** on the Ides of each month. He dared to take me to Rome.
>
> —Horace, *Satires* I.6.71–76

Pliny, who showed his interest in a practical way by contributing money to found a school in his native town of Comum, was also concerned that education should be more than book-learning:

> But now the most important thing is who gives him his instruction. Up to the present he has been at home and has had teachers there. At home there is little or no opportunity for going astray. Now his studies must be carried away from home, and we must find a teacher of Latin rhetoric in whose school we shall find a strict training along with good manners and moral standards.
>
> —Pliny, *Letters* III.3

A character in a novel of Petronius deplores the acceptance of lax standards of discipline in schools:

> What's to be done? It's the parents who are to blame for refusing to let their children benefit by severe discipline. But now boys play in school, young men are laughing-stocks in public and, what is worse than either, they refuse to admit in old age the mistakes they learned at school.
>
> —Petronius, *Satyricon* 4

*about 19 cents

Quintilian, a famous "professor" of rhetoric in Rome at the period of our story, has a very different attitude from that of the cruel schoolmaster about whom Martial wrote (see above, page 104):

> The teacher should adopt before all things the attitude of a parent toward his pupils and consider that he is taking the place of those by whom their children have been entrusted to him. He should not have faults himself, nor should he allow his pupils to have any. He should be strict but not harsh, courteous but not lax, lest the former breed hatred, the latter contempt. He should not be bad-tempered, but neither should he pass over what requires correction. When praising the speeches of his pupils, he should be neither grudging nor effusive, for the one will lead to distaste for the work, the other to over-confidence.

> —Quintilian, *Institutio oratoria* II.4–8

ST. AUGUSTINE AND PLINY ON EDUCATION

The following passages give two very personal and sharply contrasting views of education. St. Augustine, writing in the late fourth century A.D., looks back on his school days with horror. Pliny, on the other hand, writing in the early second century A.D., remembers his schooling with great fondness:

> Then I was put into school to get learning, in which I (poor wretch) did not know what use there was. And yet, if sluggish in my learning, I was beaten. What miseries and mockeries did I experience then!

> —St. Augustine, *Confessions* I.9

> Thanks to you, I am returning to school and (as it were) taking up again the sweetest part of my life; I take my seat, as I used to, with the youngsters and I experience how much respect my learning has among them.

> —Pliny, *Letters* II.18

ADDITIONAL READING:
The Romans Speak for Themselves: Book II: "Early Education in Rome,"
pages 41–49.

CHAPTER 39

A LESSON FOR SEXTUS

Postquam Marcus fīnem recitandī fēcit, grammaticus, "Illī versūs bene recitātī sunt. Nunc dīc mihi hoc! Quot sunt verba in prīmō versū?" "Quīnque." "Sed quot in secundō versū?" "Octō." "Quid dē verbō *conticuēre* mihi dīcere potes?" "*Conticuēre* est idem ac *conticuērunt*. Sīc verbum saepe scrībunt poētae."

"Bene respondistī. Et tū, Aule, dīc mihi hoc! Quī sunt 'omnēs'?" "Troiānī ūnā cum 5 rēgīnā et comitibus." "Ubi sunt hī omnēs?" "In Āfricā." "Quō in locō?" "Carthāginī." "Unde vēnit Aenēās?" "Troiā." "Quō itinere Troiā nāvigāvit?" "Prīmum ad Siciliam vēnit; deinde tempestāte Carthāginem āctus est."

"Multa tamen dē hāc fābulā omittis, nam Aenēās comitēsque multōs annōs errābant antequam ad Siciliam advēnērunt. Prīmum ad Thrāciam, deinde Dēlum, tum ad Crētam 10 nāvigāvērunt. Cūr nusquam morātus est Aenēās, Marce?" "Monitus ā dīs, Aenēās semper Hesperiam petēbat. Volēbat enim novam condere Troiam."

Omnēs discipulī grammaticum attentē audiēbant—praeter Sextum quī dormitābat. Quem ubi animadvertit grammaticus, "Sexte," clāmāvit, "Expergīscere! Dīc mihi! Ubi est Hesperia?" 15

(continued)

1 **fīnem recitandī fēcit,** *(he) made an end of reciting, (he) stopped reciting*	**Dēlos, Dēlī,** f., *Delos (small island off the eastern coast of Greece)*
2 **verbum, -ī,** n., *word, verb*	**Crēta, -ae,** f., *Crete (large island southeast of Greece)*
3 **idem ac,** *the same as*	
4 **sīc,** adv., *thus, in this way*	11 **nusquam,** adv., *nowhere*
6 **comes, comitis,** m./f., *companion*	**moneō, -ēre, -uī, -itus,** *to advise, warn*
8 **Carthāgō, Carthāginis,** f., *Carthage (city on the northern coast of Africa)*	**deus, -ī,** nom. pl., **dī,** dat., abl. pl., **dīs,** m., *god*
10 **antequam,** conj., *before*	12 **Hesperia, -ae,** f., *Hesperia (the land in the West, Italy)*
Thrācia, -ae, f., *Thrace (country northeast of Greece)*	13 **dormitō, -āre, -āvī,** *to be sleepy*

3 **conticēscō, conticēscere, conticuī,** *to become silent*
14 **animadvertō, animadvertere, animadvertī, animadversus,** *to notice*
   expergīscor, expergīscī, experrēctus sum, *to wake up*

Exercise 39a
Respondē Latīnē:
1. Quid Marcus grammaticō dīcit dē verbō *conticuēre*?
2. Quō errābat Aenēās antequam ad Siciliam advēnit?
3. Cūr Aenēās Hesperiam semper petēbat?
4. Quid faciēbat Sextus, dum cēterī discipulī grammaticum audiēbant?

"Hesperia? Nōnne est Graecia?" "Minimē, ō puer abōminande! Hesperia est Italia." "Nīl interest," mussāvit Sextus.

"At maximē interest," respondit grammaticus, īrā maximā commōtus. Ferulam sūmpsit et vōce terribilī, "Extende manum, Sexte!" clāmāvit. Cēterī discipulī conticuērunt. At Sextus grammaticō nōn pāruit. "Nōn extendam," inquit. Stupuit grammaticus. Longum   20 fuit silentium. Tandem, "Abī, puer!" clāmat. "Vocā Eucleidem paedagōgum! Ille tē domum dūcet. Satis procācitātis tuae passus sum. Tē hūc redīre vetō, nisi labōrāre volēs. Nunc abī!"

Cēterī discipulī verbīs grammaticī territī erant. Numquam anteā puer domum missus erat.

17 **interest**, *it is important*	20 **pāreō, -ēre, -uī** + dat., *to obey*
18 **ferula, -ae,** f., *cane*	

19 **extendō, extendere, extendī, extentus,** *to hold out*

Respondē Latīnē:

1. Quid respondit Sextus dē Hesperiā rogātus?
2. Quid sūmpsit grammaticus?
3. Quōmodo grammaticus "Extende manum!" dīcit?
4. Cūr Sextus ā grammaticō domum missus est?

BUILDING THE MEANING
Place Clues

Look at the following sentences:

Ad Forum festīnant.	*They hurry **to the Forum**.*
Rōmam festīnāvit.	*He hurried **to Rome**.*
Ē lūdō venit Eucleidēs.	*Eucleides comes **from the school**.*
Brundisiō discesserat Pūblius.	*Publius had departed **from Brundisium**.*
Cornēlius **in ātriō** amīcōs exspectat.	*Cornelius waits for his friends **in the atrium**.*
Pūblius **Baiīs** morābātur.	*Publius was staying **in Baiae**.*

In the first sentence of each pair, the preposition and the case of the noun give clues to the meaning of the phrase. In the second sentence of each pair, there is no preposition. This is normal with names of cities, towns, and small islands.

NOTES

1. With names of cities, towns, and small islands, the *accusative case* without a preposition indicates place *to which*:

    Rōmam festīnāvit.   *He hurried to Rome.*
    Dēlum nāvigāvit.   *He sailed to Delos.*

2. With names of cities, towns, and small islands, the *ablative case* without a preposition may indicate place *from which*:

    Brundisiō discesserat Pūblius.   *Publius had gone from Brundisium.*
    Dēlō abiit.   *He went away from Delos.*
    Baiīs profectus est.   *He set out from Baiae.*

    With names of cities, towns, and small islands, the *locative case* without a preposition indicates place *in which*. The endings of the locative case are as follows:

    a. singular nouns of the 1st and 2nd declensions: identical in spelling to the *genitive*:
       Rōm*ae* manēbat.   *He was remaining in Rome.*
       Brundisi*ī* habitat.   *He lives in Brundisium.*

    b. singular nouns of the 3rd declension: same as *ablative* (sometimes *dative*):
       Sīdōn*e* multa ēmit.   *He bought many things in Sidon.*
       Carthāgin*ī* cōmiter acceptus est.   *He was received graciously at Carthage.*

    c. plural nouns: same as *ablative*:
       Bai*īs* vīllam habet.   *He has a farm in Baiae.*
       Gād*ibus* morābātur.   *He was staying at Gades.*

3. When a noun has the same endings for both place *from which* and place *in which*, the verb will help with the meaning:

    Bai*īs* manēbat.   *He was remaining in Baiae.*
    Bai*īs* profectus est.   *He set out from Baiae.*

4. The words **domus**, *home*, and **rūs**, *country, country estate*, behave in a similar way:
    Accusative of place to which:
       Domum iit.   *He went home.*
       Rūs iit.   *He went to the country/to his country estate.*
    Ablative of place from which:
       Domō profectus est.   *He set out from home.*
       Rūre rediit.   *He returned from the country/from his country estate.*

Locative of place where:

Domī est.   *He is **at home**.*
Rūrī est.   *He is **in the country/on his country estate.***

The word **rūs, rūris** is a regular 3rd declension neuter noun; its locative is **rūrī**. The feminine noun **domus** appears as a 4th declension noun (see the forms at the left below), but some of its cases have 2nd declension alternatives (at the right below), of which the locative is one:

	Singular		Plural	
Nominative	dom**us**		dom**ūs**	
Genitive	dom**ūs**	dom**ī** (locative)	dom**uum**	dom**ōrum**
Dative	dom**uī**	dom**ō**	dom**ibus**	
Accusative	dom**um**		dom**ūs**	dom**ōs**
Ablative	dom**ū**	dom**ō**	dom**ibus**	
Vocative	dom**us**		dom**ūs**	

Omnia Rōmae cum pretiō. *Everything is available in Rome—for a price!* (Juvenal, *Satires* III.183–184)

Exercise 39b

Use each place name listed below to replace the italicized words in the following sentences. Use the prepositions **ab, in,** or **ad** *only where necessary*:

1. Mox *ad urbem* veniam.
2. Iam *ab urbe* discessī.
3. Diū *in urbe* morābar.

Āfrica, -ae, f.
Athēnae, -ārum, f. pl., *Athens*
Baiae, -ārum, f. pl.
Brundisium, -ī, n.
Carthāgō, Carthāginis, f.

Dēlos, Dēlī, f.
domus, -ūs, f.
Gādēs, Gādium, f. pl.
Gallia, -ae, f., *Gaul*

Philippī, -ōrum, m. pl.
Rōma, -ae, f.
rūs, rūris, n.
Sīdōn, Sīdōnis, f.

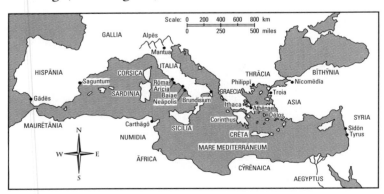

Exercise 39c

Read aloud and translate:

1. Ubi Graecī fīnem bellī fēcērunt, Ulixēs cum comitibus Troiā profectus est.
2. Domum redīre et uxōrem suam vidēre volēbat.
3. Multīs post annīs Ithacam pervēnit.
4. Cornēliī aestāte Baiīs, hieme Rōmae habitant. Nunc autem Cornēliī domī Rōmae sunt.
5. Aestāte Cornēliī domō proficīscuntur; Baiās eunt; rūrī habitant.
6. Aenēās, quī ē Siciliā profectus erat, magnā tempestāte iactātus, Carthāginem tandem advēnit.
7. Carthāginī Aenēās breve modo tempus morābātur; Carthāgine discessit quod novam urbem in Italiā condere volēbat.
8. Hannibal, ubi Saguntum, oppidum Hispāniae, cēpit, iter longum per Galliam et trāns Alpēs in Italiam fēcit.
9. Mox Quīntus Valerius, amīcus Cornēliōrum, ē Bīthȳniā Rōmam regradiētur. Tribus mēnsibus domum perveniet.

> **bellum, -ī,** n., *war*
> **multīs post annīs,** *many years afterward*
> **hiems, hiemis,** f., *winter*
> **iactō, -āre, -āvī, -ātus,** *to toss about, drive to and fro*
>
> **oppidum, -ī,** n., *town*
> **Hispānia, -ae,** f., *Spain*
> **trāns,** prep. + acc., *across*

Time Clues

1. Prepositions will be found introducing some expressions of time:

post multōs annōs	***after*** *many years*
ante prīmam lūcem	***before*** *dawn*

2. Words or phrases in the accusative or ablative cases without prepositions are found expressing other ideas of time:

   a. *Accusative of duration of time:*

mult**ōs** ann**ōs**	*throughout many years, for many years*
tōt**um** di**em**	*throughout the whole day, for the whole day*

   b. *Ablative of time when* and *ablative of time within which:*

aestāt**e**	*in summer*
e**ō** tempor**e**	*at that time*
prīm**ā** lūc**e**	*at dawn*
Īd**ibus** Mārti**īs**	*on the Ides of March*
brev**ī** tempor**e**	*within a short time, in a short time, soon*
tr**ibus** mēns**ibus**	*in three months*

3. Adverbs are found in some expressions of time:

    a. You have seen adverbs such as the following very frequently (see Chapter 13 of Level I): **crās**, *tomorrow*; **hodiē**, *today*; **iam**, *now, already*; **iterum**, *again, a second time*; **nunc**, *now*; etc. These cause no problems, but note the following:

    b. **abhinc,** *back from this point in time, ago* + accusative of duration of time:

        abhinc trēs diēs   **back from the present** *for three days* = *three days* **ago**

    c. **post,** *after(ward)* + ablative
       ante, *previously, before* + ablative:

        tribus **post** diēbus   **afterward** *by three days* = *three days* **later**
        tribus **ante** diēbus   **previously** *by three days* = *three days* **before**

Note that **post** and **ante** may be either prepositions with the accusative or adverbs with the ablative.

Exercise 39d
Select, read aloud, and translate:

1. Puerī ē lūdō (sextā hōrā/paucīs mēnsibus/decem hōrās) rediērunt.
2. Hodiē, Marce, (trēs hōrās/aestāte/ante prīmam lūcem) surrēxistī.
3. Graecī Troiam (quīnque mēnsēs/tribus annīs/decem annōs) obsidēbant.
4. Nōs apud Cornēlium (ūnum mēnsem/nōnā hōrā/tōtum diem) cēnābimus.
5. Ad vīllam (tōtum diem/duōs mēnsēs/aestāte) profectī estis.
6. Ego ad urbem (abhinc trēs diēs/octō mēnsēs/ūnō annō) advēnī.
7. Aenēās comitēsque (duōbus diēbus/multōs annōs/septem annīs) errābant.
8. Sextus iam (ūnō annō/trēs mēnsēs/quīnque hōrīs) in urbe habitat.
9. Discipulī versūs Vergiliī (tōtum diem/brevī tempore/ūnō diē) legēbant.
10. Convīvae ad domum Cornēliānam (brevī tempore/quattuor hōrās/ūnam noctem) advenient.

Exercise 39e
Using story 39 and the information on place and time clues as guides, give the Latin for:

1. When did Aeneas and his companions sail from Troy?
2. Many years later they came to Sicily.
3. They were driven to Carthage by a storm.
4. For many months they remained in Carthage; finally they returned to Sicily.
5. After a long journey they arrived at Hesperia.

Exercise 39f

Read this story of Vergil's life aloud and answer in English the questions that follow:

Pūblius Vergilius Marō, maximus poētārum Rōmānōrum, nātus est Īdibus
Octōbribus prope Mantuam, quod est oppidum Italiae septentriōnālis. Puer
Cremōnam missus, ab optimīs magistrīs ibi doctus, sextō decimō annō togam
virīlem sūmpsit. Paulisper domī in patris fundō morātus, profectus est adulēscēns
Mediolānum. Paucōs annōs et litterīs et linguae Graecae dīligentissimē studēbat.   5
Mox tamen, quod pater post bellum ē fundō suō expulsus erat, Vergilius Rōmam
cum patre migrāvit. Dum Rōmae habitat, versūs multīs dē rēbus scrīpsit et mox
praeclārus factus est poēta. In numerō amīcōrum et poētam Horātium et
prīncipem Augustum ipsum habēbat; sed (ēheu!) saepe aegrōtābat et semper
īnfirmā erat valētūdine. Interdum Neāpolī in sōlitūdine vīvēbat. Iam   10
quīnquāgintā annōs nātus dum in Graeciā iter facit, prīncipī occurrit Athēnīs.
Quī, ad Italiam rediēns, Vergilium sēcum dūxit. Athēnīs profectī ad Italiam
nāvigāvērunt. In terram ēgressus Brundisium, Vergilius aegerrimus fīēbat et in eō
oppidō mortuus est. Corpus Neāpolim lātum ab amīcīs trīstissimīs est sepultum.

2 **Mantua, -ae,** f., *Mantua* (town in
   northern Italy)
   septentriōnālis, -is, -e, *northern*
3 **Cremōna, -ae,** f., *Cremona* (town in
   northern Italy)
4 **fundus, -ī** m., *farm*
5 **Mediolānum, -ī,** n., *Milan*
   litterae, -ārum, f. pl., *letters, literature*
   lingua, -ae, f., *tongue, language*
   studeō, -ēre, -uī + dat., *to study*
7 **migrō, -āre, -āvī, -ātūrus,** *to move
   one's home*

8 **Horātius, -ī,** m., *Horace* (Roman poet)
9 **Augustus, -ī,** m., *Augustus* (first
   Roman emperor)
   aegrōtō, -āre, -āvī, -ātūrus, *to be ill*
10 **īnfirmā...valētūdine,** *in poor health*
   interdum, adv., *from time to time*
12 **rediēns,** *returning*
13 **in terram ēgressus,** *having
   disembarked*
   aeger, aegra, aegrum, *ill*

1 **nāscor, nāscī, nātus sum,** *to be born*
6 **expellō, expellere, expulī, expulsus,** *to drive out, expel*
10 **vīvō, vīvere, vīxī, victūrus,** *to live*
14 **morior, morī, mortuus sum,** *to die*
   sepeliō, sepelīre, sepelīvī, sepultus, *to bury*

1. When and where was Vergil born?
2. Where was he sent as a boy?
3. At what age did he take up the **toga
   virīlis?**
4. How long did he stay in Milan?
5. What did he study while in Milan?
6. Why did he move to Rome with his
   father?

7. Who were among his friends in Rome?
8. At what age did he take his fatal trip to
   Greece?
9. With whom did he return from Greece?
10. Where did Vergil die and where was he
   buried?

AUGUSTUS

The assassination of Julius Caesar on the Ides of March, 44 B.C., inaugurated a struggle for power in Rome that took fourteen years of war and intrigue to resolve. The ultimate struggle lay between the consul at the time of Caesar's murder, Marcus Antonius (Mark Antony), and Caesar's principal heir, adopted son, and grandnephew, Octavian. The struggle encompassed such drama and such fervor that subsequent ages have drawn upon it repeatedly for great works of art and literature. Early on in the struggle Cicero fell victim to proscriptions instituted by the Second Triumvirate, a coalition of Octavian, Antony, and Caesar's old lieutenant Lepidus, to fight their common political enemies in the name of avenging Caesar. At Antony's insistence, Cicero's severed head and hands were put on display on the Rostra in the Forum. The conclusion of the struggle was marked by Octavian's victory over Antony at the naval battle of Actium in 31 B.C. and the suicides of Antony and Cleopatra. Octavian was eighteen years old when the struggle began and thirty-two when he finally prevailed. He showed himself to be a ruthless military and political strategist and leader, but his great contributions were to begin when he took the helm in Rome in 30 B.C.

**Antony and Cleopatra
as the subjects of
Shakespeare's tragedy**
*Antony and Cleopatra by
American artist Rockwell Kent*

PAX ROMANA

After more than 100 years of political turmoil and civil wars, it seemed that a chance for a lasting peace had come to Rome. In 27 B.C., after adjusting the membership of the Senate and laying other groundwork, Octavian proclaimed the Restoration of the Republic. On the surface he appeared to have put the old constitution back in place: the Senate regained its role of leadership; the popular assemblies met as before to pass laws and elect magistrates to the offices of the **cursus honōrum**. It was in gratitude for this "restoration" that the senators awarded him the title **Augustus,** *Venerable,* by which title he is principally remembered today. In fact, however, it was he who ruled the Empire as its first emperor, and certain powers the Senate granted him assured his authority (**auctoritās**). He had the right to propose legislation in the assemblies as well as decrees in the Senate, where he ranked as senior senator, a position that allowed him to speak first with the consequence of encouraging subsequent speakers to support his proposals. He held guaranteed control over the armies, foreign affairs, and the provinces. The title he preferred for himself, however, was not **imperātor,** *commander;* hence, "emperor," but simply **prīnceps,** *first citizen,* hence, "prince." More important than any titles was his talent for convincing people to do what he wanted without seeming to order their actions.

Later in his life, Augustus personally recorded his accomplishments in his official memoirs, *The Deeds of the Deified Augustus (Res gestae Divi Augusti).* His account was published on inscriptions that were placed at his tomb in Rome and elsewhere in the empire. One inscription, which survived on the walls of a temple in Ankara, Turkey, is called, because of its location, the **Monumentum Ancyrānum.** In the text Augustus lists the offices and honors he held, his private funding of public works, and his achievements in war and peace. He also stresses that he was just in his treatment of his enemies and always acted within the legal guidelines of the republican constitution that he restored.

The remarkable **auctoritās** that Augustus possessed enabled him to lay the foundation of imperial government. Throughout the empire, professional armies loyal to the emperor enforced the **pāx Rōmāna** that he had established. In the *Res gestae* Augustus indicates his own pride in the peace when he mentions the consecration of the Altar of Augustan Peace (**Āra Pācis Augustae**) on the Campus Martius and the ceremonial closing of the doors of the Shrine of Janus Quirinus three times during his principate, a symbolic gesture of peace for Rome that had occurred only twice before since the founding of the city in 753 B.C.

On those occasions when Augustus did order the doors of the Shrine of Janus opened, the armies under his **imperium** extended the northern frontiers to the Rhine and Danube Rivers, so that communication between the eastern and western provinces was firmly protected. Late in his principate Augustus suffered one military defeat. In A.D. 9, Quinctilius Varus led three legions into a trap in the Teutoberger Forest, where the Germans slaughtered them. Augustus thereupon gave up his attempt to conquer and Romanize Germany. He expressed his displeasure by banging his head against a door in the palace and crying out, "Quinctilius Varus, give me back my legions!"

Augustus realized that he could not direct everything in the empire single-handedly; he therefore created an imperial bureaucracy, staffed by members of the senatorial and equestrian classes, to whom he delegated the responsibility of administering law and order in the provinces and in the city. The **lēgātī** who served as governors in Augustus' proconsular provinces were paid well enough so that they stayed at their posts for years and administered their duties knowledgeably and efficiently. Within the city of Rome **praefectī** and **cūrātōrēs** managed public works and agencies concerned with the citizens' welfare. The superintendent of aqueducts (**cūrātor aquārum**), for example, was in charge of the aqueducts and water supply, and the commander of watchmen (**praefectus vigilum**) commanded the companies of **vigilēs**, who dealt with fire-fighting and minor criminals.

The Roman Empire in the Age of Augustus

Under Augustus' influence, then, the Roman Empire enjoyed a sound economy, marked by increased trade and prosperity and by solvent state finances. To sense that Rome was becoming more prosperous, the citizens of Rome had only to look about them and observe the ambitious building program directed by Augustus and Marcus Agrippa, his right-hand man and son-in-law: the renovation of many old buildings, the completion of the Basilica Julia, and the construction of a new Forum. In addition, to make sure that everyone realized how great Rome, Italy, and their **prīnceps** were, the writers of the Augustan age concentrated on literary themes that glorified the Romans and their nation. Livy's impressive books on the history of Rome supported the idea that Roman character, as displayed by heroes of the past, was the source of Roman greatness. Gaius Maecenas, a wealthy equestrian businessman and a friend of Augustus, was a patron who supported several poets who helped propagandize Augustan nationalism. Horace owed him his Sabine villa and the leisure to explore patriotic themes in his *Odes* as well as the traditional topics of lyric poetry. Vergil dedicated to Maecenas his *Georgics*, poems that praised the Italian landscape and country life, where the Italian peasant farmer flourished.

Even more stirring was Vergil's epic, the *Aeneid*, in which, long before Rome was founded, Jupiter told his daughter Venus that he had granted the Romans "rule without limit" (**imperium sine fīne**) and that a Caesar, descended from the Trojans, would rise to power after many centuries and that the gates of war of the Shrine of Janus would be closed. Later in the epic, when the hero, Aeneas, visits the underworld, his father, Anchises, foretells the future greatness of Rome and specifically points out the spirit of Augustus Caesar, son of a god, who will establish again for Latium a Golden Age (**Aurea Saecula**).

Augustus and Livia
Marble statues, Ephesus Museum, Turkey

At the climax of his predictions, Anchises instructs Aeneas:

> "Tū regere imperiō populōs, Rōmāne, mementō
> (hae tibi erunt artēs) pācisque impōnere mōrem,
> parcere subiectīs et dēbellāre superbōs."
>
> — *Aeneid* VI.851–853

> "You, Roman, remember to rule nations with power
> (these will be your skills) and to impose the conditions of peace,
> to spare the conquered and to conquer the arrogant."

That, Anchises tells both Aeneas and, through Vergil's epic, the Romans of Augustus' generation, is Rome's mission.

Exercise 39g

Here are the first seven lines of Vergil's *Aeneid*. Read them aloud and translate them:

> Arma virumque canō, Troiae quī prīmus ab ōrīs
> Ītaliam fātō profugus Lāvīniaque vēnit
> lītora, multum ille et terrīs iactātus et altō
> vī superum, saevae memorem Iūnōnis ob īram,
> multa quoque et bellō passus, dum conderet urbem 5
> īnferretque deōs Latiō, genus unde Latīnum
> Albānīque patrēs atque altae moenia Rōmae.

1 **arma, -ōrum,** n. pl., *arms, weapons*
  ōra, -ae, f., *shore*
2 **fātum, -ī,** n., *fate*
  profugus, -a, -um, *exiled, fugitive*
  Lāvīnius, -a, -um, *of Lavinium (name of the town where the Trojans first settled in Italy)*
3 **lītus, lītoris,** n., *shore*
  altum, -ī, n., *the deep, the sea*
4 **superī, -ōrum,** m. pl., *the gods above*
  superum = superōrum
  saevus, -a, -um, *fierce, savage*

memor, memoris, *remembering, mindful, unforgetting*
Iūnō, Iūnōnis, f. *Juno (queen of the gods)*
ob, prep. + acc., *on account of*
5 **dum conderet...īnferretque,** *until he could found...and bring...into*
6 **Latium, -ī,** n., *Latium (the area of central Italy that included Rome)*
  genus, generis, n., *race, stock, nation*
7 **Albānus, -a, -um,** *of Alba Longa (city founded by Aeneas' son, Ascanius)*
  moenia, moenium, n. pl., *city walls*

1 **canō, canere, cecinī, cantus,** *to sing*

Mantua mē genuit, Calabrī rapuēre, tenet nunc
Parthenopē: cecinī pascua, rūra, ducēs.
Mantua gave me life, Calabria took it away, now
Naples holds me: I sang of pastures, fields, and heroes.
(Inscription on the tomb of Vergil)

Vergil reading the *Aeneid* to Augustus and his sister, Octavia, memorialized here by Ingres.
Legend has it that Octavia fainted when Vergil reached the verses about the death of her son.
Watercolor and graphite drawing, the Fogg Art Museum, Harvard University, Cambridge. Bequest of Grenville L. Winthrop

TO FATHER FROM SEXTUS

Sextus patrī suō S.P.D.

Avē, mī pater! Sī tū valēs, ego gaudeō. Sed nēmō est mē miserior. Māter mea Pompeiīs mortua est. Tū mē in Italiā relīquistī, cum in Asiam profectus es. O mē miserum!

Prīmō quidem Baiīs habitāre mē dēlectābat. Ibi ad lītus īre, in marī natāre, scaphās 5 spectāre solēbam. In silvīs quoque cum Marcō cotīdiē ambulābam; inde regressus, cum vīlicō Dāvō, quī mē maximē amat, in hortō labōrābam.

Ōlim, dum prope rīvum in silvīs ambulāmus, Cornēliam et Flāviam magnā vōce clāmantēs audīvimus. Statim accurrimus et lupum ingentem puellās petentem cōnspeximus. Tum Marcus, maximō terrōre affectus, arborem ascendit neque dēsilīre 10 ausus est. Ego tamen magnō rāmō lupum reppulī et puellās servāvī sōlus.

At abhinc paucōs mēnsēs nōs omnēs, Baiīs profectī, maximō itinere Rōmam pervēnimus. Dum autem Rōmae habitō, mē dēlectat ad Circum Maximum īre. Russātīs ego faveō quī semper vincunt.

(continued)

2 **Avē!/Avēte!** *Greetings!*
  valeō, -ēre, -uī, -itūrus, *to be strong,*
    be well
5 **prīmō,** adv., *first, at first*

  natō, -āre, -āvī, -ātūrus, *to swim*
  scapha, -ae, f., *small boat*
6 **inde,** adv., *from there, then*

10 **dēsiliō, dēsilīre, dēsiluī,** *to leap down*
11 **audeō, audēre, ausus sum,** semi-deponent + infin., *to dare (to)*
  repellō, repellere, reppulī, repulsus, *to drive off, drive back*

Exercise 40a
Respondē Latīnē:

1. Ubi nunc est Sextī pater?
2. Quid Sextus Baiīs facere solēbat?
3. Quis Sextum maximē amābat?
4. Dīcitne Sextus vēra?
5. Dīcitne Sextus vēram fābulam dē puellīs et lupō?
6. Quid Sextum Rōmae facere dēlectat?
7. Cūr Sextus russātīs favet?

    vērus, -a, -um, *true*
      vēra dīcere, *to tell the truth*

Nunc tamen miserrimus sum propter īrācundiam Palaemonis magistrī nostrī. Ille 15
enim homō īrācundissimus mē, quamquam discere semper cupiō, saepe ferulā ferōciter
verberat. Cotīdiē dē Aenēae itineribus multa mē rogat. Eī rogantī respondēre semper
cōnor. Cēterōs tamen puerōs semper facillima, mē semper difficillima rogat. Heri
quidem dē Hesperiā loquēbātur, dē quā neque ego neque cēterī puerī quidquam sciunt.
Immō vērō, etiam Aenēās ipse ignōrābat ubi esset Hesperia! Grammaticus tamen, cum 20
ego ignōrārem, īrā commōtus, ferulam rapuit et mē crūdēlissimē verberāvit. Deinde
domum statim ab Eucleide ductus sum. Cum prīmum domum advēnimus, ā Cornēliō
arcessītus sum. Eī rem tōtam explicāre cōnābar, sed mē nē loquī quidem sīvit. Iterum
igitur poenās dedī.

Ō pater, regredere, obsecrō, quam prīmum in Italiam! Ego sum miser et valdē 25
aegrōtō. Amā mē et valē!

15 **īrācundia, -ae,** f., *irritability, bad temper*
19 **neque...neque...quidquam,** *neither...nor...anything*
20 **immō vērō,** adv., *on the contrary, in fact*
ignōrō, -āre, -āvī, -ātus, *to be ignorant, not to know*
cum, conj., *since*

21 **crūdēlis, -is, -e,** *cruel*
22 **cum prīmum,** conj., *as soon as*
24 **poena, -ae,** f., *punishment, penalty*
poenās dare, *to pay the penalty, be punished*
25 **obsecrō, -āre, -āvī, -ātus,** *to beseech, beg*
quam prīmum, adv., *as soon as possible*

16 **discō, discere, didicī,** *to learn*
cupiō, cupere, cupīvī, cupītus, *to desire, want*
21 **rapiō, rapere, rapuī, raptus,** *to snatch, seize*
23 **arcessō, arcessere, arcessīvī, arcessītus,** *to summon, send for*

Respondē Latīnē:

1. Estne Palaemōn magister vērō īrācundissimus?
2. Estne rogātiō dē Hesperiā vērō facilis vel difficilis?
3. Aegrōtatne vērō Sextus?

rogātiō, rogātiōnis, f., *question*

FORMS
Semi-deponent Verbs

Some Latin verbs have regular active forms with active meanings in the present, imperfect, and future tenses but have passive forms with active meanings in the perfect, pluperfect, and future perfect:

audeō, audēre, ausus sum + infin., *to dare (to)*
gaudeō, gaudēre, gāvīsus sum, *to be glad, rejoice*
soleō, solēre, solitus sum + infin., *to be accustomed (to), be in the habit of*

These are called *semi-deponent verbs* because they are deponent (i.e., they have passive forms with active meanings) only in the perfect, pluperfect, and future perfect tenses, those made from the third principal part.

Exercise 40b
Read aloud and translate:

1. audet	9. gaudēmus	17. solent
2. audēbis	10. gāvīsae sumus	18. solitī sumus
3. ausus sum	11. gaudēbāmus	19. solēbāmus
4. audēbāmus	12. gāvīsī eritis	20. solitī eritis
5. ausī erāmus	13. gāvīsus es	21. solētis
6. audētis	14. gāvīsa eris	22. solitae erāmus
7. ausae erunt	15. gaudēbunt	23. solēbam
8. ausī sunt	16. gāvīsus eram	24. solēbitis

BUILDING THE MEANING
Present Participles

Look at the following sentence:

> Cornēliam et Flāviam **clāmantēs** audīvimus. (40:8–9)
> *We heard Cornelia and Flavia **shouting**.*

The word **clāmantēs** is a *present active participle*. As you learned in Chapter 33, participles are *verbal adjectives*, that is, adjectives made from the stems of verbs. The participle **clāmantēs** is a verbal adjective describing **Cornēliam et Flāviam**.

Here are some further examples:

> Cornēliam et Flāviam <u>magnā vōce</u> **clāmantēs** audīvimus. (40:8–9)
> *We heard Cornelia and Flavia **shouting** <u>with a loud voice/loudly</u>.*

> Lupum ingentem <u>puellās</u> **petentem** cōnspeximus. (40:9–10)
> *We caught sight of a huge wolf **attacking** <u>the girls</u>.*

Since participles are *verbal* adjectives, they can be modified by ablatives such as **magnā vōce**, and they can take direct objects such as **puellās**, as seen in the sentences above.

Translating Present Participles:

The present participle describes an action going on *at the same time* as the action of the main verb in the clause. Translation of the participle will vary according to the tense of the main verb:

> Puellās **clāmantēs** audīmus. (main verb present tense)
> *We hear the girls **shouting**.*
> *We hear the girls **who are shouting**.*

(continued)

Puellās **clāmantēs** audīvimus. (main verb perfect tense)
*We heard the girls **shouting**.*
*We heard the girls **who** <u>were</u> **shouting**.*

Present participles can sometimes best be translated into English as relative clauses (see the examples just above). Sometimes they can best be translated as clauses introduced by subordinating conjunctions:

Puerī **currentēs** dēfessī fīunt.
*The boys **when/while running** become tired.*
*The boys **because/since they are running** become tired.*

Puerī **currentēs** tamen dēfessī nōn fīunt.
*The boys, **although they are running**, nevertheless do not become tired.*

Present Participles as Substantives:

Since participles are adjectives, they can also be used *substantively*, i.e., as words that function as nouns. In Chapter 23 you learned that adjectives may be used substantively, i.e., that **multa et mīra** (neuter plural adjectives) can mean *many wonderful things*. Participles may also be used substantively:

Subitō exclāmāvit ūnus ex **adstantibus**, "Cavēte, omnēs!" (30:18)
*Suddenly one of [those] **standing near** shouted, "Watch out, everyone!"*
*Suddenly one of **the bystanders**....*

Here the participle **adstantibus** is used as a noun meaning *bystanders*.

Exercise 40c
In your reading you have already met these sentences with present participles. The participles are in boldface. Read the sentences aloud and translate them. When participles are being used as adjectives, tell what noun they modify:

1. "Cavēte!" exclāmant **adstantēs**, sed frūstrā.
2. Subitō Cornēlia duōs servōs per viam **festīnantēs** cōnspicit.
3. Nunc Cornēlia cōnspicit poētam versūs **recitantem**, nunc mendīcōs pecūniam **petentēs**.
4. Convīvae paulisper in ātriō stābant, Cornēlium **exspectantēs**.
5. Titus, ad locum suum lentē **ambulāns**, "Salvēte, amīcī omnēs!" inquit.
6. Ubi īnsulae iam appropinquābāmus, hominēs quōsdam in popīnam **intrantēs** cōnspeximus.
7. Herī vesperī Eucleidēs noster, ab urbe domum **rediēns**, duōs hominēs ē popīnā quādam **exeuntēs** vīdit.

FORMS
Present Participles

Here are the nominative and genitive singular forms of present participles of all four conjugations:

1st:	**parāns, parantis,** *preparing*	*-iō:* **iaciēns, iacientis,** *throwing*
2nd:	**habēns, habentis,** *having*	4th: **audiēns, audientis,** *hearing*
3rd:	**mittēns, mittentis,** *sending*	

The participles of deponent verbs have similar active forms and are active in meaning:

1st:	**cōnāns, cōnantis,** *trying*	*-iō:* **regrediēns, regredientis,** *returning*
2nd:	**verēns, verentis,** *fearing*	
3rd:	**loquēns, loquentis,** *speaking*	4th: **experiēns, experientis,** *testing*

NOTES
1. The nominative ends in *-ns,* and the stem, which is found by dropping the ending from the genitive singular, ends in *-nt-*.
2. The vowel preceding the letters *-ns* is always long.
3. The vowel preceding the letters *-nt-* is always short.

Present participles have 3rd declension endings. Compare the endings of present participles with those of 3rd declension nouns and adjectives and of comparative adjectives:

When the participle is used as a simple *adjective,* the ablative singular ends in *-ī,* just as do 3rd declension adjectives; when the participle is used as a true *verbal adjective* or as a *substantive,* the ablative singular ends in *-e,* just as do 3rd declension nouns, thus:

Number Case	Masc.	Fem.	Neut.
Singular			
Nominative	parāns	parāns	parāns
Genitive	parant*is*	parant*is*	parant*is*
Dative	parant*ī*	parant*ī*	parant*ī*
Accusative	parant*em*	parant*em*	parāns
Ablative	parant*ī/e*	parant*ī/e*	parant*ī/e*
Plural			
Nominative	parant*ēs*	parant*ēs*	parant*ia*
Genitive	parant*ium*	parant*ium*	parant*ium*
Dative	parant*ibus*	parant*ibus*	parant*ibus*
Accusative	parant*ēs*	parant*ēs*	parant*ia*
Ablative	parant*ibus*	parant*ibus*	parant*ibus*

Eucleidēs ā praedōne **currentī** cōnsecūtus est. (simple adjective)
*Eucleides was overtaken by the **running** robber.*

Eucleidēs ā praedōne **celerrimē currente** cōnsecūtus est. (verbal adjective)
*Eucleides was overtaken by the robber **that was running very quickly.***

(continued)

Aqua ab **adstante** ad incendium portāta est. (substantive)
*Water was brought to the fire by **a bystander**.*

The present participle of the verb **īre**, *to go*, is **iēns, euntis.** There is no present participle of the verb **esse**, *to be.*

Exercise 40d
Read aloud and translate. Locate three examples of participles used as substantives. Try translating the other participles with relative clauses or with clauses introduced by *when, while,* or *although*:

1. Aenēās Hesperiam petēns Carthāginem advēnit.
2. Marcus patrem epistulās in tablīnō scrībentem invēnit.
3. Adstantēs rogāvī ubi esset incendium.
4. Eucleidēs nocte per viās domum rediēns ā praedōnibus percussus est.
5. Dāvō in hortō labōrantī molestī erant puerī.
6. Mihi rogantī puellae nihil respondērunt.
7. Plūrimī natantium scaphās lītorī appropinquantēs vīdērunt.
8. Audīta est vōx magistrī puerōs reprehendentis.
9. Cornēlius in ātriō Eucleidem exspectāns cēterōs servōs in culīnā colloquentēs audīvit.
10. Cornēliō domō ēgredientī occurrit Titus, frāter eius.
11. Clāmōrēs gaudentium in viīs audītī sunt.
12. Cornēlius servīs fercula in trīclīnium portantibus signum dedit.
13. Cornēliī in caupōnā pernoctantēs mortem timēbant.
14. Mulierēs ad templum prōcēdentēs cōnspeximus.
15. Puellae inter sē colloquentēs multa et mīra dē puerīs nārrābant.
16. Nōs domō ēgredientēs mātrem in ātriō sedentem vīdimus.
17. Sextum arborem ascendentem dēsilīre iussī.

━━ ━━ ━━━ ━━ ━━

Quidquid id est, timeō Danaōs et dōna ferentēs. *Whatever it is, I fear the Greeks, even bearing gifts.* (Vergil, *Aeneid* II.49)
Venientī occurrite morbō! *Meet the malady as it comes!* (Persius, *Satires* III.64)
Rīdentem dīcere vērum quid vetat? *What prevents me from speaking the truth with a smile?* (Horace, *Satires* I.I.24–25)

━━ ━━ ━━━ ━━ ━━

WRITING, LETTERS, AND BOOKS

The letter that Cornelia wrote to Flavia in Chapter 36 and the one that Sextus wrote to his father in Chapter 40 would have been written either on tablets (**tabellae** or **cērae**) or on sheets of material made from papyrus. Tablets made of sheets of wood with the surface hollowed out and filled with wax **(cēra)** were widely used for everyday writing needs and in the schools. Two or more tablets could be fastened together with leather thongs laced through holes, and writing was done on the wax surfaces with a stylus (**stilus**) that was pointed at one end for writing and flat at the other end for erasing mistakes by smoothing the wax.

Letters could also be written on sheets of material made from Egyptian papyrus. This material was manufactured in Egypt and exported throughout the Mediterranean world. It was made from the pith of the triangular stalks of the papyrus plant that grew to be four or five inches thick and up to fourteen feet tall. Strips of the pith were laid out side by side, and another layer of strips was placed over them at right angles. When pressed together the papyrus strips released an adhesive agent that bonded them. The resulting sheets of material were then dried in the sun and smoothed with pumice stone as necessary. Sheets could be glued together as needed, and writing was done with pens (**pennae**) made from reeds or metal with ink made from lamp soot and vegetable gum.

If the letter was written on a pair of tablets, they could be folded together with the writing on the inside and bound with a cord that could be sealed with wax and stamped by the letter writer with his or her signet ring. The papyrus paper could be rolled up, bound, and sealed in the same way.

Books were usually produced by gluing sheets of papyrus side by side into a long strip of material that was then rolled up into what was called a **volūmen**, *roll*. The writing was usually done only on the side of the material that was rolled up inside, and it was done in columns perpendicular to the length of the material. To read a papyrus roll you would hold the roll in your right hand and unroll it with your left, rolling it up again at the left hand as you read the successive columns of text as they appeared from the roll at the right. When finished, one would rewind the material to the right so that it would be ready for the next reader to unroll it. A strip of material called a **titulus** was often attached to the edge of the last sheet of papyrus on the roll and would protrude from the roll. On it would be written the author and title of the book. Knobs might also be attached to the top and bottom of the last sheet of the roll to make it easier to roll it up. Since papyrus rolls were relatively fragile, they were often slipped into cases (**capsae** or **capsulae**) and stored in round wooden boxes or cabinets.

In the third century B.C. great libraries flourished in the centers of Greek civilization in the East, with the most famous one being in Alexandria in Egypt. In the late Republic Romans began to collect books in private libraries in their homes. Cicero, for example, had several libraries, both in his town house and at his country estates. During the reign of Augustus public libraries were established in Rome, and by the time of our story libraries were available in some of the great bathing establishments, where one could also hear recitations of literary works.

Rather than writing themselves, well-to-do Romans would usually have highly trained slaves take dictation. Copies of books could be made by individual slaves copying by sight from an original onto a new papyrus roll or by groups of slaves simultaneously taking dictation from one master reader. The book trade was only

In an age before printing, copies of books were created by a scribe, shown here as later centuries pictured him.

Oil on canvas, "A Roman Scribe" by Sir Lawrence Alma-Tadema, private collection

loosely organized, but by the time of our story there were book shops in Rome where one could buy books or have copies made. The poet Martial referred to the district in Rome called the Argiletum as a place where his poetry could be bought:

> Of course you often go down to the Argiletum. There is a shop opposite Caesar's Forum with its door-posts from top to bottom bearing advertisements, so that you can in a moment read through the list of poets. Look for me in that quarter. No need to ask Atrectus (that is the name of the shopkeeper): out of the first or second pigeon-hole he will offer you Martial smoothed with pumice and smart with purple, for five **dēnāriī**.
>
> —Martial, *Epigrams* I.117.9–17

WORD STUDY X

The Present Participial Stem

The stem of the present participle of a Latin verb sometimes becomes an English noun or adjective with a meaning closely related to that of the Latin verb. The stem of the present participle is found by dropping the ending **-is** from the genitive singular, e.g., **laudantis**, stem **laudant-**. The English word *agent* is derived from the Latin **agēns**, **agentis** (stem: **agent-**), the present participle of **agere**, *to do, drive*. Similarly, the English word *vigilant* is derived from **vigilāns, vigilantis** (stem: **vigilant-**), the present participle of **vigilāre**, *to stay awake*.

Whether the English word ends in *-ant* or *-ent* usually depends on the spelling of the Latin participle from which it is derived, as the above examples show. There are a few exceptions to this rule: they are words that came from Latin into English through Old French, which regularly changed all Latin present participial stems to *-ant*. Such English words end in *-ant*, regardless of the spelling of the original Latin participle. For example, the English word *dormant*, from Old French *dormant*, is derived from **dormiēns, dormientis** (stem: **dormient-**), the present participle of **dormīre**, *to sleep*. To be sure of the correct spelling, always consult an English dictionary.

Exercise 1

Give the English word made from the present participial stem of each of the following Latin verbs. Give the meaning of the English word, and check in a dictionary for its correct spelling:

1. servāre	4. accidere	7. occupāre
2. recipere	5. patī	8. dēfendere
3. exspectāre	6. studēre	9. repellere

Present Participial Stem + Suffix *-ia*

The suffix *-ia* may be added to the stem of the present participle of some Latin verbs. The addition of this suffix forms a first declension noun that designates the "state of," "quality of," or "act of" the meaning of the verb:

Latin Verb	Pres. Part.	P. P. Stem	Suffix	Latin Noun
convenīre, *to come together*	**conveniēns, convenientis**	**convenient-** + *-ia*		**convenientia, -ae, f.,** *agreement, harmony*
cōnstāre, *to stand firm*	**cōnstāns, cōnstantis**	**cōnstant-** + *-ia*		**cōnstantia, -ae, f.,** *steadiness*

When nouns formed in this way come into English, the letters **-tia** become *-ce* or *-cy*, e.g., *convenience, constancy*.

Exercise 2

For each English word below, give the Latin present participle (nom. sing.) and the meaning of the Latin verb from which it is derived. Give the meaning of the English word. Consult an English dictionary, as necessary:

1. audience
2. currency
3. stance
4. cadence
5. science
6. ambulance
7. sequence
8. eloquence
9. credence

Suffixes -īnus and -(i)ānus

Some Latin adjectives are formed by adding either the suffix *-īnus, -a, -um* or *-(i)ānus, -a, -um* to the base of a noun. Such adjectives mean "of" or "pertaining to" the word to which the suffix is attached:

Latin Noun	Base	Suffix	Latin Adjective
Rōma, -ae, f.	**Rōm-** +	*-ānus* =	**Rōmānus, -a, -um,** *Roman, of Rome*
mare, maris, n.	**mar-** +	*-īnus* =	**marīnus, -a, -um,** *marine, of the sea*

English words derived from this kind of Latin adjective generally end in *-ine* or *-an* (occasionally *-ane*), e.g., *marine, Roman*.

Exercise 3

For each Latin word below, give the Latin adjective ending in *-(i)ānus*. Give the English derivative and its meaning:

1. **Āfrica, -ae,** f.
2. **silva, -ae,** f.
3. **merīdiēs, -ēī,** m.
4. **Troia, -ae,** f.
5. **vetus, veteris**
6. **urbs, urbis,** f. (two English words)

The suffix *-īnus* is commonly found on Latin words for animals, e.g., **canīnus, -a, -um,** *of dogs*. The English derivative is *canine*.

Exercise 4

For each of the following animals, give the Latin adjective ending in *-īnus*. Give the English derivative and its meaning:

1. **lupus, -ī,** m.
2. **porcus, -ī,** m.
3. **equus, -ī,** m.
4. **bōs, bovis,** m./f.

Latin in Medicine

The roots of modern medicine go back to ancient Greece and Rome. The Greek physician, Hippocrates, who lived in the fifth century B.C., is considered the "father of medicine." In Roman times it was Galen, doctor to the emperor Marcus Aurelius (ruled A.D. 161–180), who expanded the frontiers of medical knowledge. His writings formed the foundation of medical science for centuries. It is no wonder that Latin and Greek are fundamental to the vocabulary of medicine.

Some Latin medical terms have become common English words, e.g., *abdomen* (belly), *cancer* (crab), *virus* (poison). Others are more obscure, e.g., *angina pectoris* (chest pain), *vena cava* ("hollow vein," vein entering the right *atrium* of the heart). Further evidence of medical Latin may be found in doctors' prescriptions, many of which use Latin abbreviations:

Rx (Recipe)	*Take*
c̄ (cum)	*with*
p.c. (post cibum)	*after eating*
t.i.d. (ter in diē)	*3 times a day*
non rep. (nōn repetātur)	*Do not repeat*

Knowledge of Latin (and Greek) can be very helpful in solving the mystery that often surrounds medical language.

Exercise 5

Replace the italicized words in each sentence with a Latin medical term of equivalent meaning, chosen from the pool below. Consult an English dictionary (or medical dictionary) for the meanings of the terms in the pool.

1. The kick Eucleides received was strong enough to break his *shinbone*.
2. Sometimes a doctor will prescribe a *substance containing no medication* in order to humor a patient whose illness is imaginary.
3. The doctor's prescription read, "Take *at bedtime*."
4. The heartbeat of the *unborn child* was normal.
5. The *small piece of tissue* that hangs down at the back of the throat is a Latin word meaning "little grape."
6. The backbone is made up of several *disk-shaped bones*.
7. The doctor wrote "*before meals*" on the prescription.
8. The *brain* is protected by the skull.
9. The ulcer was located in the *intestine measuring twelve fingers long*.
10. The *outer layer* of the adrenal gland produces important substances.
11. Lifting requires contraction of the *two-headed muscle* of the upper arm.
12. The doctor's abbreviation read, "Take *twice a day*."

biceps	vertebrae	H.S. (hōrā somnī)
cerebrum	placebo	duodenum
tibia	a.c. (ante cibum)	b.i.d. (bis in diē)
fetus	uvula	cortex

Exercise 6

Using reference material from a library or from your science teacher, make a diagram of the human skeleton, and label the bones that have Latin or Greek names.

DRAMATIC NEWS

Māne erat. Iam puerī ad lūdum profectī erant. Cornēlia sōla in domō sedēns tēlam sine studiō texēbat. Īrācunda erat quod Baiās regredī atque Flāviam amīcam suam vidēre cupiēbat. Dē multīs rēbus cōgitābat trīstis, cum māter ingressa est.

"Trīstis vidēris, Cornēlia. Aegrane es?"

"Urbs Rōma mihi nōn placet, māter," respondit Cornēlia. "Tōtum diem sōla domī 5 maneō. Mihi nōn licet forās īre. Hīc ego labōrō sōla, sed Marcus et Sextus ūnā cum multīs aliīs in lūdō student. Hīc nūllās amīcās habeō. Hīc nē canem quidem habeō. Cūr nōn Baiās regredī licet? Meam enim Flāviam rūrsus vidēre cupiō."

"Cūr Baiās regredī vīs, Cornēlia? Quīntus Valerius, adulēscēns ille optimus, hūc paucīs diēbus veniet. Nōnne eum vidēre vīs? Diū in Bīthȳniā, ut bene scīs, āfuit sed nunc 10 in Italiam regressus est. Nāve ēgressus, paulisper Brundisiī est morātus. Inde abhinc trēs diēs discessisse dīcitur; paucīs diēbus hūc adveniet. Pater tuus diū loquēbātur cum illō servō quī epistulam attulit. Quī ūnā cum dominō suō ē Bīthȳniā profectus, ē multīs itineris perīculīs vix effūgit atque, ut ipse dīcit, dominum ex hīs perīculīs ēripuit."

Cornēlia, cum hoc audīvisset, maximē gaudēbat quod Valerium vidēre valdē cupiēbat. 15 "Quantum mē dēlectat tālia audīre!" inquit. "Arcesse, obsecrō, māter, illum servum! Ipsa cum eō loquī cupiō et dē hīs perīculīs audīre."

Itaque arcessītus servus rem tōtam eīs nārrāvit.

(continued in Chapter 42)

1 **tēla, -ae,** f., *web, fabric*	**dīcitur,** *(he) is said*
2 **studium, -ī,** n., *enthusiasm*	16 **Quantum...!** adv., *How much...!*
6 **forās,** adv., *outside*	**tālia, tālium,** n. pl., *such things*
12 **discessisse,** *to have departed*	

2 **texō, texere, texuī, textus,** *to weave*

Exercise 41a
Respondē Latīnē:

1. Quid faciēbat Cornēlia sōla sedēns?
2. Cūr trīstis Cornēlia vidētur?
3. Ubi tōtum diem manet Cornēlia?
4. Puerīne quoque ibi manent?
5. Habetne in urbe amīcās Cornēlia?
6. Quem Cornēlia rūrsus vidēre cupit?
7. Quō Cornēlia regredī cupit?
8. Quis est Valerius?
9. Quandō Rōmam adveniet Valerius?
10. Ubi morātus est Valerius?
11. Unde in Italiam est Valerius regressus?
12. Quōcum Valerius iter fēcit?
13. Quis epistulam ab hōc servō accēpit?
14. Quid necesse fuit Valeriī servō in itinere facere?
15. Cūr servum Valeriī arcessī Cornēlia vult?

FORMS
Verbs: Perfect Active Infinitive

The form **discessisse**, *to have departed*, which you met in line 12 of story 41, is a *perfect active infinitive*. First look at the principal parts of this verb:

>   discēdō, discēdere, discessī, discessūrus

Two clues will help you recognize the perfect active infinitive:

>   the perfect stem, **discess-**, formed by dropping the *-ī* from the
>   third principal part

>   the ending *-isse*

The perfect active infinitive expresses an action that was completed *before* the action of the main verb:

>   Inde abhinc trēs diēs **discessisse** dīcitur. (41:11–12)
>   *He is said **to have departed** from there three days ago.*

Exercise 41b
Read aloud and translate (note that the verbs in this exercise and the next are all taken from story 41):

1. trāxisse
2. fuisse
3. cupīvisse

4. cōgitāvisse
5. placuisse
6. respondisse

7. mānsisse
8. vīdisse
9. texuisse

Exercise 41c
Give the Latin for:

1. He is said to have studied diligently.
2. . . . to have had a dog.
3. . . . to have seen Valerius in Brundisium.
4. . . . to have wanted to see him.
5. . . . to have come from Bithynia.
6. . . . to have arrived home.
7. . . . to have brought a letter.
8. . . . to have escaped from many dangers.
9. . . . to have snatched his master from these dangers.
10. . . . to have told the whole thing.

FRONTIER LIFE V
WEAVING THE TUNIC

In the previous Frontier Life section, you read how Helge and her friend Helena spun wool into yarn for weaving. In the story at the beginning of this chapter you saw Cornelia weaving fabric while daydreaming of returning to Baiae and seeing her friend Flavia. We resume our story of frontier life with a description of how Helge wove her yarn into a tunic for her husband Lucius.

To weave the wool into a tunic (Helena was making a cloak), Helge used an upright loom with the warp threads weighted down by stones with holes drilled in them. Before she could string the warp, she had to weave the starting border, which would be attached to the top bar of the loom, for the threads extending from this border would be the warp. Using the pegs of the hand loom, Helge measured off from her strongest, stoutest yarn the exact length she would need for the warp, and she then wove a short border, one finger joint wide.

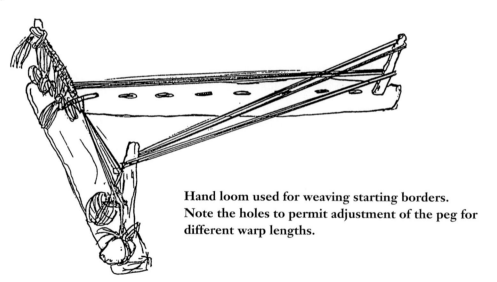

Hand loom used for weaving starting borders. Note the holes to permit adjustment of the peg for different warp lengths.

Her starting border finished, Helge was ready to begin warping her big loom. She attached the border to the round bar that was the top of her loom, taking care that none of the threads became tangled, and she took the warp-weights and arranged them in a row at the base of the loom. She tied the threads to the weights with about six threads to a stone. Weighting all the threads and preparing her loom for the weaving was a painstaking process that took skill and patience. Only then could the weaving of the cloth itself actually begin.

The poet Ovid (*Metamorphoses* VI.55–58) describes the weaving as follows:

> A reed separates the threads of the warp, and the woof is inserted through them with sharp shuttles passed quickly by the fingers, and the notched teeth of the comb pound the woof passed through the warp into place.

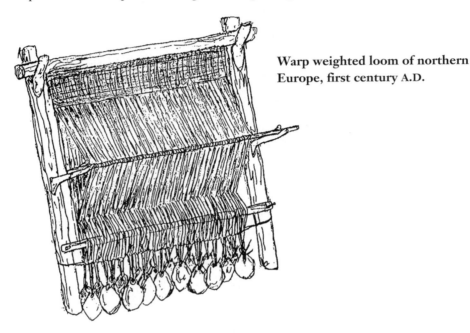

Warp weighted loom of northern Europe, first century A.D.

Since neither Helge nor her mother knew how to read or write, the way that they remembered the patterns of their complicated tartans was by verses of song, handed down from generation to generation. Although Helge was now weaving cloth of a solid color, out of habit she sang a song that told her the instructions and the colors for one of the beautiful clan plaids:

> Red, red for the color of the sun, two strands of red.
> Blue, blue, twenty strands of blue, the color of my eyes.
> Green, five strands of green, the color of the leaves of the oak.
> Red, again red, two strands.
> Yellow, the color of the sun, five strands of yellow, the color of my hair.

Helge continued singing and weaving until the tunic length was finished.

Taking a bone needle, she threaded it with the same red yarn used for the cloth, and passing it in and out she sewed a border at the bottom. She removed the starting border from the pegs at the top of the loom. Carefully folding the tunic length over her arm, she knelt on the floor and untied the warp weights. Then she repeated the whole process and wove another rectangle of material.

In comparison with the weaving, the actual sewing of the tunic was easy. Helge could not help but notice that the amount of fabric needed was just right for a tunic for her younger brother of thirteen but much, much too small for her father or any other grown man of her people; the Romans were that much smaller than the Ubians and other northern clans. Helge hemmed the two rectangles of fabric together, leaving a neck hole, and at the sides leaving openings for the arms. Looking at the finished tunic, she smiled. "Won't my soldier be pleased with his new tunic," she thought as she carefully folded it.

A SLAVE TO THE RESCUE

Quīntus Valerius, dominus meus, abhinc duōs mēnsēs ē Bīthȳniā Rōmam ā patre missus est epistulās ferēns. Ego ūnā cum dominō profectus sum. Cum quattuor diēs nāvigāvissēmus, subitō maxima tempestās coorta est. Nāvis hūc illūc ventīs iactāta in ingentī erat perīculō. Tandem cum undae et ventī nāvem ad īnsulam quandam ēgissent, nōs in terram vix ēvāsimus. Tōtam noctem in lītore morātī, prīmā lūce, quod iam vīs 5 tempestātis cecidisse vidēbātur, in nāvem regressī sumus.

Subitō complūrēs scaphās hominum plēnās cōnspeximus. Magister nāvis nostrae, cum hās scaphās cōnspexisset, "Prō dī immortālēs!" exclāmāvit. "Hī hominēs sunt pīrātae. Ēheu! effugere nōn poterimus."

Cui dominus meus, "Sī mē servāveris," inquit, "pater meus, quī est vir dīves et 10 praeclārus, magnam tibi pecūniam dabit. Haec nāvis est illīs scaphīs celerior. Pīrātae, etiam sī sequentur, nōs nōn capient."

Effugere cōnātī sumus, sed frūstrā. Pīrātae enim, cum nōs effugere cōnantēs cōnspexissent, nāvem nostram adortī sunt. Dominus meus statim gladium strīnxit et mihi clāmāns "Mē sequere!" in scapham dēsiluit. 15

Ego quidem secūtus dominum meum dēfendere coepī, nam vulnus grave accēpisse vidēbātur. Magister nāvis, cum valdē timēret, suōs vetuit nōs adiuvāre. "Sī pīrātīs resistēmus," inquit, "nōs omnēs sine dubiō necābimur." (continued)

3 **ventus, -ī,** m., *wind*	**magister, magistrī,** m., *schoolmaster;*
4 **unda, -ae,** f., *wave*	*master; captain*
7 **scapha, -ae,** f., *small boat, ship's boat*	8 **Prō dī immortālēs!** *Good heavens!*
	10 **dīves, dīvitis,** *rich*

   3 **coorior, coorīrī, coortus sum,** *to rise up, arise*
   5 **ēvādō, ēvādere, ēvāsī, ēvāsus,** *to escape*
  14 **adorior, adorīrī, adortus sum,** *to attack*
  18 **resistō, resistere, restitī** + dat., *to resist*

Exercise 42a
Respondē Latīnē:

1. Quis Quīntum Valerium ē Bīthȳniā mīsit?
2. Quot diēs nāvigāverant?
3. Quid nāvem iactāvit?
4. Quem ad locum nāvis ācta est?
5. Quō in locō Valerius et servus noctem morātī sunt?
6. Quid magister nāvis prīmā lūce cōnspexit?
7. Quid pīrātae fēcērunt cum nāvem fugientem cōnspexissent?
8. Quid servus facere coepit cum dominus vulnus accēpisset?

Tum pīrātae, cum nōs superāvissent, arma nōbīs adēmērunt et nōs ad lītus addūxērunt. Cum prīmum in terrā fuimus, pīrātae circum nōs stantēs rogābant quī 20 essēmus, unde vēnissēmus, quō iter facerēmus. Omnēs tacēbant praeter dominum meum. Ille enim, "Sī pecūniam vultis," inquit, "nūllam pecūniam hīc inveniētis. Nōs omnēs pauperēs sumus. At nisi nōs abīre sinētis, vōs omnēs poenās certē dabitis. Cīvis sum Rōmānus."

Rīsērunt pīrātae, et ūnus ex eīs exclāmāvit, "Rōmānōs nōn amō. Sī vōs nūllam 25 pecūniam habētis, vōs certē necābimus." Tum magister nāvis metū commōtus, "Hic adulēscēns," inquit, "vēra nōn dīcit. Pater eius est vir dīvitissimus. Ille magnam vōbīs pecūniam dabit." Itaque pīrātārum aliī dominum meum in casam suam trāxērunt, aliī nōs cēterōs in nāvem redūxērunt et ibi custōdiēbant.

Nocte, cum omnēs dormīrent, ego surrēxī, pūgiōne modo armātus. Clam in mare 30 dēsiluī, ad lītus natāvī, casam pīrātārum summā celeritāte petīvī. Cum casae fūrtim appropinquāvissem, per fenestram vīdī dominum meum in lectō iacentem ac duōs custōdēs vīnum bibentēs. Paulisper nihil faciēbam. Mox tamen alter ē custōdibus ē casā exiit, alter cum dominō meō manēbat. Tum ego silentiō ingressus hunc custōdem pūgiōne percussī. Deinde ē casā ēgressus ad lītus dominum portāvī, nam ille propter 35 vulnus aegrōtābat neque ambulāre poterat. Ibi scapham invēnī quam pīrātae nōn custōdiēbant. Ita ā lītore profectī ex īnsulā ēvāsimus.

Iam multōs diēs in scaphā erāmus cum ā mercātōribus quibusdam inventī sumus. Quoniam neque cibum neque aquam habēbāmus, graviter aegrōtābāmus. Sed mercātōrēs nōs cūrāvērunt et Brundisium attulērunt. Ibi dominus meus multōs diēs morātus iam 40 convaluit et paucīs diēbus aderit.

19	**superō, -āre, -āvī, -ātus,** *to overcome*	30	**pūgiō, pūgiōnis,** m., *dagger*
23	**pauper, pauperis,** *poor*		**clam,** adv., *secretly*
28	**casa, -ae,** f., *hut, cottage*	39	**quoniam,** conj., *since*

41 **convalēscō, convalēscere, convaluī,** *to grow stronger, get well*

Respondē Latīnē:

1. Quō pīrātae superātōs addūxērunt?
2. Quid pīrātae facient sī Valerius pecūniam nōn habet?
3. Quid servus nocte fēcit?
4. Quōmodo Valerius et servus ex īnsulā ēvāsērunt?

Fortī et fidēlī nihil est difficile. *Nothing is difficult for a brave and trustworthy man.*

BUILDING THE MEANING
Subordinate Clauses with the Subjunctive I

Since Chapter 40 you have been meeting subordinate clauses with their verbs in the *subjunctive*. The subjunctive (Latin, **sub-**, *under* + **iūnct-**, *joined*) is a set of Latin verb forms that are often used in subordinate clauses. Here are examples from the story at the beginning of this chapter:

1. Magister nāvis, cum valdē **timēret**, suōs vetuit nōs adiuvāre. (42:17)
   *The captain of the ship, since/because **he was** very **frightened**, forbade his own men to help us.*

2. Cum quattuor diēs **nāvigāvissēmus**, subitō maxima tempestās coorta est. (42:2–3)
   *When **we had sailed** four days, suddenly a very great storm arose.*

The verb **timēret** in the first sentence above is an *imperfect subjunctive* and is translated *was....*

The verb **nāvigāvissēmus** in the second sentence above is a *pluperfect subjunctive* and is translated *had....*

Exercise 42b
Read aloud and translate these two sentences from story 42, both of which contain verbs in the subjunctive (in boldface):

1. Nocte, cum omnēs **dormīrent**, ego surrēxī, pūgiōne modo armātus.
2. Cum casae fūrtim **appropinquāvissem**, per fenestram vīdī dominum meum in lectō iacentem ac duōs custōdēs vīnum bibentēs.

FORMS
Verbs: Imperfect and Pluperfect Subjunctive Active
Imperfect Subjunctive Active

The imperfect subjunctive active is formed by adding the personal endings to the present active infinitive:

Active Voice

		1st Conjugation	2nd Conjugation	3rd Conjugation		4th Conjugation
Singular	1	portāre*m*	movēre*m*	míttere*m*	iácere*m*	audīre*m*
	2	portāre*s*	movēre*s*	míttere*s*	iácere*s*	audīre*s*
	3	portāre*t*	movēre*t*	míttere*t*	iácere*t*	audīre*t*
Plural	1	portārē*mus*	movērē*mus*	mitterē*mus*	iacerē*mus*	audīrē*mus*
	2	portārē*tis*	movērē*tis*	mitterē*tis*	iacerē*tis*	audīrē*tis*
	3	portāre*nt*	movēre*nt*	míttere*nt*	iácere*nt*	audīre*nt*

		ésse
Singular	1	éssem
	2	éssēs
	3	ésset
Plural	1	essḗmus
	2	essḗtis
	3	éssent

So also the irregular verbs **posse, velle, nōlle, īre,** and **ferre.**

Be sure to learn these forms thoroughly.

Note that the *e* at the end of the infinitive lengthens to *ē* except before *-m, -t,* and *-nt.*

Pluperfect Subjunctive Active

The pluperfect subjunctive active is formed by adding the personal endings to the perfect active infinitive:

		1st Conjugation	2nd Conjugation	3rd Conjugation		4th Conjugation
Singular	1	portāvíssem	mōvíssem	mīsíssem	iēcíssem	audīvíssem
	2	portāvíssēs	mōvíssēs	mīsíssēs	iēcíssēs	audīvíssēs
	3	portāvísset	mōvísset	mīsísset	iēcísset	audīvísset
Plural	1	portāvissḗmus	mōvissḗmus	mīsissḗmus	iēcissḗmus	audīvissḗmus
	2	portāvissḗtis	mōvissḗtis	mīsissḗtis	iēcissḗtis	audīvissḗtis
	3	portāvíssent	mōvíssent	mīsíssent	iēcíssent	audīvíssent

		ésse
Singular	1	fuíssem
	2	fuíssēs
	3	fuísset
Plural	1	fuissḗmus
	2	fuissḗtis
	3	fuíssent

So also the irregular verbs **posse (potuisse*m*), velle (voluisse*m*), nōlle (nōluisse*m*), īre (īsse*m*),** and **ferre (tulisse*m*).**

Note again that the *e* at the end of the infinitive lengthens to *ē* except before *-m, -t,* and *-nt.* Be sure to learn these forms thoroughly.

Exercise 42c

In story 42, locate four verbs in the imperfect subjunctive and seven in the pluperfect subjunctive.

Exercise 42d

Give the imperfect and pluperfect subjunctives, 3rd person plural, of the following verbs:

1. superō, -āre, -āvī, -ātus

2. ēvādō, ēvādere, ēvāsī, ēvāsus

BUILDING THE MEANING
Subordinate Clauses with the Subjunctive II

1. **Cum** Causal Clauses

   Subordinate clauses that are introduced by the conjunction **cum** may be *cum causal clauses*; **cum** is translated as *since* or *because*. Such clauses state the reason for the action of the main clause:

   > Magister nāvis, <u>cum valdē **timēret**</u>, suōs vetuit nōs adiuvāre. (42:17)
   > *The captain of the ship, <u>since/because **he was very frightened**</u>, forbade his own men to help us.*

2. **Cum** Circumstantial Clauses

   Subordinate clauses that are introduced by the conjunction **cum** may also be *cum circumstantial clauses*; **cum** is translated as *when*. Such clauses describe the circumstances that accompanied or preceded the action of the main clause:

   > <u>Cum quattuor diēs **nāvigāvissēmus**</u>, subitō maxima tempestās coorta est. (42:2–3)
   > <u>*When **we had sailed** four days*</u>, *suddenly a very great storm arose.*

   Often only the context and sense will tell you whether **cum** is to be translated *since/because* or *when*.

3. Indirect Questions

   > Pīrātae rogābant <u>quī **essēmus**</u>, <u>unde **vēnissēmus**</u>, <u>quō iter **facerēmus**</u>. (42:20–21)
   > *The pirates were asking <u>who **we were**, from where **we had come**, [and] to where **we were making** a journey</u>.*

   Look at these pairs of sentences:

   a. Direct question: Quī estis?
       Who are you?

   b. Indirect question: Pīrātae rogābant <u>quī **essēmus**.</u>
       *The pirates were asking <u>who **we were**</u>.*

   a. Direct question: Unde vēnistis?
       From where have you come?

   b. Indirect question: Pīrātae rogābant <u>unde **vēnissēmus**</u>.
       *The pirates were asking <u>from where **we had come**</u>.*

(continued)

a.	Direct question:	Quō iter facitis? *To where are you making a journey?*
b.	Indirect question:	Pīrātae rogābant <u>quō iter</u> **facerēmus**. *The pirates were asking <u>to where</u> **we were making a journey**.*

After the introductory words **Pīrātae rogābant**, the direct questions (a) are stated indirectly in subordinate clauses (b, underlined), and their verbs are in the subjunctive. These subordinate clauses are called *indirect questions*.

Exercise 42e

Read aloud and translate; be sure to decide whether **cum** clauses are circumstantial or causal and be sure that your translation reflects the tense of each verb in the subjunctive:

1. Cum prope rīvum ambulārēmus, Cornēliam et Flāviam clāmantēs audīvimus.
2. Grammaticus Marcum rogāvit unde vēnisset Aenēās.
3. Grammaticus Sextum rogāvit ubi esset Hesperia.
4. Grammaticus mē, cum dē Hesperiā ignōrārem, verberāvit.
5. Pīrātae Valerium rogāvērunt quis esset.
6. Magister nāvis, cum pīrātās timēret, dē patre Valeriī vēra dīcere cōnstituit.
7. Servus, cum in mare dēsiluisset, ad lītus celeriter natāvit.
8. Cum casae appropinquāvissem, dominum vīdī.
9. Cum casam intrāvisset, custōdem pūgiōne percussit.
10. Cum neque cibum neque aquam habērent, aegerrimī erant.

Exercise 42f

Using story 42 and the material above on the subjunctive as guides, give the Latin for the following (use subjunctives in all subordinate clauses):

1. When the force of the storm had subsided, we returned onto the ship.
2. Since the men were pirates, we were afraid to resist.
3. When my master had drawn his sword, he leaped down into the boat.
4. We asked why the pirates had captured us poor men.
5. Since my master was ill on account of his wound, he was not able to walk.

PIRACY

Piracy was a constant threat to travel and trade by sea in the ancient world. Merchant ships were often seized by pirates and their goods sold, and sailors and travelers caught by pirates would be sold as slaves at the great slave markets such as that on the island of Delos in the Aegean Sea. Pirates would also attack coastal towns and coastal roads, ruthlessly killing or capturing men, women, and children to ransom or to sell as slaves.

In 74 B.C. Julius Caesar was captured by pirates. The historian Suetonius tells the story:

> While crossing to Rhodes, after the winter season had already begun, he was taken by pirates near the island of Pharmacussa and remained in their custody for nearly forty days in a state of intense vexation, attended only by a single physician and two body-servants; for he had sent off his traveling companions and the rest of his attendants at the outset, to raise money for his ransom. Once he was set on shore on payment of fifty talents, he did not delay then and there to launch a fleet and pursue the departing pirates, and the moment they were in his power to inflict on them the punishment which he had often threatened when joking with them.
>
> —Suetonius, *Julius Caesar* 4.1–2

In 66 B.C., Cicero enumerated the troubles that pirates had caused the Romans in the recent past, claiming that the sea had been virtually closed to Rome's allies, that envoys had been captured, that ransom had been paid for Rome's ambassadors, that the sea had been unsafe for merchants, that Roman lictors had been captured by pirates, that whole cities had fallen into their hands, that the harbors of the Romans and their trading partners had been held by pirates, and that a fleet commanded by a Roman had been captured and destroyed by pirates. Cicero reported that all of these troubles had been ended the previous year, when the Roman general Pompey the Great (**Pompeius Magnus**) was given a fleet and empowered to rid the sea of pirates. Cicero tells what happened:

> Pompeius, though the sea was still unfit for navigation, visited Sicily, explored Africa, sailed to Sardinia and, by means of strong garrisons and fleets, made secure those three sources of our country's grain supply. After that he returned to Italy, secured the two provinces of Spain together with Transalpine Gaul, dispatched ships to the coast of the Illyrian Sea, to Achaea and the whole of Greece, and so provided the two seas of Italy with mighty fleets and strong garrisons; while he himself, within forty-nine days of starting from Brundisium, added all

Cilicia to the Roman Empire. All the pirates, wherever they were, were either captured or put to death; or they surrendered to his power and authority and to his alone.

—Cicero, *On the Manilian Law* 12.34–35

Augustus established a permanent fleet to keep the seas safe from pirates, but the menace remained, and a traveler such as Valerius in our story could easily be captured by pirates while sailing from Asia Minor to Brundisium.

REVIEW IX: CHAPTERS 38-42

Exercise IXa: Place

Select, read aloud, and translate:

1. Mercātōrēs Rōmānī _____ morābantur.   Gādēs/Gādium/Gādibus
2. Cornēliī _____ profectī sunt.   Rōma/Rōmae/Rōmā
3. Cornēliī _____ sērō advēnērunt.   Baiae/Baiārum/Baiās
4. Cornēliī _____ profectī sunt.   domus/domī/domō
5. Mīles Rōmānus _____ discessit.   Carthāginī/Carthāginem/Carthāgine
6. Amīcus mīlitis adhūc _____ habitat.   Carthāginī/Carthāginem/Carthāgō
7. Cornēlia _____ manet.   domī/domum/domō
8. Cornēliī _____ diū manēbant.   Rōmae/Rōmam/Rōmā
9. Cornēliī _____ diū manēbunt.   rūs/rūrī
10. Cornēliī _____ semper aestāte redeunt.   rūs/rūrī

Exercise IXb: Time

Read aloud, supplying the Latin words for the English cues, and translate:

1. Cornēliī in vīllā rūsticā _____ _____ morābantur. (for many months)
2. Ad urbem Rōmam _____ _____ regredientur. (in a few days)
3. Pseudolus _____ _____ _____ porcum ēmit. (three days ago)
4. Cornēliī ad vīllam rūsticam_____ _____ _____ regressī sunt. (after a few months)
5. Puerī in lūdō_____ _____ sedēbant. (for the whole day)
6. Valerius Brundisiō ēgressus Rōmam _____ _____ _____ adveniet. (several days later)

Exercise IXc: Present Participles

Read aloud and translate. Identify all present participles and tell what word they modify, unless they are being used as substantives:

1. Valerius iter ad Italiam faciēns tempestāte ad īnsulam āctus est.
2. Pīrātae celeriter sequentēs nāvem Valeriī cōnsecūtī sunt.
3. Nāvis Valeriī ā sequentibus capta est.
4. Servus Valeriī pīrātās in casā dormientēs adortus est.
5. Custōs ā servō Valeriī in casam ingrediente pugiōne percussus est.
6. Graviter aegrōtantēs ā mercātōribus inveniuntur.

Exercise IXd: Present Participles
Select, read aloud, and translate:

1. Sextum domum _____ audīvit Cornēlius.   intrantī/intrante/intrantem
2. Nāvis Valeriī pīrātās _____ effugere   sequentēs/sequentibus/sequentium
   nōn poterat.
3. Magistrō _____ ūnus ē discipulīs bene   rogantem/rogantī/rogantis
   respondit.
4. Aenēās Hesperiam _____ tempestāte   petentem/petente/petēns
   Carthāginem āctus est.
5. Cornēlius ā frātre nimis vīnī _____   bibentem/bibentis/bibente
   vexātus est.

Exercise IXe: Numbers
Match the cardinal numbers at the left with the corresponding ordinal
numbers at the right and give the meaning of the numbers in each pair:

1. quīnque   a. octāvus
2. octō   b. duodecimus
3. duo   c. quīngentēsimus
4. quīngentī   d. secundus
5. duodecim   e. quīntus
6. centum   f. septimus
7. trēs   g. quīnquāgēsimus
8. novem   h. tertius
9. quīnquāgintā   i. centēsimus
10. septem   j. nōnus

Exercise IXf: Semi-deponent Verbs
Translate into Latin, using semi-deponent verbs:

1. You (sing.) dare.   7. We are accustomed.
2. You (sing.) will be glad.   8. We will dare.
3. You (sing.) were daring.   9. We were daring.
4. You (sing.) dared.   10. We dared.
5. You (sing.) had been glad.   11. We had been accustomed.
6. You (sing.) will have dared.   12. We will have been glad.

Exercise IXg: Perfect Active Infinitives

Give and translate the present and perfect active infinitives of the following verbs:

1. laudō
2. habeō
3. currō
4. iaciō
5. dormiō

Exercise IXh: Imperfect and Pluperfect Subjunctives

Give the imperfect and pluperfect subjunctives of the verbs in Exercise IXg in the following persons and numbers:

1. Second person singular
2. First person plural

Exercise IXi: Subordinate Clauses with the Subjunctive

Read aloud and translate. Identify the tense of each verb in the subjunctive, and identify **cum** causal clauses, **cum** circumstantial clauses, and indirect questions:

1. Cum Vergilius Cremōnam advēnisset, ab optimīs magistrīs doctus est.
2. Scīvistīne ubi Vergilius togam virīlem sūmpsisset?
3. Cum Vergilius Mediolānum vēnisset, litterīs et linguae Graecae dīligentissimē studēbat.
4. Cum mīlitēs patrem Vergiliī ē fundō expulissent, Vergilius et pater Rōmam migrāvērunt.
5. Cum Vergilius Rōmae optimōs versūs scrīberet, poēta praeclārus factus es.
6. Cum Vergilius Rōmae habitāret, saepe aegrōtābat.
7. Cum in Graeciā iter faceret, prīncipī occurrit Athēnīs.
8. Cum prīnceps ad Italiam redīret, Vergilium sēcum dūxit.
9. Cum Brundisium advēnissent, Vergilius aegerrimus factus est.
10. Scīvistīne ubi amīcī Vergilium sepelīvissent?

Exercise IXj: Reading Comphrehension

Read the following passage and answer the questions below in English:

LIFE OF AUGUSTUS

A.d. ix Kal. Oct., M. Cicerōne et C. Antōniō cōnsulibus, nātus est C. Octāvius, quī
posteā prīmus prīnceps Rōmānus factus est. Cum quattuor annōs complēvisset, pater
mortuus est; Gaius igitur a mātre Atiā alēbātur. Avunculus magnus quoque, C. Iūlius
Caesar, eum multa docuisse dīcitur.

Ubi Caesar ā coniūrātīs necātus est, Octāvius iam XVIII annōs nātus aberat in 5
Illyricō. Rōmam quam celerrimē regressus, hērēs Caesaris testāmentō adoptātus est
atque, cum cognōvisset quī Caesarem necāvissent, statim cōnstituit avunculum mortuum,
ut patrem, ōlim ulcīscī. Eō tempore tamen, quod nūllum exercitum habēbat, nihil facere
poterat.

Intereā, quod M. Antōnius populum Rōmānum excitāverat, coniūrātī ex urbe fugere 10
coāctī sunt. Dum tamen Antōnius coniūrātōs per Italiam persequēbātur, M. Tullius
Cicerō, ōrātor ille praeclārissimus, ōrātiōnēs habuit in quibus dīcēbat Antōnium esse
hostem reī pūblicae. Tum Octāvius, dīvitiīs ūsus quās testāmentō Caesaris accēperat,
senātuī persuāsit ut sē cōnsulem creāret. Eōdem tempore nōminātus est Gaius Iūlius
Caesar Octāviānus. Volēbant senātōrēs Octāviānum contrā Antōnium, quem iam 15
timēbant, urbem Rōmam dēfendere. Octāviānus tamen cum Antōniō se coniūnxit.

Prīmō Octāviānus et Antōnius ūnā coniūrātōs in Graeciā cōnsecūtī, proeliō
dēbellāvērunt. Deinde, cum coniūrātōs superāvissent, cōnstituērunt Octāviānus et
Antōnius imperium Rōmānum inter sē dīvidere. Rōmam regressus est Octāviānus; ad
Aegyptum profectus est Antōnius. Rēgīna autem Aegyptiōrum erat Cleopatra, quam 20
pulcherrimam statim amāvit Antōnius. Mox Antōnius et Cleopatra tōtum imperium
Rōmānum regere volēbant. Quae cum ita essent, Octāviānō necesse fuit bellum Antōniō
īnferre. Proelium ad Actium factum est; Cleopatra Antōniusque victī sē necāvērunt. Octāviānus
tōtam Aegyptum bellō captam imperiō Rōmānō addidit. Tum Iānum Quirīnum clausit
atque pācem tōtum per imperium prōnūntiāvit. Ipse prīnceps Rōmānōrum factus est. 25

Multa et optima et ūtilissima populō Rōmānō ab eō īnstitūta sunt atque
imperium Rōmānum auctum stabilītumque est. Multī etiam poētae—Vergilius, Horātius,
Propertius, Ovidius—rēs Rōmānās versibus laudābant. Inter multōs honōrēs quōs
senātus eī dedit maximus certē erat cognōmen Augustus, quod eī dēlātum est a.d. XVII
Kal. Feb. annō DCCXXVII, A.U.C. Ex hōc tempore mēnsis Sextīlis nōminātus est 30
Augustus.

Bis uxōrem dūxit sed nūllum fīlium habēbat. Generum autem Marcellum in animō
habēbat hērēdem adoptāre. Hic tamen annō DCCXXXI A.U.C. trīstissimē morbō
mortuus est. Augustus igitur Tiberium, fīlium Līviae uxōris secundae, hērēdem
adoptāvit. 35

Cum annum septuāgēsimum sextum paene complēvisset, dum iter in Campāniā facit,
trīstissimē morbō a.d. XIV Kal. Sept. mortuus est. Corpus Rōmam relātum ingentī in
sepulcrō sepultum est atque ūnō post mēnse senātus, quī Augustum iam dīvīnum esse
prōnūntiāverat, eum cum avunculō inter deōs numerāvit.

1 **M. = Marcus**
  C. = Gaius
3 **avunculus, -ī,** m., *maternal uncle*
5 **coniūrātus, -ī,** m., *conspirator*
6 **hērēs, hērēdis,** m., *heir*
8 **ōlim,** adv., *at some future time, one day*
  exercitus, -ūs, m., *army*
10 **populus, -ī,** m., *people*
13 **hostis, hostis,** gen. pl., **hostium,** m.,
  enemy
  rēs pūblica, reī pūblicae, f., *republic,
  the state*
  dīvitiae, -ārum, f. pl., *riches*
14 **ut sē cōnsulem creāret,** *to make him
  consul*
15 **contrā,** prep. + acc., *against*
16 **coniungō, coniungere, coniūnxī,
  coniūnctus,** *to join*

17 **proelium, -ī,** n., *battle*
18 **dēbellō, -āre, -āvī, -ātus,** *to defeat*
19 **imperium, -ī,** n., *power, empire*
20 **Aegyptus, -ī,** f., *Egypt*
22 **bellum īnferre** + dat., *to make war upon*
24 **Iānus Quirīnus, -ī,** m., *shrine of
  Janus Quirinus*
25 **pāx, pācis,** f., *peace*
  prōnūntiō, -āre, -āvī, -ātus, *to proclaim*
27 **stabiliō, -īre, -īvī, -ītus,** *to steady,
  make firm*
32 **bis,** adv., *twice*
  uxōrem dūcere, *to marry*
  gener, generī, m., *son-in-law*
33 **morbus, -ī,** m., *illness*
39 **numerō, -āre, -āvī, -ātus,** *to number,
  include*

2 **compleō, complēre, complēvī, complētus,** *to fill, complete*
3 **alō, alere, aluī, altus,** *to rear*
7 **cognōscō, cognōscere, cognōvī, cognitus,** *to learn*
8 **ulcīscor, ulcīscī, ultus sum,** *to avenge*
11 **cōgō, cōgere, coēgī, coāctus,** *to compel, force*
  persequor, persequī, persecūtus sum, *to pursue*
13 **ūtor, ūtī, ūsus sum** + abl., *to use*
22 **regō, regere, rēxī, rēctus,** *to rule*
26 **īnstituō, īnstituere, īnstituī, īnstitūtus,** *to establish*
27 **augeō, augēre, auxī, auctus,** *to increase*
29 **dēferō, dēferre, dētulī, dēlātus,** irreg., *to award, grant*
37 **referō, referre, retulī, relātus,** irreg., *to bring back*

1. On what day of what month was Gaius Octavius born?
2. How old was he when his father died?
3. Who were responsible for his rearing and education?
4. Where was Octavius when Caesar was assassinated?
5. What did Octavius decide to do when he learned who had assassinated Caesar?
6. Why was he unable to do anything at the time?
7. Why were the conspirators forced to flee from Rome?
8. Who pursued them?
9. What attitude did Cicero take toward Antony?
10. How did Octavius persuade the Senate to make him consul?

(continued)

11. Who overtook the conspirators in Greece and defeated them?
12. Where did the victors go?
13. What were Antony and Cleopatra's plans?
14. Who defeated whom at the battle of Actium?
15. What new province did Octavian add to the Roman empire?
16. What kind of a ruler was Octavian?
17. What was the greatest honor that the Senate gave him?
18. Whom did he want to succeed him as ruler?
19. Why was that not possible?
20. What honor did the Senate confer upon Augustus after his death?

FORMS

The following charts show the forms of typical Latin nouns, adjectives, pronouns, and verbs. As an aid in pronunciation, markings of long vowels and of accents are included.

I. Nouns

Number Case	1st Declension Fem.	2nd Declension Masc.	Masc.	Masc.	Neut.	3rd Declension Masc.	Fem.	Neut.
Singular								
Nominative	puéll*a*	sérv*us*	púer	áger	bácul*um*	páter	vōx	nṓmen
Genitive	puéll*ae*	sérv*ī*	púer*ī*	ágr*ī*	bácul*ī*	pátr*is*	vṓc*is*	nṓmin*is*
Dative	puéll*ae*	sérv*ō*	púer*ō*	ágr*ō*	bácul*ō*	pátr*ī*	vṓc*ī*	nṓmin*ī*
Accusative	puéll*am*	sérv*um*	púer*um*	ágr*um*	bácul*um*	pátr*em*	vṓc*em*	nṓmen
Ablative	puéll*ā*	sérv*ō*	púer*ō*	ágr*ō*	bácul*ō*	pátr*e*	vṓc*e*	nṓmin*e*
Vocative	puéll*a*	sérv*e*	púer	áger	bácul*um*	páter	vōx	nṓmen
Plural								
Nominative	puéll*ae*	sérv*ī*	púer*ī*	ágr*ī*	bácul*a*	pátr*ēs*	vṓc*ēs*	nṓmin*a*
Genitive	puell*árum*	serv*órum*	puer*órum*	agr*órum*	bacul*órum*	pátr*um*	vṓc*um*	nṓmin*um*
Dative	puéll*īs*	sérv*īs*	púer*īs*	ágr*īs*	bácul*īs*	pátr*ibus*	vṓc*ibus*	nōmín*ibus*
Accusative	puéll*ās*	sérv*ōs*	púer*ōs*	ágr*ōs*	bácul*a*	pátr*ēs*	vṓc*ēs*	nṓmin*a*
Ablative	puéll*īs*	sérv*īs*	púer*īs*	ágr*īs*	bácul*īs*	pátr*ibus*	vṓc*ibus*	nōmín*ibus*
Vocative	puéll*ae*	sérv*ī*	púer*ī*	ágr*ī*	bácul*a*	pátr*ēs*	vṓc*ēs*	nṓmin*a*

Number Case	4th Declension Masc.	Neut.	5th Declension Masc.	Fem.
Singular				
Nominative	árc*us*	gén*ū*	dí*ēs*	r*ēs*
Genitive	árc*ūs*	gén*ūs*	di*éī*	r*éī*
Dative	árc*uī*	gén*ū*	di*éī*	r*éī*
Accusative	árc*um*	gén*ū*	dí*em*	r*em*
Ablative	árc*ū*	gén*ū*	dí*ē*	r*ē*
Vocative	árc*us*	gén*ū*	dí*ēs*	r*ēs*
Plural				
Nominative	árc*ūs*	gén*ua*	dí*ēs*	r*ēs*
Genitive	árc*uum*	gén*uum*	di*érum*	r*érum*
Dative	árc*ibus*	gén*ibus*	di*ébus*	r*ébus*
Accusative	árc*ūs*	gén*ua*	dí*ēs*	r*ēs*
Ablative	árc*ibus*	gén*ibus*	di*ébus*	r*ébus*
Vocative	árc*ūs*	gén*ua*	dí*ēs*	r*ēs*

II. Adjectives

Number Case	1st and 2nd Declension			3rd Declension		
	Masc.	Fem.	Neut.	Masc.	Fem.	Neut.
Singular						
Nominative	mágn*us*	mágn*a*	mágn*um*	ómn*is*	ómn*is*	ómn*e*
Genitive	mágn*ī*	mágn*ae*	mágn*ī*	ómn*is*	ómn*is*	ómn*is*
Dative	mágn*ō*	mágn*ae*	mágn*ō*	ómn*ī*	ómn*ī*	ómn*ī*
Accusative	mágn*um*	mágn*am*	mágn*um*	ómn*em*	ómn*em*	ómn*e*
Ablative	mágn*ō*	mágn*ā*	mágn*ō*	ómn*ī*	ómn*ī*	ómn*ī*
Vocative	mágn*e*	mágn*a*	mágn*um*	ómn*is*	ómn*is*	ómn*e*
Plural						
Nominative	mágn*ī*	mágn*ae*	mágn*a*	ómn*ēs*	ómn*ēs*	ómn*ia*
Genitive	magn*órum*	magn*árum*	magn*órum*	ómn*ium*	ómn*ium*	ómn*ium*
Dative	mágn*īs*	mágn*īs*	mágn*īs*	ómn*ibus*	ómn*ibus*	ómn*ibus*
Accusative	mágn*ōs*	mágn*ās*	mágn*a*	ómn*ēs*	ómn*ēs*	ómn*ia*
Ablative	mágn*īs*	mágn*īs*	mágn*īs*	ómn*ibus*	ómn*ibus*	ómn*ibus*
Vocative	mágn*ī*	mágn*ae*	mágn*a*	ómn*ēs*	ómn*ēs*	ómn*ia*

III. Comparative Adjectives

Number Case	Masc.	Fem.	Neut.
Singular			
Nominative	púlchrior	púlchrior	púlchrius
Genitive	pulchrió*ris*	pulchrió*ris*	pulchrió*ris*
Dative	pulchrió*rī*	pulchrió*rī*	pulchrió*rī*
Accusative	pulchrió*rem*	pulchrió*rem*	púlchrius
Abative	pulchrió*re*	pulchrió*re*	pulchrió*re*
Vocative	púlchrior	púlchrior	púlchrius
Plural			
Nominative	pulchrió*rēs*	pulchrió*rēs*	pulchrió*ra*
Genitive	pulchrió*rum*	pulchrió*rum*	pulchrió*rum*
Dative	pulchrió*ribus*	pulchrió*ribus*	pulchrió*ribus*
Accusative	pulchrió*rēs*	pulchrió*rēs*	pulchrió*ra*
Ablative	pulchrió*ribus*	pulchrió*ribus*	pulchrió*ribus*
Vocative	pulchrió*rēs*	pulchrió*rēs*	pulchrió*ra*

Adjectives have *positive*, *comparative*, and *superlative* forms. You can usually recognize the comparative by the letters **-ior(-)** and the superlative by *-issimus*, *-errimus*, or *-illimus*:

ignávus, -a, -um, *lazy*	ignávior, ignávius	ignavíssimus, -a, -um
púlcher, púlchra, púlchrum, *beautiful*	púlchrior, púlchrius	pulchérrimus, -a, -um
fácilis, -is, -e, *easy*	facílior, facílius	facíllimus, -a, -um

Some very common adjectives are irregular in the comparative and superlative:

Positive	Comparative	Superlative
bónus, -a, -um, *good*	**mélior, mélius,** *better*	**óptimus, -a, -um,** *best*
málus, -a, -um, *bad*	**péior, péius,** *worse*	**péssimus, -a, -um,** *worst*
mágnus, -a, -um, *big*	**máior, máius,** *bigger*	**máximus, -a, -um,** *biggest*
párvus, -a, -um, *small*	**mínor, mínus,** *smaller*	**mínimus, -a, -um,** *smallest*
múltus, -a, -um, *much*	**plūs,*** *more*	**plúrimus, -a, -um,** *most, very much*
múltī, -ae, -a, *many*	**plúrēs, plúra,** *more*	**plúrimī, -ae, -a,** *most, very many*

*Note that **plūs** is not an adjective but a neuter substantive, usually found with a partitive genitive, e.g., Titus **plūs vīnī** bibit. *Titus drank **more (of the) wine**.*

IV.   Present Participles

Number Case	Masc.	Fem.	Neut.
Singular			
Nominative	párāns	párāns	párāns
Genitive	paránt*is*	parántis	parántis
Dative	parántī	parántī	parántī
Accusative	parántem	parántem	párāns
Ablative	parántī/e	parántī/e	parántī/e
Plural			
Nominative	parántēs	parántēs	parántia
Genitive	parántium	parántium	parántium
Dative	parántibus	parántibus	parántibus
Accusative	parántēs	parántēs	parántia
Ablative	parántibus	parántibus	parántibus

V. Numbers

Case	Masc.	Fem.	Neut.	Masc.	Fem.	Neut.	Masc.	Fem.	Neut.
Nom.	únus	úna	únum	dúo	dúae	dúo	trēs	trēs	tría
Gen.	únīus	únīus	únīus	duórum	duárum	duórum	tríum	tríum	tríum
Dat.	únī	únī	únī	duóbus	duábus	duóbus	tríbus	tríbus	tríbus
Acc.	únum	únam	únum	dúōs	dúās	dúo	trēs	trēs	tría
Abl.	únō	únā	únō	duóbus	duábus	duóbus	tríbus	tríbus	tríbus

	Cardinal	Ordinal
I	únus, -a, -um, *one*	prímus, -a, -um, *first*
II	dúo, -ae, -o, *two*	secúndus, -a, -um, *second*
III	trēs, trēs, tría, *three*	tértius, -a, -um, *third*
IV	quáttuor, *four*	quártus, -a, -um
V	quínque, *five*	quíntus, -a, -um
VI	sex, *six*	séxtus, -a, -um
VII	séptem, *seven*	séptimus, -a, -um
VIII	óctō, *eight*	octávus, -a, -um
IX	nóvem, *nine*	nónus, -a, -um
X	décem, *ten*	décimus, -a, -um
XI	úndecim, *eleven*	ūndécimus, -a, -um
XII	duódecim, *twelve*	duodécimus, -a, -um
XIII	trédecim, *thirteen*	tértius décimus, -a, -um
XIV	quattuórdecim, *fourteen*	quártus décimus, -a, -um
XV	quíndecim, *fifteen*	quíntus décimus, -a, -um
XVI	sédecim, *sixteen*	séxtus décimus, -a, -um
XVII	septéndecim, *seventeen*	séptimus décimus, -a, -um
XVIII	duodēvīgíntī, *eighteen*	duodēvīcésimus, -a, -um
XIX	ūndēvīgíntī, *nineteen*	ūndēvīcésimus, -a, -um
XX	vīgíntī, *twenty*	vīcésimus, -a, -um
L	quīnquāgíntā, *fifty*	quīnquāgésimus, -a, -um
C	céntum, *a hundred*	centésimus, -a, -um
D	quīngéntī, -ae, -a, *five hundred*	quīngentésimus, -a, -um
M	mílle, *a thousand*	mīllésimus, -a, -um

N.B. The cardinal numbers from **quattuor** to **centum** do not change their form to indicate case and gender.

VI. Personal Pronouns

Number Case	1st	2nd	3rd Masc.	Fem.	Neut.
Singular					
Nominative	égo	tū	is	éa	id
Genitive	méī	túī	éius	éius	éius
Dative	míhi	tíbi	éī	éī	éī
Accusative	mē	tē	éum	éam	id
Ablative	mē	tē	éō	éā	éō
Plural					
Nominative	nōs	vōs	éī	éae	éa
Genitive	nóstrī	véstrī	eórum	eárum	eórum
	nóstrum	véstrum			
Dative	nóbīs	vóbīs	éīs	éīs	éīs
Accusative	nōs	vōs	éōs	éās	éa
Ablative	nóbīs	vóbīs	éīs	éīs	éīs

Note: The forms of **is, ea, id** may also serve as demonstrative adjectives.

VII. Reflexive Pronoun

Singular	
Nominative	——
Genitive	súī
Dative	síbi
Accusative	sē
Ablative	sē
Plural	
Nominative	——
Genitive	súī
Dative	síbi
Accusative	sē
Ablative	sē

VIII. Relative Pronoun

Number Case	Masc.	Fem.	Neut.
Singular			
Nominative	quī	quae	quod
Genitive	cúius	cúius	cúius
Dative	cui	cui	cui
Accusative	quem	quam	quod
Ablative	quō	quā	quō
Plural			
Nominative	quī	quae	quae
Genitive	quórum	quárum	quórum
Dative	quíbus	quíbus	quíbus
Accusative	quōs	quās	quae
Ablative	quíbus	quíbus	quíbus

IX. Interrogative Pronoun

Number Case	Masc.	Fem.	Neut.
Singular			
Nominative	quis	quis	quid
Genitive	cúius	cúius	cúius
Dative	cui	cui	cui
Accusative	quem	quem	quid
Ablative	quō	quō	quō
Plural	Same as the plural of the relative pronoun above.		

X. Indefinite Adjective

Number Case	Masc.	Fem.	Neut.
Singular			
Nominative	quídam	quaédam	quóddam
Genitive	cuiúsdam	cuiúsdam	cuiúsdam
Dative	cúidam	cúidam	cúidam
Accusative	quéndam	quándam	quóddam
Ablative	quódam	quádam	quódam
Plural			
Nominative	quídam	quaédam	quaédam
Genitive	quōrúndam	quārúndam	quōrúndam
Dative	quibúsdam	quibúsdam	quibúsdam
Accusative	quósdam	quásdam	quaédam
Ablative	quibúsdam	quibúsdam	quibúsdam

XI. Demonstrative Adjectives and Pronouns

Number Case	Masc.	Fem.	Neut.	Masc.	Fem.	Neut.
Singular						
Nominative	hic	haec	hoc	ílle	ílla	íllud
Genitive	húius	húius	húius	illíus	illíus	illíus
Dative	húic	húic	húic	íllī	íllī	íllī
Accusative	hunc	hanc	hoc	íllum	íllam	íllud
Ablative	hōc	hāc	hōc	íllō	íllā	íllō
Plural						
Nominative	hī	hae	haec	íllī	íllae	ílla
Genitive	hórum	hárum	hórum	illórum	illárum	illórum
Dative	hīs	hīs	hīs	íllīs	íllīs	íllīs
Accusative	hōs	hās	haec	íllōs	íllās	ílla
Ablative	hīs	hīs	hīs	íllīs	íllīs	íllīs

Number Case	Masculine	Feminine	Neuter
Singular			
Nominative	ípse	ípsa	ípsum
Genitive	ipsíus	ipsíus	ipsíus
Dative	ípsī	ípsī	ípsī
Accusative	ípsum	ípsam	ípsum
Ablative	ípsō	ípsā	ípsō
Plural			
Nominative	ípsī	ípsae	ípsa
Genitive	ipsórum	ipsárum	ipsórum
Dative	ípsīs	ípsīs	ípsīs
Accusative	ípsōs	ípsās	ípsa
Ablative	ípsīs	ípsīs	ípsīs

Number Case	Masc.	Fem.	Neut.	Masc.	Fem.	Neut.
Singular						
Nominative	is	éa	id	ídem	éadem	ídem
Genitive	éius	éius	éius	eiúsdem	eiúsdem	eiúsdem
Dative	éī	éī	éī	eídem	eídem	eídem
Accusative	éum	éam	id	eúndem	eándem	ídem
Ablative	éō	éā	éō	eódem	eádem	eódem
Plural						
Nominative	éī	éae	éa	eídem	eaédem	éadem
Genitive	eórum	eárum	eórum	eōrúndem	eārúndem	eōrúndem
Dative	éīs	éīs	éīs	eísdem	eísdem	eísdem
Accusative	éōs	éās	éa	eósdem	eásdem	éadem
Ablative	éīs	éīs	éīs	eísdem	eísdem	eísdem

XII. Adverbs

Latin adverbs may be formed from adjectives of the 1st and 2nd declensions by adding *-ē* to the base of the adjective, e.g., **strēnuē**, *strenuously*, from **strēnuus, -a, -um**. To form an adverb from a 3rd declension adjective, add *-iter* to the base of the adjective or *-er* to bases ending in **-nt-**, e.g., **breviter**, *briefly*, from **brevis, -is, -e**, and **prūdenter**, *wisely*, from **prūdēns, prūdentis**.

laétē, *happily*	laétius	laetíssimē
fēlíciter, *luckily*	fēlícius	fēlīcíssimē
celériter, *quickly*	celérius	celérrimē
prūdénter, *wisely*	prūdéntius	prūdentíssimē

Note the following as well:

díū, *for a long time*	diútius	diūtíssimē
saépe, *often*	saépius	saepíssimē
sḗrō, *late*	sḗrius	sēríssimē

Some adverbs are irregular:

béne, *well*	**mélius**, *better*	**óptimē**, *best*
mále, *badly*	**péius**, *worse*	**péssimē**, *worst*
fácile, *easily*	**facílius**, *more easily*	**facíllimē**, *most easily*
magnópere, *greatly*	**mágis**, *more*	**máximē**, *most*
paúlum, *little*	**mínus**, *less*	**mínimē**, *least*
múltum, *much*	**plūs**, *more*	**plúrimum**, *most*

XIII. Regular Verbs Active: Infinitive, Imperative, Indicative

				1st Conjugation	2nd Conjugation	3rd Conjugation		4th Conjugation
Infinitive				par*áre*	hab*ére*	mítt*ere*	iác*ere (-iō)*	aud*íre*
Imperative				pár*á*	háb*é*	mítt*e*	iác*e*	aúd*í*
				par*áte*	hab*éte*	mítt*ite*	iác*ite*	aud*íte*
Present	Singular		1	pár*ō*	hábe*ō*	mítt*ō*	iáci*ō*	aúdi*ō*
			2	pár*ās*	háb*ēs*	mítt*is*	iác*is*	aúd*īs*
			3	pára*t*	hábe*t*	mítt*it*	iáci*t*	aúdi*t*
	Plural		1	par*ámus*	hab*émus*	mítt*imus*	iác*imus*	audí*mus*
			2	par*átis*	hab*étis*	mítt*itis*	iác*itis*	aud*ítis*
			3	pára*nt*	hábe*nt*	mítt*unt*	iáci*unt*	aúdi*unt*
Imperfect	Singular		1	par*ábam*	hab*ébam*	mitt*ébam*	iaci*ébam*	audi*ébam*
			2	par*ábās*	hab*ébās*	mitt*ébās*	iaci*ébās*	audi*ébās*
			3	par*ábat*	hab*ébat*	mitt*ébat*	iaci*ébat*	audi*ébat*
	Plural		1	par*ābámus*	hab*ēbámus*	mitt*ēbámus*	iaci*ēbámus*	audi*ēbámus*
			2	par*ābátis*	hab*ēbátis*	mitt*ēbátis*	iaci*ēbátis*	audi*ēbátis*
			3	par*ábant*	hab*ébant*	mitt*ébant*	iaci*ébant*	audi*ébant*
Future	Singular		1	par*ábō*	hab*ébō*	mítt*am*	iáci*am*	aúdi*am*
			2	par*ábis*	hab*ébis*	mítt*ēs*	iáci*ēs*	aúdi*ēs*
			3	par*ábit*	hab*ébit*	mítt*et*	iáci*et*	aúdi*et*
	Plural		1	par*ábimus*	hab*ébimus*	mitt*émus*	iaci*émus*	audi*émus*
			2	par*ábitis*	hab*ébitis*	mitt*étis*	iaci*étis*	audi*étis*
			3	par*ábunt*	hab*ébunt*	mítt*ent*	iáci*ent*	aúdi*ent*
Perfect	Singular		1	par*ávī*	háb*uī*	mís*ī*	iéc*ī*	audí*vī*
			2	par*ávístī*	hab*uístī*	mis*ístī*	iēc*ístī*	audiv*ístī*
			3	par*ávit*	háb*uit*	mís*it*	iéc*it*	audí*vit*
	Plural		1	par*ávimus*	hab*úimus*	mís*imus*	iéc*imus*	audí*vimus*
			2	par*ávistis*	hab*uístis*	mis*ístis*	iēc*ístis*	audiv*ístis*
			3	parāv*érunt*	hab*uérunt*	mis*érunt*	iēc*érunt*	audiv*érunt*
Pluperfect	Singular		1	par*áveram*	hab*úeram*	mís*eram*	iéc*eram*	audí*veram*
			2	par*áverās*	hab*úerās*	mís*erās*	iéc*erās*	aud*éverās*
			3	par*áverat*	hab*úerat*	mís*erat*	iéc*erat*	audí*verat*
	Plural		1	parāv*erámus*	hab*uerámus*	mis*erámus*	iēc*erámus*	audiv*erámus*
			2	parāv*erátis*	hab*uerátis*	mis*erátis*	iēc*erátis*	audiv*erátis*
			3	par*áverant*	hab*úerant*	mís*erant*	iéc*erant*	audí*verant*
Future Perfect	Singular		1	par*áverō*	hab*úerō*	mís*erō*	iéc*erō*	audí*verō*
			2	par*áveris*	hab*úeris*	mís*eris*	iéc*eris*	audí*veris*
			3	par*áverit*	hab*úerit*	mís*erit*	iéc*erit*	audí*verit*
	Plural		1	parāv*érimus*	hab*uérimus*	mis*érimus*	iēc*érimus*	audiv*érimus*
			2	parāv*éritis*	hab*uéritis*	mis*éritis*	iēc*éritis*	audiv*éritis*
			3	par*áverint*	hab*úerint*	mís*erint*	iéc*erint*	audí*verint*

XIV. Regular Verbs Passive: Infinitive, Imperative, Indicative

			1st Conjugation	2nd Conjugation	3rd Conjugation		4th Conjugation
Infinitive			port*árī*	mov*érī*	mítt*ī*	iác*ī*	aud*írī*
Imperative			port*áre*	mov*ére*	mítt*ere*	iác*ere*	aud*íre*
			port*ámini*	mov*émini*	mitt*ímini*	iac*ímini*	aud*ímini*
Present	Singular	1	pórto*r*	móveo*r*	mítto*r*	iácio*r*	aúdio*r*
		2	portá*ris*	mové*ris*	mítte*ris*	iáce*ris*	audí*ris*
		3	portá*tur*	mové*tur*	mítti*tur*	iáci*tur*	audí*tur*
	Plural	1	portá*mur*	mové*mur*	mítti*mur*	iáci*mur*	audí*mur*
		2	portá*mini*	mové*mini*	mittí*mini*	iací*mini*	audí*mini*
		3	portá*ntur*	mové*ntur*	mittú*ntur*	iaciú*ntur*	audiú*ntur*
Imperfect	Singular	1	portā*bar*	movē*bar*	mittē*bar*	iaciē*bar*	audiē*bar*
		2	portā*báris*	movē*báris*	mittē*báris*	iaciē*báris*	audiē*báris*
		3	portā*bátur*	movē*bátur*	mittē*bátur*	iaciē*bátur*	audiē*bátur*
	Plural	1	portā*bámur*	movē*bámur*	mittē*bámur*	iaciē*bámur*	audiē*bámur*
		2	portā*bámini*	movē*bámini*	mittē*bámini*	iaciē*bámini*	audiē*bámini*
		3	portā*bántur*	movē*bántur*	mittē*bántur*	iaciē*bántur*	audiē*bántur*
Future	Singular	1	portá*bor*	mové*bor*	mítt*ar*	iáci*ar*	aúdi*ar*
		2	portá*beris*	mové*beris*	mitt*éris*	iaci*éris*	audi*éris*
		3	portá*bitur*	mové*bitur*	mitt*étur*	iaci*étur*	audi*étur*
	Plural	1	portá*bimur*	mové*bimur*	mitt*émur*	iaci*émur*	audi*émur*
		2	portá*bímini*	mové*bímini*	mitt*émini*	iaci*émini*	audi*émini*
		3	portá*búntur*	movē*búntur*	mitt*éntur*	iaci*éntur*	audi*éntur*

		Perfect Passive		Pluperfect Passive		Future Perfect Passive	
Singular	1	portátus, -a	sum	portátus, -a	éram	portátus, -a	érō
	2	portátus, -a	es	portátus, -a	érās	portátus, -a	éris
	3	portátus, -a, -um	est	portátus, -a, -um	érat	portátus, -a, -um	érit
Plural	1	portátī, -ae	súmus	portátī, -ae	erámus	portátī, -ae	érimus
	2	portátī, -ae	éstis	portátī, -ae	erátis	portátī, -ae	éritis
	3	portátī, -ae, -a	sunt	portátī, -ae, -a	érant	portátī, -ae, -a	érunt

XV. Regular Verbs: Infinitives

	Present		Perfect
	Active	Passive	Active
1	portáre	portárī	portāvísse
2	movére	movérī	mōvísse
3	míttere	míttī	mīsísse
iō	iácere	iácī	iēcísse
4	audíre	audírī	audīvísse

XVI. Deponent Verbs: Infinitive, Imperative, Indicative

			1st Conjugation	2nd Conjugation	3rd Conjugation		4th Conjugation
Present Infinitive			cōn*árī*	ver*érī*	lóqu*ī*	régred*ī*	exper*írī*
Imperative			cōn*áre*	ver*ére*	lóqu*ere*	regréd*ere*	exper*íre*
			cōn*áminī*	ver*éminī*	loqu*íminī*	regred*íminī*	exper*íminī*
Present	Singular	1	cón*or*	vére*or*	lóqu*or*	regréd*ior*	expér*ior*
		2	cōn*áris*	ver*éris*	ióqu*eris*	regréd*eris*	exper*íris*
		3	cōn*átur*	ver*étur*	lóqu*itur*	regréd*itur*	exper*ítur*
	Plural	1	cōn*ámur*	ver*émur*	lóqu*imur*	regréd*imur*	exper*ímur*
		2	cōn*áminī*	ver*éminī*	loqu*íminī*	regred*íminī*	exper*íminī*
		3	cōn*ántur*	ver*éntur*	loqu*úntur*	regredi*úntur*	experi*úntur*
Imperfect	Singular	1	cōn*ábar*	ver*ébar*	loqu*ébar*	regredi*ébar*	experi*ébar*
		2	cōn*abáris*	ver*ebáris*	loqu*ebáris*	regredi*ebáris*	experi*ebáris*
		3	cōn*abátur*	ver*ebátur*	loqu*ebátur*	regredi*ebátur*	experi*ebátur*
Future	Singular	1	cōn*ábor*	ver*ébor*	lóqu*ar*	regréd*iar*	expér*iar*
		2	cōn*áberis*	ver*éberis*	loqu*éris*	regredi*éris*	experi*éris*
		3	cōn*ábitur*	ver*ébitur*	loqu*étur*	regredi*étur*	experi*étur*
Perfect		1	cōnátus sum	véritus sum	locútus sum	regréssus sum	expértus sum
Pluperfect		1	cōnátus éram	véritus éram	locútus éram	regréssus éram	expértus éram
Future Perfect		1	cōnátus érō	véritus érō	locútus érō	regréssus érō	expértus érō

XVII. Regular and Irregular Verbs Active: Subjunctive

Imperfect

			Active Voice				
			1st Conjugation	2nd Conjugation	3rd Conjugation		4th Conjugation
Singular		1	portáre*m*	movére*m*	míttere*m*	iácere*m*	audíre*m*
		2	portáré*s*	movére*s*	mítteré*s*	iácere*s*	audíré*s*
		3	portáre*t*	movére*t*	míttere*t*	iácere*t*	audíre*t*
Plural		1	portāré*mus*	movēré*mus*	mitteré*mus*	iaceré*mus*	audīré*mus*
		2	portāré*tis*	movēré*tis*	mitteré*tis*	iaceré*tis*	audīré*tis*
		3	portáre*nt*	movére*nt*	míttere*nt*	iácere*nt*	audíre*nt*

			esse
Singular		1	ésse*m*
		2	éssē*s*
		3	ésse*t*
Plural		1	essé*mus*
		2	essé*tis*
		3	ésse*nt*

So also the irregular verbs **posse, velle, nōlle, īre,** and **ferre.**

Pluperfect

			1st Conjugation	2nd Conjugation	3rd Conjugation		4th Conjugation
Pluperfect	Singular	1	portāvíssem	mōvíssem	mīsíssem	iēcíssem	audīvíssem
		2	portāvíssēs	mōvíssēs	mīsíssēs	iēcíssēs	audīvíssēs
		3	portāvísset	mōvísset	mīsísset	iēcísset	audīvísset
	Plural	1	portāvissḗmus	mōvissḗmus	mīsissḗmus	iēcissḗmus	audīvissḗmus
		2	portāvissḗtis	mōvissḗtis	mīsissḗtis	iēcissḗtis	audīvissḗtis
		3	portāvíssent	mōvíssent	mīsíssent	iēcíssent	audīvíssent

		esse
Singular 1	fuíssem
2	fuíssēs
3	fuísset
Plural 1	fuissḗmus
2	fuissḗtis
3	fuíssent

So also the irregular verbs **posse (potuissem)**, **velle (voluissem)**, **nōlle (nōluissem)**, **īre (īssem)**, and **ferre (tulissem)**.

XVIII.   Irregular Verbs: Infinitive, Imperative, Indicative

Infinitive			ésse	pósse	vélle	nṓlle
Imperative			es	—	—	nṓlī
			éste	—	—	nōlíte
Present	Singular	1	sum	póssum	vólō	nṓlō
		2	es	pótes	vīs	nōn vīs
		3	est	pótest	vult	nōn vult
	Plural	1	súmus	póssumus	vólumus	nṓlumus
		2	éstis	potéstis	vúltis	nōn vúltis
		3	sunt	póssunt	vólunt	nṓlunt
Imperfect	Singular	1	éram	póteram	volḗbam	nōlḗbam
		2	érās	póterās	volḗbās	nōlḗbās
		3	érat	póterat	volḗbat	nōlḗbat
	Plural	1	erḗmus	poterḗmus	volēbḗmus	nōlēbḗmus
		2	erḗtis	poterḗtis	volēbḗtis	nōlēbḗtis
		3	érant	póterant	volḗbant	nōlḗbant
Future	Singular	1	érō	póterō	vólam	nṓlam
		2	éris	póteris	vólēs	nṓlēs
		3	érit	póterit	vólet	nṓlet
	Plural	1	érimus	potérimus	volḗmus	nōlḗmus
		2	éritis	potéritis	volḗtis	nōlḗtis
		3	érunt	póterunt	vólent	nṓlent

Infinitive			férre	férrī	íre
Imperative			fer	férre	ī
			férte	férimini	íte
Present	Singular	1	férō	féror	éō
		2	fers	férris	īs
		3	fert	fértur	it
	Plural	1	férimus	férimur	ímus
		2	fértis	feríminī	ítis
		3	férunt	ferúntur	éunt
Imperfect	Singular	1	ferébam	ferébar	íbam
		2	ferébās	ferēbáris	íbās
		3	ferébat	ferēbátur	íbat
	Plural	1	ferēbámus	ferēbámur	ībámus
		2	ferēbátis	ferēbámini	ībátis
		3	ferébant	ferēbántur	íbant
Future	Singular	1	féram	férar	íbō
		2	férēs	feréris	íbis
		3	féret	ferétur	íbit
	Plural	1	ferémus	ferémur	íbimus
		2	ferétis	feréminī	íbitis
		3	férent	feréntur	íbunt

XIX. Irregular Verbs: Perfect, Pluperfect, Future Perfect Indicative

Full charts are not supplied for these forms because (except for the perfect of **eō**, for which see below) they are not irregular in any way. They are made in the same way as the perfect, pluperfect, and future perfect tenses of regular verbs, by adding the perfect, pluperfect, and future perfect endings to the perfect stem. The perfect stem is found by dropping the *-ī* from the third principal part. The first three principal parts of the irregular verbs are as follows (the perfect stem is underlined):

sum, esse, <u>fu</u>ī	volō, velle, <u>volu</u>ī	ferō, ferre, <u>tul</u>ī
possum, posse, <u>potu</u>ī	nōlō, nōlle, <u>nōlu</u>ī	eō, īre, <u>i</u>ī or <u>īv</u>ī

Examples:

Perfect: fuistī, voluērunt, tulimus
Pluperfect: fueram, potuerant, nōluerāmus
Future Perfect: fuerō, volueris, tulerimus

The perfect forms of **eō** made from the stem **i-** are as follows:

Singular: iī, īstī, iit   Plural: iimus, īstis, iērunt

Note that the stem vowel (**i-**) contracts with the *-i* of the endings *-istī* and *-istis* to give ī- (**īstī, īstis**). Thus also the perfect infinitive: **īsse** (for **iisse**).

The perfect forms of **eō** made from the stem **īv-** are regular, as follows:

Singular: īvī, īvistī, īvit   Plural: īvimus, īvistis, īvērunt

REFERENCE GRAMMAR

I. NOUNS

    A. Nominative Case
        1. Subject
        A noun or pronoun in the nominative case may be the subject of
        a verb:

        In pictūrā est **puella**.... (1:1)
        *A **girl** is in the picture....*

        2. Complement
        A linking verb may be accompanied by a complement in the nom-
        inative case:

        Cornēlia est **puella**.... (1:1)   Cornēlia est **laeta**.... (1:2–3)
        *Cornelia is a **girl**....*   *Cornelia is **happy**....*

        While the verb **esse** is the most common linking verb, the verbs
        in the following sentences are also classed as linking verbs and
        have complements in the nominative case:

        "Quam **scelestus** ille caupō <u>vidētur</u>!" (21:22)
        *"How **wicked** that innkeeper <u>seems</u>!"*

        "'Nōn sine causā tū <u>vocāris</u> **Pseudolus**.'" (31:23)
        *"'Not without reason <u>are you called</u> **Pseudolus**.'"*

        "Quis <u>creābitur</u> **arbiter** bibendī?" (34:4)
        *"Who <u>will be chosen</u> **master** of the drinking?"*

        <u>Fit</u> in diēs **molestior**. (34h:16)
        *"He <u>becomes</u> **more troublesome** every day."*

    B. Genitive Case (see Book I-A, page 80)
    The genitive case usually relates or attaches one noun to another.
        1. Genitive of Possession

        ...vīlicus ipse <u>vīllam</u> **dominī** cūrat. (11:3)
        *...the overseer himself looks after the <u>country house</u> **of the master**.*

        2. Genitive with Adjectives
        Words or phrases in the genitive case may be found with certain
        adjectives, especially those having to do with fullness:

        Brevī tempore ārea est <u>plēna</u> **servōrum** et **ancillārum**.... (11:4)
        *In a short time the threshing-floor is <u>full</u> **of slaves** and **slave-women**....*

3. Partitive Genitive

A word or phrase in the genitive case may indicate the whole of which something is a part (see Book I-B, page 95):

"<u>Nihil</u> **malī**," inquit. (21:7)
"<u>*Nothing*</u> ***of a bad thing***," *he said.*
"*Nothing bad*" or "*There is nothing wrong.*"

Crās <u>satis</u> **temporis** habēbimus. (23f:14)
Tomorrow we will have <u>enough</u> (of) time.

With numbers and the words **paucī,** *a few,* **quīdam,** *a certain,* and **nūllus,** *no, no one,* the preposition **ex** or **dē** with the ablative is used:

<u>ūnus</u> **ē praedōnibus** (26:24)   <u>*one*</u> ***of the robbers***

The partitive genitive is used with superlative adjectives and adverbs (see Book II-A, pages 64 and 76):

Titus erat bibendī arbiter <u>pessimus</u> **omnium.** (34:24)
*Titus was the <u>worst</u> master of the drinking **of all.***

Hic puer <u>optimē</u> **omnium** scrībit. (35h:2)
*This boy writes <u>best</u> **of all.***

4. Genitive of Indefinite Value

The genitive case may be found in statements or questions of the general value of something (compare this with the ablative of price, below):

"'**Quantī,**' inquit Pseudolus, 'est illa perna?'" (31:7–8)
"'***How much,***' *says Pseudolus, 'is that ham?'*"

C. Dative Case

1. Indirect Object of Transitive Verbs

A word or phrase in the dative case may indicate the indirect object of transitive verbs, especially verbs of "giving," "telling," or "showing" (see Book I-B, pages 52–53 and 55 and Exercise 22c):

...servī cistās Cornēliōrum **raedāriō** <u>trādidērunt</u>. (22:2)
*...the slaves <u>handed</u> the chests of the Cornelii <u>over</u> **to the coachman.***

2. Dative with Intransitive Verbs

Intransitive verbs and verbs that may be transitive but are used without a direct object may be accompanied by words or phrases in the dative case (see Book I-B, page 55):

Aulus **Septimō** <u>clāmāvit</u>. (21:8–9) *Aulus <u>shouted</u> **to Septimus.***

3. Dative with Intransitive Compound Verbs
   Many intransitive compound verbs are accompanied by words or phrases in the dative case (see Book I-B, pages 78–79):

   Iam **urbī** <u>appropinquābant</u>. (22:12)
   *Already <u>they were coming near to/approaching</u> **the city**.*

4. Dative with Special Intransitive Verbs (see Book I-B, page 119)
   The dative case is used with special intransitive verbs such as **cōnfīdere**, *to trust*, **favēre**, *to (give) favor (to)*, *to (give) support (to)*, **nocēre**, *to do harm (to)*, and **placēre**, *to please*:

   Ego **russātīs** <u>favēbō</u>. (27:25)
   *I <u>will give favor</u> **to the reds**.*   *I <u>will favor</u> **the reds**.*

5. Dative with Impersonal Verbal Phrases and Impersonal Verbs
   The dative case is found with impersonal verbal phrases such as **necesse est** and with impersonal verbs (see Book I-B, page 56):

   "**Nōbīs** <u>necesse est</u> statim discēdere." (9:13–14)
   "*<u>It is necessary</u> **for us** to leave immediately.*"

   "<u>Licet</u>ne **nōbīs**," inquit Marcus, "hīc cēnāre?" (20:7)
   "*<u>Is it allowed</u> **for us**,*" said Marcus, "*to eat here?*"
   "*May we eat here?*"

6. Dative with Verbs of Taking Away or Depriving
   A word in the dative case sometimes denotes the person or thing from which something is taken:

   Mihi <u>est adēmptum</u> baculum…. (35:20)
   *(My) stick <u>was taken away</u> **from me**….*

7. Dative of Possession
   When found with a form of the verb **esse,** the dative case may indicate possession; the thing possessed is the subject of the clause and the person who possesses it is in the dative:

   …servus quīdam **cui** nōmen <u>est</u> Pseudolus. (31:5–6)
   *…a certain slave, **to whom** the name <u>is</u> Pseudolus.*
   …whose name is Pseudolus.
   …who has the name Pseudolus.

D. Accusative Case
   1. Direct Object
      A word or phrase in the accusative case may be the direct object of a transitive verb (see Book I-A, pages 20 and 40–41):

      Sextus…semper **Cornēliam** <u>vexat</u>. (4:1)   *Sextus…<u>is</u> always <u>annoying</u> **Cornelia**.*

2. Double or Predicate Accusative
Verbs of naming, electing, making, and asking often take two accusatives, the first the direct object and the second a predicate to that object:

Cēterōs...puerōs semper **facillima**, **mē** semper **difficillima** <u>rogat</u>. (40:18)

*He always (<u>asks</u>) **the other boys very easy things**, **me** he always <u>asks</u> **very difficult things**.*

3. Accusative with Prepositions
The accusative case is used with certain prepositions, especially those expressing motion toward or into or through (see Book I-A, page 64):

<u>ad</u> **vīllam**, *<u>to/toward</u> **the country house*** (2:7)
<u>in</u> **piscīnam**, *<u>into</u> **the fishpond*** (3:8)
<u>per</u> **agrōs**, *<u>through</u> **the fields*** (9:1)

Prepositional phrases with the accusative case may also indicate the vicinity in which someone or something is located:

<u>prope</u> **rīvum** (5:3)
*<u>near</u> **the stream***
...iānitor <u>ad</u> **iānuam** vīllae dormit. (9:3)
*...the doorkeeper sleeps <u>near/at</u> **the door** of the country house.*

4. Accusative of Place to Which without a Preposition
With names of cities, towns, small islands, and the words **domus** and **rūs**, the idea of place to which is expressed by the accusative case without a preposition (see Book II-A, pages 118–120):

Rōmam festīnāvit.
*He hurried **to Rome**.*

Domum iit.
*He went **home**.*

Rūs proficīscitur.
*He sets out **for the country**.*

5. Accusative of Duration of Time
Words or phrases in the accusative case without a preposition may indicate duration of time (see Book II-A, page 121):

Iam **multōs diēs** in scaphā erāmus.... (42:38)
*We had already been in the boat **for many days**....*

6. Adverbial Accusative
A word in the accusative case may be used as an adverb:

Multum et diū clāmat lanius, sed Pseudolus **nihil**
respondet. (31:25)
*The butcher shouts **a lot** and for a long time, but Pseudolus makes
no reply.*

7. Exclamatory Accusative
The accusative case is used in exclamations:

"**Ō mē miseram!**" (9:18)
"*Poor me!*"

8. For the accusative and infinitive, see IX.D below.

E. Ablative Case
1. Ablative of Respect
A noun or phrase in the ablative may denote that with respect to
which something is or is done:

In pictūrā est puella, **nōmine** Cornēlia. (1:1)
*In the picture is a girl, Cornelia **with respect to her name**.*
*In the picture is a girl, Cornelia **by name/called** Cornelia.*

2. Ablative of Time When
A noun or phrase in the ablative case without a preposition may
indicate time when:

Etiam in pictūrā est vīlla rūstica ubi Cornēlia **aestāte**
habitat. (1:2)
*Also in the picture is the country house and farm where Cornelia lives
in summer.*

3. Ablative of Time within Which
A noun or phrase in the ablative case without a preposition may
indicate time within which:

Brevī tempore Cornēlia est dēfessa. (2:4–5)
In/Within a short time Cornelia is tired.

4. Ablative of Instrument, Means, or Cause
A word or phrase in the ablative case without a preposition may
indicate the means by which, the instrument with which, or the
cause on account of which an action is carried out or a person or
thing is in a certain state (see Book I-A, page 91, Book I-B, page
79, and Book II-A, pages 34–35):

Dāvus eum **tunicā** <u>arripit</u> et **baculō** <u>verberat</u>. (means, instrument, 12:17–18)
*Davus <u>grabs hold of</u> him **by the tunic** and <u>beats</u> him **with his stick**.*

Tuā culpā raeda <u>est in fossā</u>. (cause, 14:7)
Because of your fault *the carriage <u>is in the ditch</u>.*
It's your fault that the carriage is in the ditch.

The ablative of instrument, means, or cause is often used with passive verbs (see Book II-A, page 35):

...nam interdiū nihil intrā urbem **vehiculō** <u>portātur</u>. (29:3–4)
*...for during the day nothing <u>is carried</u> **by a vehicle** within the city.*

5. Ablative of Agent
   If the action of a passive verb is carried out by a person, the ablative of agent is used, consisting of the preposition **ā** or **ab** with the ablative case (see Book II-A, page 35):

   ...māter et fīlia **ā servīs** per urbem <u>ferēbantur</u>. (29:1–2)
   *...the mother and her daughter <u>were being carried</u> through the city **by slaves**.*

6. Ablative of Manner
   A phrase consisting of a noun and adjective in the ablative case may be used with or without the preposition **cum** to indicate how something happens or is done (see Book II-A, page 34):

   Tum venit Dāvus ipse et, "Tacēte, omnēs!" **magnā vōce/magnā cum vōce** <u>clāmat</u>. (11:6)
   *Then Davus himself comes, and <u>he shouts</u> **in a loud voice**, "Be quiet, everyone!"*

   The ablative of manner may consist of a single noun with **cum**:

   Caupō iam **cum rīsū** <u>clāmāvit</u>.... (19:17)
   *Now **with a laugh/jokingly** the innkeeper <u>shouted</u>....*

   Occasionally the ablative of manner may consist of a noun in the ablative case without an accompanying adjective or **cum**:

   Tum ego **silentiō** ingressus.... (42:34)
   *Then I having entered **silently**....*

7. Ablative of Price
   The ablative case is used to refer to the specific price of something (compare this with the genitive of indefinite value, above):

   "'Itaque tibi **decem dēnāriīs** eum vēndam.'" (31:17–18)
   *"'Therefore I will sell it to you **for ten denarii**.'"*

8. Ablative of Comparison
   The ablative of comparison may be found with comparative adjectives and adverbs (see Book II-A, pages 72 and 76):

   Mārtiālis **Eucleide** est multō prūdentior. (35d:4)
   *Mārtial is much _wiser_ **than** Eucleides.*

   Sextus paulō celerius **Marcō** currere potest. (35h:4)
   *Sextus can run a little _faster_ **than** Marcus.*

9. Ablative of Degree of Difference
   The ablative case is used to express the degree of difference with comparative adjectives, adverbs, and other words implying comparison (see Book II-A, pages 72 and 76):

   "Quam libenter eum rūrsus vidēbō! Sānē tamen **multō** libentius tē vidēbō ubi tū Rōmam veniēs!" (36:10–11)
   *"How gladly I will see him again! But of course I will see you **much** _more gladly/more gladly_ **by much** when you come to Rome!"*

   Multīs post annīs...pervēnit. (39c:3)
   *"He arrived...**many years** _later/later_ **by many years**.*

10. Ablative of Separation
    Verbs or adjectives implying separation are often accompanied by words or phrases in the ablative, sometimes with **ab** or **ex** and sometimes without a preposition, to express the thing from which something is separated or free:

    ...vir **vīnō** abstinentissimus! (34h:28) *...a man _most abstinent_ **from wine!***

11. Ablative with Prepositions
    The ablative case is used with certain prepositions, especially those expressing motion from or out of, place where, and accompaniment (see Book I-A, pages 64 and 90):

    ab urbe, _from_ **the city** (13:12)   in pictūrā, _in_ **the picture** (1:1)
    ē silvā, _out of_ **the woods** (5:12)   sub arbore, _under_ **the tree** (1:3)
    ex agrīs, _out of_ **the fields** (2:7)   cum canibus, _with_ **dogs** (12:9)

12. Ablative of Place from Which without a Preposition
    With names of cities, towns, small islands, and the words **domus** and **rūs**, the idea of place from which is expressed by the ablative case without a preposition (see Book II-A, page 119):

    Brundisiō...proficīscētur.... (36:8–9)
    *He will set out **from Brundisium**....*

    Domō/Rūre profectus est.
    *He set out **from home/from the country**.*

13. Ablative of Description
   A noun and adjective in the ablative case may be used without a preposition to describe another noun:

   [Vergilius] semper **īnfirmā** erat **valētūdine**. (39f: 9–10)
   *[Vergil] was always **of weak health**.*

F. Vocative Case
   The vocative case is used when addressing a person or persons directly (see Book I-A, page 56):

   "Dēscende, **Sexte**!" (4:6)
   *"Come down, **Sextus**!"*

   "Abīte, **molestī**!" (3:8–9)
   *"Go away, **pests**!"*

G. Locative Case
   The locative case is used to indicate place where with names of cities, towns, and small islands and with the words **domus** and **rūs** (see Book II-A, pages 119–120):

   Rōmae *at Rome*, **Brundisiī** *at Brundisium*, **Carthāginī** *at Carthage*, **Baiīs** *at Baiae*, **domī** *at home*, and **rūrī** *in the country*

II. ADJECTIVES

A. Agreement
   Adjectives agree with the nouns they modify in gender, number, and case (see Book I-B, pages 5–6)

B. Adjectives Translated as Adverbs
   Adjectives may sometimes best be translated as adverbs:

   Brevī tempore, ubi Marcus advenit, eum **laetae** excipiunt. (5:12–13)
   *In a short time, when Marcus arrives, they welcome him **happily**.*

C. Adjectives as Substantives
   Adjectives may be used as substantives, i.e., as nouns (see Book I-B, page 66):

   "Abīte, **molestī**!" (3:8–9)
   *"Go away, **pests**!"*

   Multa et **mīra** vidēbunt puerī. (23:12)
   *The boys will see **many** (and) **wonderful (things)**.*

D. Comparison of Adjectives

Adjectives occur in positive, comparative, and superlative degrees (see Book II-A, pages 64 and 65). For an example of a comparative adjective, see **prūdentior** in I.E.8 above, and for an example of a superlative adjective, see **pessimus** in I.B.3 above.

Instead of following the rules given in Book II-A, page 65, a few adjectives form their comparative and superlative degrees with the adverbs **magis** and **maximē:**

Paulātim igitur fīēbat **magis ēbrius?** (34h:21)
*Did he therefore gradually become **more drunk?***

Statim factus est **maximē ēbrius**.... (34h:22)
*Suddenly he became **very drunk.***

Comparative adjectives may be used with **quam** or with the ablative case to express the comparison (see Book II-A, pages 64 and 72):

"Quis enim est prūdentior **quam** Gaius?" (34:7)
"Quis enim est prūdentior **Gaiō**?"
*"For who is wiser **than** Gaius?"*

Mārtiālis est multō prūdentior **quam** Eucleidēs.
Mārtiālis **Eucleide** est multō prūdentior. (35d:4)
*Martial is much wiser **than** Eucleides.*

Superlative adjectives may be used with the partitive genitive, see I.B.3 above.

III. ADVERBS

A. Adverbs may modify verbs, other adverbs, or adjectives (see Book I-A, pages 100–101):

Laeta est Flāvia quod Cornēlia **iam** in vīllā <u>habitat</u>. (1:5)
*Flavia is happy because Cornelia <u>is</u> **now** <u>living</u> in the country house.*

Scrībe **quam** <u>saepissimē</u>. (36:25)
*Write **as** <u>often</u> **as possible.***

"**Valdē** <u>dēfessī</u>," respondit Cornēlius. (23:9)
*"**Very** <u>tired</u>," replied Cornelius.*

B. Comparison of Adverbs

Adverbs occur in positive, comparative, and superlative degrees (see Book II-A, pages 74–76). For an example of a comparative adverb, see **celerius** in I.E.8 above, and for an example of a superlative adverb, see **optimē** in I.B.3 above.

The comparative adverb may be used with **quam** or with the ablative case:

Nēmō celerius **quam** frāter meus currere potest. (35h:3)
*No one is able to run faster **than** my brother.*

Sextus celerius **Marcō** currere potest. (35h:4)
*Sextus is able to run faster **than** Marcus.*

The superlative adverb may be used with a partitive genitive, see I.B.3 above.

IV. VERBS

A. Function
Verbs may be divided into three types according to their function in the sentence or clause:

1. Linking verbs connect a subject with a predicate noun or adjective:

   Cornēlia **est** puella Rōmāna. (1:1)   *Cornelia **is** a Roman girl.*

   For other examples, see I.A.2 above.

2. Intransitive verbs describe actions that do not take direct objects:

   Cornēlia…in Italiā **habitat.** (1:1–2)   *Cornelia **lives** in Italy.*

3. Transitive verbs describe actions that take direct objects:

   Sextus…semper Cornēliam **vexat.** (4:1)
   *Sextus…always **annoys** Cornelia.*

B. Voice

1. Active and Passive
   Verbs may be either active or passive in voice. In the active voice the subject performs the action of the verb; in the passive voice the subject receives the action of the verb (see Book II-A, pages 23–24, 33, and 42–43):

   Incolae omnia **agunt.** (active, Book II-A, page 23)
   *The tenants **are doing** everything.*

   Ab incolīs omnia **aguntur.** (passive, Book II-A, page 23)
   *Everything **is being done** by the tenants.*

2. Deponent Verbs
   Some verbs, called deponent, are passive in form but active in meaning (see Book II-A, pages 98–100):

   Subitō **collāpsus est.** (34:22)   *Suddenly **he collapsed**.*

3. Semi-deponent Verbs
   Some verbs, such as **audeō, audēre, ausus sum**, have regular active forms with active meanings in the present, imperfect, and future tenses but have passive forms with active meanings in the perfect, pluperfect, and future perfect tenses (see Book II-A, pages 132–133):

   Tum Marcus arborem ascendit neque dēsilīre **ausus est**.
   (40:10–11)
   *Then Marcus climbed a tree and **did** not **dare** jump down.*

4. Impersonal Verbs
   See IX, Uses of the Infinitive, below.

C. Tenses of the Indicative
   1. Present
      The present tense describe an action or a state of being in present time (see Book I-A, page 73):

      In pictūrā **est** puella...quae in Italiā **habitat**. (1:1–2)
      *In the picture **is** a girl...who **lives** in Italy.*

   2. Vivid or Historic Present
      Sometimes a writer will switch to the present tense while describing past events; this is called the vivid or historic present and helps make the reader feel personally involved in the narrative (see Book II-A, page 23).

   3. Imperfect
      The imperfect tense (see Book I-A, page 106) describes a continuing, repeated, or habitual action or state of being in past time:

      Ego et Marcus **spectābāmus** cisium. (continuing action, 14:10)
      *Marcus and I **were watching** the carriage.*

      Cornēlius...Syrum identidem **iubēbat** equōs incitāre. (repeated action, 13:1–2)
      *Cornelius **kept ordering** Syrus again and again to spur on the horses.*

      Dāvus in Britanniā **habitābat**. (habitual action)
      *Davus **used to live** in Britain.*

      The imperfect tense may also indicate the beginning of an action in past time (see Book I-A, page 107):

      Equōs ad raedam nostram **dēvertēbat**. (14:11)
      *He **began to turn** the horses **aside** in the direction of our carriage.*

The imperfect tense with **iam** and an expression of duration of time is often best translated in English with a pluperfect:

Iam <u>multōs diēs</u> in scaphā **erāmus** cum ā mercātōribus quibusdam inventī sumus. (42:38)
*We **had already been** in the boat <u>for many days</u> when we were found by certain merchants.*

4. Future
The future tense indicates an action that will take place at some time subsequent to the present (see Book I-B, page 67):

"Brevī tempore ad Portam Capēnam **adveniēmus**...." (22:26)
*"In a short time **we will arrive** at the Porta Capena...."*

5. Perfect System
The perfect, pluperfect, and future perfect tenses are formed from the perfect stem, which is derived from the third principal part of the verb.

   a. The perfect tense refers to an action that happened or that someone did in past time or to an action completed as of present time (see Book I-B, pages 16–17):

   Eō ipsō tempore ad iānuam caupōnae **appāruit** homō obēsus.... (18:12)
   *At that very moment a fat man **appeared** at the door of the inn....*

   "Servī meī alium lectum tibi **parāvērunt**." (19:17–18)
   *"My slaves **have prepared** another bed for you."*

   b. The pluperfect tense describes an action that was completed prior to some other action in the past (see Book I-B, page 79):

   Titus in itinere mōnstrāvit puerīs mīra aedificia quae prīncipēs in Palātīnō **aedificāverant**. (24:19–20)
   *Along the way Titus showed the boys the wonderful buildings that the emperors **had built** on the Palatine.*

   c. The future perfect tense describes an action that will have been completed before another action in future time begins (see Book I-B, page 84):

   "Cum **intrāverimus**, tandem aurīgās ipsōs spectābimus." (26:17–18)
   *"When we **enter/will have entered**, we will finally watch the charioteers themselves."*

D. Mood

    1. Indicative Mood

    The term *indicative mood* refers to a set of verb forms that are used to express statements or questions of fact in main clauses and statements of fact in many subordinate clauses:

    "Cum **intrāverimus**, tandem aurīgās ipsōs **spectābimus**." (26:17–18)
    *"When **we enter/will have entered**, we **will** finally **watch** the charioteers themselves."*

    2. Imperative Mood

    The imperative mood is used to express a command (see Book I-A, page 74):

    "**Abīte**, molestī!" (3:8–9)
    *"**Go away**, pests!"*

    A negative command is expressed by **nōlī/nōlīte** and the infinitive:

    "**Nōlī** servōs **excitāre**!" (9:9)
    *"**Don't wake up** the slaves!"*

    3. Subjunctive Mood

    The term *subjunctive mood* refers to a set of verb forms that you have seen used in certain types of subordinate clauses: **cum** causal clauses, **cum** circumstantial clauses, and indirect questions (see below). This mood gets its name from the Latin elements **sub-**, *under*, and **iūnct-**, *joined*, because verbs in this mood are often found in subordinate clauses, i.e., clauses that are "joined under" the main clause. In such clauses the subjunctive is often not translated any differently from the way a verb in the corresponding tense of the indicative would be translated. (For examples, see below.)

V. PARTICIPLES

    A. Present Participles (see Book II-A, pages 133–134)

        1. Participles as Verbal Adjectives

        Participles are verbal adjectives and may modify nouns:

        Nunc cōnspicit poētam versūs **recitantem**. (29:5)
        *Now she catches sight of a poet **reciting** verses.*

        Since the participle is a verbal adjective, it may take a direct object of its own; in the sentence above **versūs** is the object of the participle **recitantem**.

2. Participles as Substantives
Present active participles are frequently used as substantives (nouns) (see Book II-A, page 134):

"Cavēte!" exclāmant **adstantēs**.... (29:9–10)
*"Watch out!" shout **the bystanders**....*

B. Perfect Participles as Adjectives
Perfect participles often modify the subject of the verb of the clause (see Book II-A, pages 50–51):

Itaque coquus **vocātus** ab omnibus laudātus est. (33:26)
*Therefore the cook, **having been summoned**, was praised by everyone.*
See Book II-A, page 51 for alternative translations.

...inde **regressus**...in hortō labōrābam. (40:6–7)
*...**having returned** from there...I worked in the garden.*

VI. GERUNDS

The gerund is a neuter verbal noun that appears in the genitive, dative, accusative, and ablative singular only. It will be formally introduced in Book III. Gerunds are translated as verbal nouns in English:

"Quis creābitur arbiter **bibendī**?" (34:4)
*"Who will be made master **of the drinking**?"*

VII. SENTENCES

A. Agreement
The subject and verb of a sentence must agree in number; a singular subject takes a singular verb, and a plural subject, a plural verb:

Cornēlia <u>est</u> puella Rōmāna.... (1:1)   *Cornelia <u>is</u> a Roman girl....*

Cornēlia et Flāvia <u>sunt</u> puellae Rōmānae.... (2:1–2)
***Cornelia and Flavia** <u>are</u> Roman girls....*

B. Questions
1. Questions may be introduced by many interrogative words:

   Quid facit Cornēlia?   ***What** is Cornelia doing?*

2. Questions may also be introduced by the particle **-ne** attached to the end of the first word (often the verb) of the question:

   Est**ne** puer ignāvus? (5:4)   *Is the boy cowardly?*

3. Questions that expect the answer "yes" are introduced with **nōnne**:

   "**Nōnne** cēnāre vultis?" (19:2)   *"**Surely** you want to eat, **don't you?**"*

C. Coordinating Conjunctions

Conjunctions are words that join together (Latin **con-,** *together* + **iungere,** *to join*) sentences or elements within a sentence. Coordinating conjunctions join elements that are simply added to one another and are of equal grammatical importance (Latin **co-,** *together, same* + **ōrdō,** *order, rank*):

Cornēlia sedet **et** legit. (1:3)   *Cornelia sits **and** reads.*

Etiam Sextus dormit **neque** Cornēliam vexat. (6:2)
*Even Sextus is sleeping **and** is **not** annoying Cornelia.*

Marcus **neque** ignāvus **neque** temerārius est. (5:5–6)
*Marcus is **neither** cowardly **nor** rash.*

Hodiē puellae nōn sedent **sed** in agrīs ambulant. (2:2–3)
*Today the girls are not sitting **but** are walking in the fields.*

Servī in vīllā sedent, **nam** dēfessī sunt. (8c:8)
*The slaves are sitting in the country house, **for** they are tired.*

Sextus est puer molestus quī semper Cornēliam vexat. Cornēlia **igitur** Sextum nōn amat. (4:1–2)
*Sextus is an annoying boy who always annoys Cornelia. Cornelia, **therefore**, does not like Sextus.*

VIII. **SUBORDINATE CLAUSES**

A clause is a group of words containing a verb. The following sentence contains two clauses, each of which is said to be a main clause because each could stand by itself as a complete sentence:

Rīdent Marcus et Cornēlia, sed nōn rīdet Sextus. (4:10–11)
Marcus and Cornelia laugh, but Sextus does not laugh.

Subordinate (Latin **sub-,** *below* + **ōrdō,** *order, rank*) clauses are clauses that are of less grammatical importance than the main clause in a sentence. They are sometimes called dependent (Latin **dē-,** *down from* + **pendēre,** *to hang*) clauses because they hang down from the main clause and cannot stand by themselves. They are joined to the main clause by pronouns, adverbs, or subordinating conjunctions.

A. Adjectival Subordinate Clauses with Verbs in the Indicative

Subordinate clauses are modifiers. They may be descriptive, like adjectives, and modify nouns:

Cornēlia est puella Rōmāna <u>**quae** in Italiā habitat</u>. (1:1–2)
*Cornelia is a Roman girl, <u>**who** lives in Italy</u>.*

Etiam in pictūrā est vīlla rūstica <u>**ubi** Cornēlia aestāte habitat</u>. (1:2)
*Also in the picture is a country house and farm <u>**where** Cornelia lives in the summer</u>.*

The relative pronoun (**quī, quae, quod**) introduces relative clauses, as in the first example above, and agrees with its antecedent in number and gender; its case depends on its use in its own clause (see Book II-A, pages 4–5):

Deinde īrā commōtus servum petit ā **quō** porcus aufūgit. (29:11–12)
*Then in a rage he goes after the slave from **whom** the pig escaped.*

The relative pronoun **quō** is masculine and singular because of the gender and number of its antecedent, **servus**; it is ablative because of its use with the preposition **ā** in its own clause.

Omnia **quae** videt Cornēlia eam dēlectant. (29:5)
*Everything **that** Cornelia sees pleases her.*

The relative pronoun **quae** is neuter and plural because of the gender and number of its antecedent, **omnia**; it is accusative because of its use as the direct object of **videt** in its own clause.

"...īre ad mercātōrem quendam **cuius** taberna nōn procul abest...." (28:10)
*"...to go to a certain merchant **whose** shop is not far away...."*

The relative pronoun **cuius** is masculine and singular because of the gender and number of its antecedent, **mercātōrem quendam**; it is genitive because of its use as a possessive within its own clause (*whose shop*).

B. Adverbial Subordinate Clauses with Verbs in the Indicative
In contrast to adjectival subordinate clauses described above, most subordinate clauses are adverbial, that is, they modify the verb of the main clause or the action of the main clause as a whole and are introduced by subordinating conjunctions that express ideas such as the following:

sī, condition:

> **Sī** tū puer strēnuus es, ascende arborem!
> *If you are an energetic boy, climb a tree!*

quamquam, concession:

> **Quamquam** dominus abest, necesse est nōbīs strēnuē labōrāre. (11:7)
> *Although the master is away, it is necessary for us to work hard.*

dum, ubi, cum, etc., time:

> **Dum** Cornēlia legit, Flāvia scrībit. (1:4–5)
> *While Cornelia reads, Flavia writes.*

Dum per viam ībant, Aurēlia et Cornēlia spectābant rūstīcōs quī in agrīs labōrābant. (13:3–4)
(**Dum** with the imperfect tense = *while/as long as*.)
While/As long as they were going along the road, Aurelia and Cornelia were looking at the peasants who were working in the fields.

Dum puerī cibum dēvorant, subitō intrāvit mīles quīdam. (20:13)
While the boys were devouring their food, a certain soldier suddenly entered.
(Here the present tense verb in the **dum** clause is to be translated with the English past tense that describes ongoing action.) (See Book I-B, page 27.)

Puerī, **ubi** clāmōrem audiunt, statim ad puellās currunt. (5:10)
*The boys, **when they hear the shout**, immediately run to the girls.*

Crās, **ubi surgētis**, puerī, clāmōrem et strepitum audiētis.
*Tomorrow, **when you get up/will get up**, boys, you will hear shouting and noise.*

Cum intrāverimus, tandem aurīgās ipsōs spectābimus. (26:17–18)
When we enter/will have entered, we will finally watch the charioteers themselves.

(While the verbs of the subordinate clauses are in the future, **surgētis,** and future perfect, **intrāverimus,** we translate them into English as presents; see Book I-B, page 84. The use of the tenses is more exact in Latin.)

quod, cause:

Cornēlia est laeta **quod** iam in vīllā habitat. (1:2–3)
*Cornelia is happy **because** she now lives in the country house.*

Conjunctions you have met that may introduce adverbial subordinate clauses with their verbs in the indicative are:

dum, *as long as* (15:1)
dum, *while* (20:13)
nisi, *if not, unless* (18:16)
postquam, *after* (21:10)
quamquam, *although* (11:7)
quod, *because* (1:3)
simulac, *as soon as* (24:1)
sī, *if* (5:1)
ubi, *when* (5:10)
ut, *as* (16:17)

C. Adverbial Subordinate Clauses with Verbs in the Subjunctive
1. **Cum** Causal Clauses
Subordinate clauses that are introduced by the conjunction **cum** and have their verbs in the subjunctive may be **cum** causal clauses; **cum** is translated as *since* or *because*. Such clauses are adverbial and state the reason for the action of the main clause (see Book II-A, page 153):

Magister nāvis, **cum valdē timēret**, suōs vetuit nōs adiuvāre. (42:17)
*The captain of the ship, **since/because he was very frightened**, forbade his own men to help us.*

2. **Cum** Circumstantial Clauses
Subordinate clauses that are introduced by the conjunction **cum** and have their verbs in the subjunctive may also be **cum** circumstantial clauses; **cum** is translated as *when*. Such clauses are adverbial and describe the circumstances that prevailed at the time of the action of the main clause (see Book II-A, page 153):

Cum quattuor diēs **nāvigāvissēmus**, subitō maxima tempestās coorta est. (42:2–3)
***When we had sailed** four days, suddenly a very great storm arose.*

Often only the context and sense will tell you whether **cum** is to be translated *since/because* or *when*.

D. Substantive Subordinate Clauses with Verbs in the Subjunctive
a. Indirect Questions (see Book II-A, pages 153–154)
Indirect questions are substantive or noun clauses that may serve as the object of the main verb of the sentence; their verbs are in the subjunctive.

Pīrātae rogābant **quī essēmus, unde vēnissēmus,** quō iter **facerēmus**. (42:20–21)
*The pirates were asking **who we were, from where we had come, [and] to where we were making** a journey.*

IX. USES OF THE INFINITIVE

A. Complementary Infinitive
The meaning of verbs and verbal phrases such as **velle, nōlle, posse, parāre, solēre, timēre,** and **in amimō habēre** is often completed by a complementary infinitive (see Book I-A, page 26):

Cūr Marcus arborēs **ascendere** nōn vult? (5:4)
*Why does Marcus not want **to climb** trees?*

B. Infinitive as Subject

The infinitive may be used as the subject of the verb **est**, with a neuter singular complement (see Book I-B, page 28):

"Etiam in caupōnā **pernoctāre** saepe <u>est</u> <u>perīculōsum</u>." (20:19)
*"**To spend the night** in an inn <u>is</u> also often <u>dangerous</u>."*
*"<u>It is</u> also often <u>dangerous</u> **to spend the night** in an inn."*

C. Infinitive with Impersonal Verbal Phrases and Impersonal Verbs

Impersonal verbal phrases and impersonal verbs are often used with infinitives (see Book I-B, page 28):

Nōbīs igitur <u>necesse est</u> statim **discēdere.** (9:13–14)
***To leave** immediately <u>is necessary</u> for us.*
*<u>It is necessary</u> for us **to leave** immediately.*

"<u>Licet</u>ne nōbīs," inquit Marcus, "hīc **cēnāre**?" (20:7)
*"<u>Is it allowed</u> for us," Marcus said, "**to dine** here?"*
"May we dine here?"

Strictly speaking, the infinitive is the subject of the impersonal verbal phrase or impersonal verb, but we usually supply *it* as the subject in English and translate the infinitive after the verb.

D. Accusative and Infinitive (see Book I-A, page 72, and Book I-B, page 28):

The verbs **docēre**, *to teach,* **iubēre**, *to order,* and **vetāre**, *to forbid,* are used with an accusative and infinitive:

Aurēlia **Cornēliam** <u>docet</u> vīllam **cūrāre.** (6:11)
*Aurelia <u>teaches</u> **Cornelia** (how) **to take care of** the country house.*

Ancillam <u>iubet</u> aliās tunicās et stolās et pallās in cistam **pōnere.** (10:2)
*<u>She orders</u> **the slave woman to put** other tunics and stolas and pallas into a chest.*

Cūr pater meus **nōs exīre** <u>vetat</u>? (26:12)
*Why <u>does</u> my father <u>forbid</u> **us to go out**?*

LATIN TO ENGLISH VOCABULARY

Numbers in parentheses at the end of entries refer to the chapters in which the words appear in vocabulary entries or in Building the Meaning or Forms sections. Roman numerals refer to Review chapters.

A

ā or **ab**, prep. + abl., *from, by* (13, 29, 31)

ábeō, abíre, ábiī or **abívī, abitúrus**, irreg., *to go away* (3, 9)

abhínc, adv., *ago, previously* (25, 39)

abōminándus, -a, -um, *detestable, horrible* (39)

ábstinēns, abstinéntis + abl., *refraining from* (34)

ábstulī (see **aúferō**)

ábsum, abésse, áfuī, āfutúrus, irreg., *to be away, be absent, be distant* (11, 25)

ac, conj., *and* (30)
   ídem ac, *the same as* (39)

áccidit, accídere, áccidit, *it happens* (14, 26)

accípiō, accípere, accépī, accéptus, *to receive, get, welcome* (31)

accúmbō, accúmbere, accúbuī, accubitúrus, *to recline (at table)* (32)

accúrrō, accúrrere, accúrrī, accursúrus, *to run toward/up to* (29)

accúsō, -áre, -ávī, -átus, *to accuse* (21)

ácer, ácris, ácre, *keen* (34)

ad, prep. + acc., *to, toward, at, near* (2, 9)
   ad témpus, *on time* (37)

áddō, áddere, áddidī, ádditus, *to add* (31)

addúcō, addúcere, addúxī, addúctus, *to lead on, bring* (29)

adhúc, adv., *still, as yet* (5, 13)

ádimō, adímere, adémī, adémptus + dat., *to take away (from)* (35)

ádiuvō, adiuváre, adiúvī, adiútus, *to help* (6, 21)

admóveō, admovére, admóvī, admótus, *to move toward* (22)

adóptō, -áre, -ávī, -átus, *to adopt* (IX)

adórior, adorírī, adórtus sum, *to attack* (42)

adstántēs, adstántium, m. pl., *bystanders* (29)

ádsum, adésse, ádfuī, adfutúrus, irreg., *to be present, be near* (26)

aduléscēns, adulēscéntis, m., *young man, youth* (36)

advéniō, adveníre, advénī, adventúrus, *to reach, arrive (at)* (5, 23)

advesperáscit, advesperáscere, advesperávit, *it gets dark* (17)

aedifícium, -ī, n., *building* (17)

aedíficō, -áre, -ávī, -átus, *to build* (24)

aéger, aégra, aégrum, *ill* (39)

aegrótō, -áre, -ávī, -átúrus, *to be ill* (39)

Aenéās, Aenéae, m., *Aeneas (son of Venus and Anchises and legendary ancestor of the Romans)* (38)

Aenéis, Aenéidis, f., *the* Aeneid (38)

aéstās, aestátis, f., *summer* (1, 12)

aéstus, -ūs, m., *heat* (24, 25)

afféctus, -a, -um, *affected, overcome* (35)

áfferō, afférre, áttulī, allátus, irreg., *to bring, bring to, bring in* (29, 32)

África, -ae, f., *Africa* (38)

áger, ágrī, m., *field, territory, land* (2)

agnóscō, agnóscere, agnóvī, ágnitus, *to recognize* (18)

ágō, ágere, égī, áctus, *to do, drive* (8, 14, 23)
   Áge!/Ágite! Come on! (8)
   Grátiās tíbi ágō! *I thank you! Thank you!* (26)
   Quid ágis? *How are you?* (18)

Albánus, -a, -um, *of Alba Longa (city founded by Aeneas' son, Ascanius)* (39)

albátus, -a, -um, *white* (27)

áliquī, -ae, -a, *some* (38)

áliquid, *something* (25)

áliter, adv., *otherwise* (26)

álius, ália, áliud, *another, other, one… another* (10)
   áliī… áliī…, *some…others…* (9)

Álpēs, Álpium, f. pl., *the Alps* (39)

álter, áltera, álterum, *a/the second, one (of two), the other (of two), another* (1)

    álter...álter, *the one...the other* (16)

áltus, -a, -um, *tall, high, deep* (38)

    áltum, -ī, n., *the deep, the sea* (39)

ámbulō, -áre, -ávī, -atúrus, *to walk* (2)

amíca, -ae, f., *friend* (2)

amícus, -ī, m., *friend* (3)

ámō, -áre, -ávī, -átus, *to like, love* (4)

ámor, amóris, m., *love* (34)

amphitheátrum, -ī, n., *amphitheater* (25)

ancílla, -ae, f., *slave-woman* (6)

ánima, -ae, f., *soul, "heart"* (33)

animadvértō, animadvértere, animadvértī, animadvérsus, *to notice* (39)

ánimus, -ī, m., *mind* (16)

    ánimum recuperáre, *to regain one's senses, be fully awake* (21)

    Bónō ánimō es!/éste! *Be of good mind! Cheer up!* (32)

    in ánimō habére, *to intend* (16)

ánnus, -ī, m., *year* (38)

    múltīs post ánnīs, *many years afterward* (39)

ánte, prep. + acc., *before, in front of* (36, 39)

ánte, adv., *previously, before* (39)

ánteā, adv., *previously, before* (20)

ántequam, conj., *before* (39)

antíquus, -a, -um, *ancient* (26)

apériō, aperíre, apéruī, apértus, *to open* (16, 26)

ápium, -ī, n., *parsley* (34)

appáreō, -ére, -uī, -itúrus, *to appear* (15, 18)

appéllō, -áre, -ávī, -átus, *to call, name* (21)

appropínquō, -áre, -ávī, -atúrus + dat. or **ad** + acc., *to approach, come near (to)* (4, 22)

Aprílis, -is, -e, *April* (36)

ápud, prep. + acc., *with, at the house of, in front of, before* (16, 26)

áqua, -ae, f., *water* (6)

aquaedúctus, -ūs, m., *aqueduct* (23, 25)

aránea, -ae, f., *cobweb* (34)

árbiter, árbitrī, m., *master* (34)

    árbiter bibéndī, *master of the drinking* (34)

árbor, árboris, f., *tree* (1)

arcéssō, arcéssere, arcessívī, arcessítus, *to summon, send for* (40)

árcus, -ūs, m., *arch* (24, 25)

área, -ae, f., *open space, threshing-floor* (11)

árma, -órum, n. pl., *arms, weapons* (39)

armátus, -a, -um, *armed* (42)

arrípiō, arrípere, arrípuī, arréptus, *to grab hold of, snatch, seize* (5, 19, 26)

ars, ártis, gen. pl., **ártium,** f., *skill* (14)

ascéndō, ascéndere, ascéndī, ascēnsúrus, *to climb, climb into (a carriage)* (4, 22)

Ásia, -ae, f., *Asia Minor* (21)

aspáragus, -ī, m., *asparagus* (33)

aspérsus, -a, -um, *sprinkled* (33)

at, conj., *but* (23)

Athénae, -árum, f. pl., *Athens* (39)

átque, conj., *and, also* (22)

átrium, -ī, n., *atrium, main room* (26)

atténtē, adv., *attentively, closely* (20)

attónitus, -a, -um, *astonished, astounded* (24)

audáx, audácis, *bold* (36)

áudeō, audére, aúsus sum, semi-deponent + infin., *to dare (to)* (40)

áudiō, -íre, -ívī, -ítus, *to hear, listen to* (4, 20)

aúferō, auférre, ábstulī, ablátus, irreg., *to carry away, take away* (29, 32)

aufúgiō, aufúgere, aufúgī, *to run away, escape* (29)

Augústus, -a, -um, *August* (36)

Augústus, -ī, m., *Augustus (first Roman emperor)* (39)

aúreus, -a, -um, *golden* (25)

auríga, -ae, m., *charioteer* (13)

aúrum, -ī, n., *gold* (21)

aut, conj., *or* (26)

    aut...aut, conj., *either...or* (26)

aútem, conj., *however, but, moreover* (31)

auxílium, -ī, n., *help* (5, 15)

    Fer/Férte auxílium! *Bring help! Help!* (5)

Ávē!/Avéte! *Hail! Greetings!* (40)

B

báculum, -ī, n., *stick, staff* (10, 15)

béllum, -ī, n., *war* (39)

béne, adv., *well* (22, 35)

bíbō, bíbere, bíbī, *to drink* (31)

Bīthýnia, -ae, f., *Bithynia (province in Asia Minor)* (39)

bōlétus, -ī, m., *mushroom* (33)

bónus, -a, -um, *good* (12, 34)

   bóna, -órum, n. pl., *goods, possessions* (26)

   Bónō ánimō es!/éste! *Be of good mind!*
     Cheer up! (32)

bōs, bóvis, m./f., *ox, cow* (15)

brévis, -is, -e, *short* (2, 34)

   bréviter, adv., *briefly* (35)

Británnia, -ae, f., *Britain* (8)

Británnicus, -a, -um, *British* (3)

Brundísium, -ī, n., *Brundisium* (36)

   Brundísiī, *at Brundisium* (36)

   Brundísiō, *from Brundisium* (36)

   Brundísium, *to Brundisium* (36)

C

cachínnus, -ī, m., *laughter* (30)

cádō, cádere, cécidī, cāsúrus, *to fall* (3, 22)

caélum, -ī, n., *sky, heaven* (17)

Caésar, Caésaris, m., *Caesar, emperor* (27)

cálidus, -a, -um, *warm* (5)

Calígula, -ae, m., *Caligula (emperor, A.D. 37–41)* (27)

candēlábrum, -ī, n., *candelabrum, lamp-stand* (32)

cándidus, -a, -um, *white, fair-skinned, beautiful* (34)

cánis, cánis, m./f., *dog, the lowest throw of the knucklebones* (12, 34)

cánō, cánere, cécinī, cántus, *to sing* (39)

cántō, -áre, -ávī, -átus, *to sing* (21)

cápiō, cápere, cépī, cáptus, *to take, catch, capture* (21)

captívus, -ī, m., *captive, prisoner* (26)

cáput, cápitis, n., *head* (25)

cáreō, carére, cáruī, caritúrus + abl., *to need, lack* (33)

cāríssimus, -a, -um, *dearest* (16)

cárō, cárnis, f., *meat, flesh* (31)

Carthágō, Cartháginis, f., *Carthage (city on the northern coast of Africa)* (39)

cása, -ae, f., *hut* (42)

castígō, -áre, -ávī, -átus, *to rebuke, reprimand* (37)

cásū, *by chance, accidentally* (32)

caúda, -ae, f., *tail* (18)

caúpō, caupónis, m., *innkeeper* (17)

caupóna, -ae, f., *inn* (17, 20)

caúsa, -ae, f., *reason* (25)

   quā dē caúsā, *for this reason* (32)

   Quam ob caúsam...? *For what reason...?* (28)

cáveō, cavére, cávī, caútus, *to be careful, watch out for, beware* (4, 13, 23)

céleber, célebris, célebre, *famous* (31)

céler, céleris, célere, *swift* (34)

   celériter, adv., *quickly* (8, 13, 35)

   celérius, adv., *more quickly* (35)

   celérrimē, adv., *very fast, very quickly* (14)

   celérrimus, -a, -um, *fastest, very fast* (29)

   quam celérrimē, adv., *as quickly as possible* (34)

celéritās, celeritátis, f., *speed* (29)

   súmmā celeritáte, *with the greatest speed, as fast as possible* (29)

célō, -áre, -ávī, -átus, *to hide, conceal* (11)

céna, -ae, f., *dinner* (19)

cénō, -áre, -ávī, -átus, *to dine, eat dinner* (19)

centésimus, -a, -um, *hundredth* (38)

céntum, *a hundred* (15, 38)

Cérberus, -ī, m., *Cerberus (three-headed dog guarding the underworld)* (32)

cértus, -a, -um, *certain* (35)

   cértē, adv., *certainly* (19, 35)

céssō, -áre, -ávī, -ātúrus, *to be idle, do nothing, delay* (14)

céterī, -ae, -a, *the rest, the others* (33)

Chárōn, Charónis, m., *Charon (ferryman in the underworld)* (32)

cíbus, -ī, m., *food* (6)

circénsis, -is, -e, *in the circus* (27)

   lūdī circénsēs, lūdórum circénsium, m. pl., *chariot-racing* (27)

círcum, prep. + acc., *around* (32)

circúmeō, circumíre, circúmiī or **circúmīvī, circúmitus**, irreg., *to go around* (24)

Círcus Máximus, -ī, m., *Circus Maximus (a stadium in Rome)* (23)

císium, -ī, n., *light two-wheeled carriage* (14, 15)

císta, -ae, f., *trunk, chest* (10)

cívis, cívis, gen. pl., **cívium**, m./f., *citizen* (13)

clam, adv., *secretly* (42)

clámō, -áre, -ávī, -atū́rus, *to shout* (3)

clámor, clāmṓris, m., *shout, shouting* (5)

claúdō, claúdere, claúsī, claúsus, *to shut* (26)

claúsus, -a, -um, *shut, closed* (24)

clíēns, cliéntis, m., *client, dependent* (25)

coépī, *I began* (38)

cṓgitō, -áre, -ávī, -átus, *to think* (21)

cognṓmen, cognṓminis, n., *surname (third or fourth name of a Roman)* (IX)

collábor, collábī, collápsus sum, *to collapse* (34, 37)

cóllis, cóllis, gen. pl., **cóllium**, m., *hill* (35)

collóquium, -ī, n., *conversation* (26)

cólloquor, cólloquī, collocū́tus sum, *to converse, speak together* (37)

cólō, cólere, cóluī, cúltus, *to cultivate* (23)

cómes, cómitis, m./f., *companion* (39)

cómiter, adv., *courteously, graciously, in a friendly way* (32)

commissátiō, commissātiṓnis, f., *drinking party* (34)

commóveō, commovḗre, commṓvī, commṓtus, *to move, upset* (29, 30)

commṓtus, -a, -um, *moved* (14)

cómparō, -áre, -ávī, -átus, *to buy, obtain, get ready* (32)

cómpleō, complḗre, complḗvī, complḗtus, *to fill, complete* (33)

compléxus, -ūs, m., *embrace* (9, 25)

complū́rēs, -ēs, -a, *several* (32)

cóncidō, concídere, cóncidī, *to fall down* (14)

concúrrō, concúrrere, concúrrī, concursū́rus, *to run together, rush up* (35)

concúrsō, -áre, -ávī, -átus, *to run to and fro, run about* (29)

cóndō, cóndere, cóndidī, cónditus, *to found, establish* (36, 39)

condū́cō, condū́cere, condū́xī, condū́ctus, *to hire* (23)

cōnfíciō, cōnfícere, cōnfḗcī, cōnféctus, *to accomplish, finish* (25, 32)

cōnfī́dō, cōnfī́dere, cōnfísus sum + dat., *to give trust (to), trust* (26)

coníciō, conícere, coniḗcī, coniéctus, *to throw* (21)

cóniūnx, cóniugis, m./f., *husband, wife* (26)

cónor, -árī, -átus sum, *to try* (36, 37)

cónsequor, cónsequī, cōnsecū́tus sum, *to catch up to, overtake* (35, 37)

cōnsī́dō, cōnsī́dere, cōnsḗdī, *to sit down* (23)

cōnspíciō, cōnspícere, cōnspḗxī, cōnspéctus, *to catch sight of* (4, 21)

cōnstítuō, cōnstitúere, cōnstítuī, cōnstitū́tus, *to decide* (23)

cónsul, cónsulis, m., *consul* (36)

cónsulō, cōnsúlere, cōnsúluī, cōnsúltus, *to consult* (7)

conticḗscō, conticḗscere, contícuī, *to become silent* (38, 39)

cóntrā, adv., *in return* (34)

convalḗscō, convalḗscere, convā́luī, *to grow stronger, get well* (42)

convī́va, -ae, m., *guest (at a banquet)* (31)

convī́vium, -ī, n., *feast, banquet* (34)

cónvocō, -áre, -ávī, -átus, *to call together* (12)

coórior, cooírī, coórtus sum, *to rise up, arise* (42)

cóquō, cóquere, cóxī, cóctus, *to cook* (6, 32)

cóquus, -ī, m., *cook* (33)

Cornēliā́nus, -a, -um, *belonging to Cornelius* (10)

Cornéliī, -ṓrum, m. pl., *the members of the family of Cornelius* (22)

corṓna, -ae, f., *garland, crown* (34)

corṓnō, -áre, -ávī, -átus, *to crown* (34)

córpus, córporis, n., *body* (21)

corrípiō, corrípere, corrípuī, corréptus, *to seize, grab* (35)

cotī́diē, adv., *daily, every day* (37)

crās, adv., *tomorrow* (10, 13)

crḗdō, crḗdere, crḗdidī, crḗditus + dat., *to trust, believe* (35)

Cremṓna, -ae, f., *Cremona (town in northern Italy)* (39)

creō, -áre, -ávī, -átus, *to appoint* (34)

Crḗta, -ae, f., *Crete (large island southeast of Greece)* (39)

crī́nēs, crī́nium, m. pl., *hair* (28)

crótalum, -ī, n., *castanet* (21)

crūdḗlis, -is, -e, *cruel* (40)

cubículum, -ī, n., *room, bedroom* (8, 15)

cúbitum íre, *to go to bed* (19)

Cúius…? *Whose…?* (22)

culína, -ae, f., *kitchen* (21)

cúlpa, -ae, f., *fault, blame* (14)

cum, prep. + abl., *with* (12)

cum, conj., *when, since* (22, 40)

   cum prímum, *as soon as* (40)

cúnctī, -ae, -a, *all* (14)

Cupídō, Cupídinis, m., *Cupid (the son of Venus)* (34)

cúpiō, cúpere, cupívī, cupítus, *to desire, want* (40)

Cūr…? *Why…?* (1)

cúra, -ae, f., *care* (34)

Cúria, -ae, f., *Senate House* (23)

cúrō, -áre, -ávī, -átus, *to look after, take care of* (6)

currículum, -ī, n., *race track* (27)

cúrrō, cúrrere, cucúrrī, cursúrus, *to run* (2, 23)

custódiō, -íre, -ívī, -ítus, *to guard* (17)

cústōs, custódis, m., *guard* (26)

cýathus, -ī, m., *small ladle, measure (of wine)* (34)

D

dē, prep. + abl., *down from, concerning, about* (16)

débeō, -ére, -uī, -itus, *to owe*; + infin., *ought* (26)

décem, *ten* (15, 38)

Decémber, Decémbris, Decémbre, *December* (36)

décimus, -a, -um, *tenth* (38)

dédicō, -áre, -ávī, -átus, *to dedicate* (33)

dēféndō, dēféndere, dēféndī, dēfénsus, *to defend* (I, 35)

dēféssus, -a, -um, *tired* (2)

dēíciō, dēícere, dēiécī, dēiéctus, *to throw down; pass., to fall* (32)

deínde, adv., *then, next* (8, 13)

dēléctō, -áre, -ávī, -átus, *to delight, amuse* (29)

déleō, dēlére, dēlévī, dēlétus, *to destroy* (38)

Délos, -ī, f., *Delos (small island off the eastern coast of Greece)* (39)

dēmónstrō, -áre, -ávī, -átus, *to show* (24)

dēnárius, -ī, m., *denarius (silver coin)* (31)

dēpónō, dēpónere, dēpósuī, dēpósitus, *to lay down, put aside, set down* (31)

dērídeō, dērīdére, dērísī, dērísus, *to laugh at, get the last laugh* (33)

dēscéndō, dēscéndere, dēscéndī, dēscēnsúrus, *to come/go down, climb down* (4, 23)

dēsíderō, -áre, -ávī, -átus, *to long for, desire, miss* (26)

dēsíliō, dēsilíre, dēsíluī, *to leap down* (40)

déus, -ī, nom. pl., **dī**, dat., abl. pl., **dīs**, m., *god* (35, 39)

   Dī immortálēs! *Immortal Gods! Good heavens!* (33)

   Prō dī immortálēs! *Good heavens!* (42)

dēvértō, dēvértere, dēvértī, dēvérsus, *to turn aside* (14, 27)

dévorō, -áre, -ávī, -átus, *to devour* (20)

dī (nom. pl. of **déus**) (33, 39)

dícō, dícere, díxī, díctus, *to say, tell* (20, 21)

   dícitur, *(he/she/it) is said* (41)

   salútem dícere, *to send greetings* (36)

   véra dícere, *to tell the truth* (40)

Dídō, Dīdónis, f., *Dido (queen of Carthage)* (38)

díēs, diḗī, m., *day* (5, 13, 25)

   in díēs, *every day, day by day* (34)

difficilis, -is, -e, *difficult* (34)

difficúltās, difficultátis, f., *difficulty* (35)

díligēns, dīligéntis, *diligent, painstaking, thorough* (35)

   dīligénter, adv., *carefully* (19)

discédō, discédere, discéssī, discessúrus, *to go away, depart* (9, 22, 41)

discípulus, -ī, m., *pupil* (38)

díscō, díscere, dídicī, *to learn* (40)

dissímilis, -is, -e, *dissimilar* (34)

díū, adv., *for a long time* (15, 35)

   diūtíssimē, adv., *longest* (35)

   diútius, adv., *longer* (35)

díves, dívitis, *rich* (42)

dívidō, dīvídere, dīvísī, dīvísus, *to divide* (IX)

dīvínus, -a, -um, *divine* (IX)

dō, dáre, dédī, dátus, *to give* (21)

   poénās dáre, *to pay the penalty, be punished* (40)

   sē quiḗtī dáre, *to rest* (23)

dóceō, docére, dócuī, dóctus, *to teach* (6, 21)

dóleō, -ére, -uī, -itúrus, *to be sorry, be sad* (18)

dólor, dolóris, m., *grief* (38)

dómina, -ae, f., *mistress, lady of the house* (17)

dóminus, -ī, m., *master, owner* (11)

dómus, -ūs, f., *home* (23, 25, 39)

    dómī, *at home* (26, 39)

    dómō, *from home* (23, 39)

    dómum, *homeward, home* (23, 39)

dónec, conj., *until* (33)

dónō, -áre, -ávī, -átus, *to give* (34)

dórmiō, -íre, -ívī, -ītúrus, *to sleep* (4)

dórmitō, -áre, -ávī, *to be sleepy* (39)

dúbium, -ī, n., *doubt* (30)

dúcō, dúcere, dúxī, dúctus, *to lead, take, bring* (7, 19, 20)

dum, conj., *while, as long as* (1)

dúo, dúae, dúo, *two* (15, 38)

duódecim, *twelve* (38)

duodécimus, -a, -um, *twelfth* (38)

duodēvīgíntī, *eighteen* (38)

duodēvīcésimus, -a, -um, *eighteenth* (38)

E

ē or **ex,** prep. + abl., *from, out of* (2, 5, 9)

ébrius, -a, -um, *drunk* (34)

Écce! *Look! Look at…!* (1)

édō, ésse, édī, ésus, irreg., *to eat* (33)

éfferō, efférre, éxtulī, ēlátus, irreg., *to carry out, bring out* (30)

effúgiō, effúgere, effúgī, *to flee, run away, escape* (11, 21, 29)

effúndō, effúndere, effúdī, effúsus, *to pour out;* pass., *to spill* (32)

égo, *I* (5, 27)

ēgrédior, ēgredī, ēgréssus sum, *to go out, leave* (37, 39)

Éheu! *Alas!* (7)

Ého! *Hey!* (25)

ēíciō, ēícere, ēiécī, ēiéctus, *to throw out, wash overboard* (30)

élegāns, ēlegántis, *elegant, tasteful* (29)

ēmíttō, ēmíttere, ēmísī, ēmíssus, *to send out* (30)

émō, émere, émī, émptus, *to buy* (21, 31)

énim, conj., *for* (20)

éō, íre, íī or **ívī, itúrus,** irreg., *to go* (7, 17, 19, 20, 21)

    cúbitum íre, *to go to bed* (19)

éō, adv., *there, to that place* (23)

epístula, -ae, f., *letter* (7)

équus, -ī, m., *horse* (10)

ērípiō, ērípere, ērípuī, ēréptus, *to snatch (from), rescue* (29)

érrō, -áre, -ávī, -ātúrus, *to wander, be mistaken* (5, 18)

ērudítus, -a, -um, *learned, scholarly* (37)

ērúptiō, ēruptiónis, f., *eruption* (26)

ésse (see **sum** or **édō**)

Éstō! *All right! So be it!* (20)

ēsúriō, -íre, -ívī, -ītúrus, *to be hungry* (19)

et, conj., *and, also* (1)

    et…et, conj., *both… and*

étiam, adv., *also, even* (1, 6, 13)

etiámsī, conj., *even if* (37)

Éuge! *Hurray!* (33)

Éugepae! *Hurray!* (7)

Eurydicē, -ēs, f., *Eurydice (wife of Orpheus)* (VII)

ēvádō, ēvádere, ēvásī, ēvásus, *to escape* (42)

ēvértō, ēvértere, ēvértī, ēvérsus, *to overturn, upset* (32)

ex or **ē,** prep. + abl., *from, out of* (2, 5, 9)

excípiō, excípere, excépī, excéptus, *to welcome, receive, catch* (5, 16, 22)

éxcitō, -áre, -ávī, -átus, *to rouse, wake (someone) up* (8)

    excitátus, -a, -um, *wakened, aroused* (25)

exclámō, -áre, -ávī, -átus, *to exclaim, shout out* (10)

excúsō, -áre, -ávī, -átus, *to forgive, excuse* (33)

    sē excūsáre, *to apologize* (33)

éxeō, exíre, éxiī or **exívī, exitúrus,** irreg., *to go out* (5, 23)

expéllō, expéllere, éxpulī, expúlsus, *to drive out, expel* (39)

expergíscor, expergíscī, experréctus sum, *to wake up* (39)

expérior, experírī, expértus sum, *to test, try* (37)

éxplicō, -áre, -ávī, -átus, *to explain* (19)

    rem explicáre, *to explain the situation* (19)

exspéctō, -áre, -ávī, -átus, *to look out for, wait for* (15)

éxstāns, exstántis, *standing out, towering* (23)

exstínguō, exstínguere, exstínxī, exstínctus, *to put out, extinguish* (30)

exténdō, exténdere, exténdī, exténtus, *to hold out* (18, 39)

éxtrā, prep. + acc., *outside* (23)

éxtrahō, extráhere, extráxī, extráctus, *to drag out, take out* (14, 21)

éxuō, exúere, éxuī, exútus, *to take off* (33)

F

fábula, -ae, f., *story* (20)

fácilis, -is, -e, *easy* (34)
  fácile, adv., *easily* (35)

fáciō, fácere, fḗcī, fáctus, *to make, do* (1, 23)
  íter fácere, *to travel* (13)

fáctiō, factiónis, f., *company (of charioteers)* (27)

fátum, -ī, n., *fate* (39)

fátuus, -a, -um, *stupid* (13)

fáveō, favḗre, fā́vī, fautū́rus + dat., *to give favor (to), favor, support* (27)

Februárius, -a, -um, *February* (36)

fḗlēs, fḗlis, gen. pl., **fḗlium**, f., *cat* (21)

fḗlīx, fēlícis, *lucky* (34)
  fēlíciter, adv., *well, happily, luckily* (35)

fḗmina, -ae, f., *woman* (3)

fenéstra, -ae, f., *window* (30)

férculum, -ī, n., *dish, tray* (33)

fēriátus, -a, -um, *celebrating a holiday* (27)

fériō, -íre, -ívī, -ítus, *to hit, strike* (16)

férō, férre, túlī, látus, irreg., *to bring, carry, bear* (5, 12, 17, 21)
  Fer/Férte auxílium! *Bring help! Help!* (5)

férōx, ferócis, *fierce* (35)
  feróciter, adv., *fiercely* (13)

férula, -ae, f., *cane* (39)

festínō, -áre, -ávī, -ātū́rus, *to hurry* (9)

fidélis, -is, -e, *faithful* (31, 34)

fília, -ae, f., *daughter* (11)

fílius, -ī, m., *son* (11)

fíniō, -íre, -ívī, -ítus, *to finish* (21)

fínis, fínis, gen. pl., **fínium**, m., *end* (29)

fíō, fíerī, fáctus sum, irreg., *to become, be made, be done, happen* (34)

flámma, -ae, f., *flame* (29)

flōs, flóris, m., *flower* (34)

foédus, -a, -um, *filthy, disgusting* (34)

fórās, adv., *outside* (41)

fortásse, adv., *perhaps* (15)

fórte, adv., *by chance* (33)

fórtis, -is, -e, *brave, strong* (18)
  fortíssimē, adv., *most/very bravely* (35)
  fórtiter, adv., *bravely* (35)

Fórum, -ī, n., *the Forum (town center of Rome)* (25)

fóssa, -ae, f., *ditch* (12)

frágor, fragóris, m., *crash, noise, din* (4)

fráter, frátris, m., *brother* (11)

frígidus, -a, -um, *cool, cold* (5)

fritíllus, -ī, m., *cylindrical box* (34)

frōns, fróntis, f., *forehead* (12)

frū́strā, adv., *in vain* (14)

frústum, -ī, n., *scrap* (33)

fúgiō, fúgere, fū́gī, fugitū́rus, *to flee* (18, 25)

fúī (see **sum**)

fū́mus, -ī, m., *smoke* (29)

fúndus, -ī, m., *farm* (39)

fū́rtim, adv., *stealthily* (4, 13)

fū́stis, fū́stis, gen. pl., **fū́stium**, m., *club, cudgel* (35)

G

Gā́dēs, Gā́dium, f. pl., *Gades (Cadiz, a town in Spain)* (21)

Gállia, -ae, f., *Gaul* (39)

gaúdeō, gaudḗre, gāvísus sum, *to be glad, rejoice* (14, 40)

gaúdium, -ī, n., *joy* (23)

gémō, gémere, gémuī, gémitus, *to groan* (3)

génus, géneris, n., *race, stock, nation* (39)

gérō, gérere, géssī, géstus, *to wear* (10)

gládius, -ī, m., *sword* (21, 26)
  gládium stríngere, *to draw a sword* (26)

glīs, glíris, m., *dormouse* (28)

glória, -ae, f., *fame, glory* (27)

grácilis, -is, -e, *slender* (34)

Graécia, -ae, f., *Greece* (21)

Graécus, -a, -um, *Greek* (17)
  Graécī, -órum, m. pl., *the Greeks* (I)

grammáticus, -ī, m., *secondary school teacher* (37)

grátia, -ae, f., *gratitude, thanks* (26)

    Grátiās tíbi ágō, *I thank you! Thank you!* (26)

grátīs, adv., *free, for nothing* (31)

grávis, -is, -e, *heavy, serious* (35)

grúnniō, -íre, *to grunt* (29)

gustátiō, gustātiónis, f., *hors d'oeuvre, first course* (33)

H

habénae, -árum, f. pl., *reins* (22)

hábeō, -ére, -uī, -itus, *to have, hold* (10, 20, 26)

    in ánimō habére, *to intend* (16)

    ōrātiónem habére, *to deliver a speech* (26)

hábitō, -áre, -ávī, -átus, *to live, dwell* (1)

haéreō, haerére, haésī, haesúrus, *to stick* (14)

haúriō, hauríre, haúsī, haústus, *to drain* (34)

hédera, -ae, f., *ivy* (34)

Hérculēs, Hérculis, m., *Hercules (Greek hero)* (34)

héri, adv., *yesterday* (20)

Hespéria, -ae, f., *Hesperia (the land in the West, Italy)* (39)

hīc, adv., *here* (9, 13)

hic, haec, hoc, *this, the latter* (18, 19, 20, 25, 26, 31)

híems, híemis, f., *winter* (39)

Hispánia, -ae, f., *Spain* (39)

hódiē, adv., *today* (2, 13)

hólus, hóleris, n., *vegetable* (32)

hómō, hóminis, m., *man* (18)

    hóminēs, hóminum, m. pl., *people* (15, 36)

hónor, honóris, m., *honor* (IX)

hóra, -ae, f., *hour* (9)

    Quóta hóra est? *What time is it?* (38)

Horátius, -ī, m., *Horace (Roman poet)* (39)

hórtus, -ī, m., *garden* (3)

hóspes, hóspitis, m., *guest, host, friend, a person related to one of another city by ties of hospitality* (16)

hūc, adv., *here, to here* (36)

    hūc illúc, adv., *here and there, this way and that* (23)

húmī, *on the ground* (27)

húmilis, -is, -e, *humble* (34)

I

iáceō, -ére, -uī, -itúrus, *to lie, be lying down* (26)

iáciō, iácere, iécī, iáctus, *to throw* (10, 20)

iáctō, -áre, -ávī, -átus, *to toss about, drive to and fro* (39)

iam, adv., *now, already* (1, 8, 13)

    nōn iam, adv., *no longer* (2, 13)

iánitor, iānitóris, m., *doorkeeper* (9)

iánua, -ae, f., *door* (9)

Iānuárius, -a, -um, *January* (36)

íbi, adv., *there* (5, 13)

id (see **is**)

ídem, éadem, ídem, *the same* (3, 31)

    ídem ac, *the same as* (39)

idéntidem, adv., *again and again, repeatedly* (13)

Ídūs, Íduum, f. pl., *the Ides* (36)

iēntáculum, -ī, n., *breakfast* (37)

ígitur, conj., *therefore* (4)

ignávus, -a, -um, *cowardly, lazy* (5)

ígnis, ígnis, gen. pl., **ígnium**, m., *fire* (32)

ignórō, -áre, -ávī, -átus, *to be ignorant, not to know* (40)

ílle, ílla, íllud, *that; he, she, it; the former; that famous* (11, 15, 16, 20, 22, 25, 26, 31)

illúc, adv., *there, to that place* (23)

    hūc illúc, adv., *here and there, this way and that* (23)

ímber, ímbris, gen. pl., **ímbrium**, m., *rain* (23)

ímmemor, immémoris + gen., *forgetful* (22)

ímmō, adv., *rather, on the contrary* (31)

    ímmō vérō, adv., *on the contrary, in fact* (40)

immóbilis, -is, -e, *motionless* (12)

immortális, -is, -e, *immortal* (27)

    Dī immortálēs! *Immortal Gods! Good heavens!* (33)

    Prō dī immortálēs! *Good heavens!* (42)

impédiō, -íre, -ívī, -ítus, *to hinder, prevent* (11)

in, prep. + abl., *in, on, among* (1, 9, 28)

    in ánimō habére, *to intend* (16)

in, prep. + acc., *into, against* (3, 9)

    in díēs, *every day, day by day* (34)

    in quíbus, *among whom* (28)

incéndium, -ī, n., *fire* (30)

incéndō, incéndere, incéndī, incénsus, *to burn, set on fire* (38)

íncitō, -áre, -ávī, -átus, *to spur on, urge on, drive* (10)

íncola, -ae, m./f., *inhabitant, tenant* (30)

incólumis, -is, -e, *unhurt, safe and sound* (14)

índe, adv., *from there, then* (38, 40)

índuō, indúere, índuī, indútus, *to put on* (8, 23)

íneō, iníre, íniī or **inívī, ínitus**, irreg., *to go into, enter* (28)

īnfándus, -a, -um, *unspeakable* (38)

īnfāns, īnfántis, m./f., *infant, young child* (30)

ínferī, -órum, m. pl., *the underworld* (32)

ínferō, īnférre, íntulī, illátus, irreg., *to bring in* (39)

īnfírmus, -a, -um, *weak, shaky, frail* (4, 30)

íngēns, ingéntis, *huge* (22)

ingrédior, íngredī, ingréssus sum, *to go in, enter* (37)

innocéntia, -ae, f., *innocence* (21)

ínquit, *(he/she) says, said* (7)

īnspíciō, īnspícere, īnspéxī, īnspéctus, *to examine* (21)

ínsula, -ae, f., *island, apartment building* (30)

inténtus, -a, -um, *intent, eager* (38)

ínter, prep. + acc., *between, among* (33)

intérdiū, adv., *during the day, by day* (23)

intérdum, adv., *from time to time* (39)

intéreā, adv., *meanwhile* (10, 13)

ínterest, *it is important* (39)

interpéllō, -áre, -ávī, -átus, *to interrupt* (14)

íntrā, prep. + acc., *inside* (22)

íntrō, -áre, -ávī, -átus, *to enter, go into* (8, 19)

inúrō, inúrere, inússī, inústus, *to brand* (12)

invéniō, inveníre, invénī, invéntus, *to come upon, find* (12, 21)

invítō, -áre, -ávī, -átus, *to invite* (28, 32)

invítus, -a, -um, *unwilling* (21)

ínvocō, -áre, -ávī, -átus, *to invoke, call upon* (34)

iócus, -ī, m., *joke, funny story, prank* (16)
   per iócum, *as a prank/joke* (16)

ípse, ípsa, ípsum, *himself, herself, itself, themselves, very* (6, 10, 29, 31)

íra, -ae, f., *anger* (11)

īrācúndia, -ae, f., *irritability, bad temper* (40)

īrācúndus, -a, -um, *irritable, in a bad mood* (40)

īrátus, -a, -um, *angry* (3, 33)

íre (see **éō**) (7, 17)

irrúmpō, irrúmpere, irrúpī, irrúptus, *to burst in* (33)

is, éa, id, *he, she, it; this, that* (27, 31)

íta, adv., *thus, so, in this way* (3, 13, 21)
   Íta vérō! adv., *Yes! Indeed!* (3, 13)

Itália, -ae, f., *Italy* (1)

ítaque, adv., *and so, therefore* (16)

íter, itíneris, n., *journey, route* (10, 13, 15)
   íter fácere, *to travel* (13)

íterum, adv., *again, a second time* (8, 13)

Íthaca, -ae, f., *Ithaca (island home of Ulysses)* (39)

iúbeō, iubére, iússī, iússus, *to order, bid* (10, 19, 21)

Iúlius, -a, -um, *July* (36)

Iúnius, -a, -um, *June* (36)

Iúnō, Iūnónis, f., *Juno (queen of the gods)* (39)

iússa, -órum, n. pl., *commands, orders* (32)

K

Kaléndae, -árum, f. pl., *the Kalends (first day in the month)* (36)

L

lábor, labóris, m., *work, toil* (24)

labórō, -áre, -ávī, -átus, *to work* (3)

lácrimō, -áre, -ávī, -átus, *to weep, cry* (9)

laétus, -a, -um, *happy, glad* (1)
   laétē, adv., *happily* (35)

lána, -ae, f., *wool* (6)
   lánam tráhere, *to spin wool* (6)

lánius, -ī, m., *butcher* (31)

lantérna, -ae, f., *lantern* (37)

lapídeus, -a, -um, *of stone, stony* (33)

lápis, lápidis, m., *stone* (25)

Latínus, -a, -um, *Latin* (39)

Látium, -ī, n., *Latium (the area of central Italy that included Rome)* (39)

lātrátus, -ūs, m., *a bark, barking* (25)

látrō, -áre, -ávī, -ātúrus, *to bark* (12)

laúdō, -áre, -ávī, -átus, *to praise* (18)

Lāvínius, -a, -um, *of Lavinium (name of the town where the Trojans first settled in Italy)* (39)

lávō, laváre, lávī, laútus, *to wash* (20)

lectíca, -ae, f., *litter* (23)

lectīcárius, -ī, m., *litter-bearer* (23)

léctus, -ī, m., *bed, couch* (19)

lēgátus, -ī, m., *envoy* (18)

légō, légere, légī, léctus, *to read* (1, 24)

léntus, -a, -um, *slow* (35)
  léntē, adv., *slowly* (2, 13)

lépus, léporis, m., *hare* (31)

libénter, adv., *gladly* (36)

líber, líbrī, m., *book* (24)

líberī, -órum, m. pl., *children* (10, 11)

lībértās, līberátis, f., *freedom* (21)

lībértus, -ī, m., *freedman* (29)

lícet, licére, lícuit + dat., *it is allowed* (20, 24, 52)
  lícet nóbīs, *we are allowed, we may* (20)

lígō, -áre, -ávī, -átus, *to bind up* (35)

língua, -ae, f., *tongue, language* (39)

liquámen, liquáminis, n., *garum (a sauce made from fish, used to season food)* (33)

líttera, -ae, f., *letter (of the alphabet)* (12)
  lítterae, -árum, f. pl., *letter, epistle, letters, literature* (39)

lítus, lítoris, n., *shore* (39)

lócus, -ī, m., *place* (33)

lóngus, -a, -um, *long* (15)
  lóngē, adv., *far* (35)

lóquor, lóquī, locútus sum, *to speak, talk* (37)

lúcet, lucére, lúxit, *it is light, it is day* (6)

lúdō, lúdere, lúsī, lūsúrus, *to play* (16)
  pílā lúdere, *to play ball* (16)

lúdus, -ī, m., *game, school* (26, 37)
  lúdī, -órum, m. pl., *games* (24)
  lúdī circénsēs, lūdórum circénsium, m. pl., *chariot-racing* (27)

lúna, -ae, f., *moon* (33)

lúpa, -ae, f., *she-wolf* (II)

lúpus, -ī, m., *wolf* (5)

lútum, -ī, n., *mud* (26)

lūx, lúcis, f., *light* (21)
  prímā lúce, *at dawn* (21)

M

mágis, adv., *more* (34, 35)

magíster, magístrī, m., *schoolmaster, master, captain* (37, 42)

magníficus, -a, -um, *magnificent* (24)

magnópere, adv., *greatly* (31, 35)

mágnus, -a, -um, *big, great, large, loud (voice, laugh)* (4, 34)

máior, máior, máius, gen., **maióris**, *bigger* (34)

Máius, -a, um, *May* (36)

málum, -ī, n., *apple* (32)

málus, -a, -um, *bad, evil* (21, 34)
  mále, adv., *badly* (35)

mandátum, -ī, n., *order, instruction* (22)

máne, adv., *early in the day, in the morning* (21)

máneō, manére, mánsī, mānsúrus, *to remain, stay, wait* (9, 20, 23)

Mántua, -ae, f., *Mantua (town in northern Italy)* (39)

mánus, -ūs, f., *hand* (18, 25)

máppa, -ae, f., *napkin* (27)

máre, máris, gen. pl., **márium**, n., *sea* (38)

Mártius, -a, -um, *March* (36)

máter, mátris, f., *mother* (6, 11)

máximus, -a, -um, *biggest, greatest, very great, very large* (23, 34)
  maximē, adv., *most, very much, very* (34, 35)

mē, *me* (4)
  mécum, *with me* (9)

médicus, -ī, m., *doctor* (33)

Mediolánum, -ī, n., *Milan* (39)

médius, -a, -um, *mid-, middle of* (20)
  média nox, médiae nóctis, f., *midnight* (20)

Mégara, -ae, f., *Megara (a city in Greece)* (21)

Mehércule! *By Hercules! Goodness me!* (18)

mélior, mélior, mélius, gen., **melióris**, *better* (19, 34)
  mélius, adv., *better* (35)

mémor, mémoris, *remembering, mindful, unforgetting* (39)

memória, -ae, f., *memory* (30)
  memóriā tenére, *to remember* (37)

mendícus, -ī, m., *beggar* (29)

ménsa, -ae, f., *table* (29)

   secúndae ménsae, -árum, f. pl., *second course, dessert* (33)

ménsis, ménsis, m., *month* (38)

mercátor, mercātóris, m., *merchant* (22)

Mercúrius, -ī, m., *Mercury (messenger god)* (32)

merídiē, adv., *at noon* (33)

mérus, -a, -um, *pure* (34)

   mérum, -ī, n., *undiluted wine* (34)

méta, -ae, f., *mark, goal, turning post* (27)

métus, -ūs, m., *fear* (26)

méus, -a, -um, *my, mine* (7)

mígrō, -áre, -ávī, -ātúrus, *to move one's home* (39)

míles, mílitis, m., *soldier* (20)

mílle, *a thousand* (15, 38)

mīllésimus, -a, -um, *thousandth* (38)

mínimus, -a, -um, *very small, smallest* (34)

   minímē, adv., *least* (35)

   Mínimē (vérō)! adv., *No! Not at all! No indeed!* (3, 13)

mínor, mínor, mínus, gen., **minóris,** *smaller* (34)

   mínus, adv., *less* (35)

mínuō, minúere, mínuī, minútus, *to lessen, reduce, decrease* (31)

mírus, -a, -um, *wonderful, marvelous, strange* (23)

mísceō, miscére, míscuī, míxtus, *to mix* (34)

míser, mísera, míserum, *unhappy, miserable, wretched* (9)

miserábilis, -is, -e, *miserable, wretched* (30)

míttō, míttere, mísī, míssus, *to send* (9, 20, 31)

módo, adv., *only* (18)

módus, -ī, m., *way, method* (34)

moénia, moénium, n. pl., *walls* (39)

mólēs, mólis, gen. pl., **mólium,** f., *mass, huge bulk* (24)

moléstus, -a, -um, *troublesome, annoying* (4)

   moléstus, -ī, m., *pest* (3)

móneō, -ére, -uī, -itus, *to advise, warn* (39)

mōns, móntis, gen. pl., **móntium,** m., *mountain, hill* (24)

   Mōns Vesúvius, Móntis Vesúviī, m., *Mount Vesuvius (a volcano in southern Italy)* (26)

mónstrō, -áre, -ávī, -átus, *to show* (22)

mórior, mórī, mórtuus sum, *to die* (39)

móror, -árī, -átus sum, *to delay, remain, stay* (36, 37)

mors, mórtis, gen. pl., **mórtium,** f., *death* (21)

mórtuus, -a, -um, *dead* (16)

móveō, movére, móvī, mótus, *to move* (14, 24)

mox, adv., *soon, presently* (6, 13)

múlier, mulíeris, f., *woman* (27)

múlsum, -ī, n., *wine sweetened with honey* (33)

multitúdō, multitúdinis, f., *crowd* (23)

múltus, -a, -um, *much* (31, 34)

   múltum, adv., *greatly, much* (31, 35)

   múltī, -ae, -a, *many* (3, 34)

   múltīs post ánnīs, *many years afterward* (39)

múrmur, múrmuris, n., *murmur, rumble* (15)

múrus, -ī, m., *wall* (23)

mūs, múris, m., *mouse* (21)

Músa, -ae, f., *Muse (goddess of song and poetry)* (VII)

mússō, -áre, -ávī, -átúrus, *to mutter* (11)

N

nam, conj., *for* (8)

nārrátor, nārrātóris, m., *narrator* (8)

nárrō, -áre, -ávī, -átus, *to tell (a story)* (20)

   nārrátus, -a, -um, *told* (20)

náscor, náscī, nátus sum, *to be born* (39)

násus, -ī, m., *nose* (33)

nátō, -áre, -ávī, -átúrus, *to swim* (40)

návigō, -áre, -ávī, -átus, *to sail* (38)

návis, návis, gen. pl., **návium,** f., *ship* (38)

-ne (indicates a question) (3)

nē…quídem, adv., *not even* (34)

Neápolis, Neápolis, acc., **Neápolim,** f., *Naples* (15)

necésse, adv. or indecl. adj., *necessary* (6, 13)

nécō, -áre, -ávī, -átus, *to kill* (20)

néglegēns, neglegéntis, *careless* (28)

   neglegénter, adv., *carelessly* (28)

neglegéntia, -ae, f., *carelessness* (28)

némō, néminis, m./f., *no one* (9)

néque, conj., *and…not* (6)

   néque…néque, conj., *neither…nor* (5)

   néque…néque…quídquam, *neither…nor…anything* (40)

nésciō, -íre, -ívī, -ítus *to be ignorant, not to know* (9)

níger, nígra, nígrum, *black* (33)

níhil, *nothing* (4)

  nīl, *nothing* (34)

nímis, adv., *too much* (34)

nísi, conj., *unless, if…not, except* (18, 26)

nóceō, -ére, -uī, -itúrus + dat., *to do harm (to), harm* (26)

noctúrnus, -a, -um, *happening during the night* (22)

nólō, nólle, nóluī, irreg., *to be unwilling, not to wish, refuse* (5, 17, 21)

  Nólī/Nólíte + infin., *Don't…!* (9)

nómen, nóminis, n., *name* (1, 15)

nōn, adv., *not* (2, 13)

  nōn iam, adv., *no longer* (2, 13)

Nónae, -árum, f. pl., *Nones* (36)

nóndum, adv., *not yet* (6, 13)

Nónne…? (introduces a question that expects the answer "yes") (19)

nōnnúmquam, adv., *sometimes* (26)

nónus, -a, -um, *ninth* (16, 38)

nōs, *we, us* (8, 27)

nóster, nóstra, nóstrum, *our* (14, 27)

nótus, -a, -um, *known* (31)

nóvem, *nine* (15, 38)

Novémber, Novémbris, Novémbre, *November* (36)

nóvus, -a, -um, *new* (16)

nox, nóctis, gen. pl., **nóctium**, f., *night* (11)

  média nox, médiae nóctis, f., *midnight* (20)

núbēs, núbis, gen. pl., **núbium**, f., *cloud* (15)

núllus, -a, -um, *no, none* (9)

númerō, -áre, -ávī, -átus, *to count* (33)

númerus, -ī, m., *number* (11)

númquam, adv., *never* (20)

nunc, adv., *now* (6, 13)

núntius, -ī, m., *messenger* (7)

núsquam, adv., *nowhere* (39)

O

ō (used with vocative and in exclamations) (9)

ob, prep. + acc., *on account of* (39)

obdórmiō, -íre, -ívī, -itúrus, *to go to sleep* (21)

obésus, -a, -um, *fat* (18)

obscúrō, -áre, -ávī, -átus, *to hide* (30)

óbsecrō, -áre, -ávī, -átus, *to beseech, beg* (40)

obsérvō, -áre, -ávī, -átus, *to watch* (6)

obsídeō, obsidére, obsédī, obséssus, *to besiege* (38)

occupátus, -a, -um, *busy* (7)

occúrrō, occúrrere, occúrrī, occursúrus + dat., *to meet* (24)

octávus, -a, -um, *eighth* (36, 38)

óctō, *eight* (15, 38)

Octóber, Octóbris, Octóbre, *October* (36)

óculus, -ī, m., *eye* (26)

óleum, -ī, n., *oil* (32)

olfáciō, olfácere, olfécī, olfáctus, *to catch the scent of, smell, sniff* (12, 18)

ólim, adv., *once (upon a time)* (18)

olíva, -ae, f., *olive* (33)

olīvétum, -ī, n., *olive grove* (14, 15)

omíttō, omíttere, omísī, omíssus, *to leave out, omit* (39)

ómnis, -is, -e, *all, the whole, every, each* (6, 18)

ónus, óneris, n., *load, burden* (15)

óppidum, -ī, n., *town* (39)

ópprimō, opprímere, oppréssī, oppréssus, *to overwhelm* (30)

  oppréssus, -a, -um, *crushed* (25)

óptimus, -a, -um, *best, very good, excellent* (20, 31, 34)

  óptimē, adv., *best, very well, excellently* (34, 35)

  vir óptime, *sir* (20)

óra, -ae, f., *shore* (39)

ōrátiō, ōrātiónis, f., *oration, speech* (26)

  ōrātiónem habére, *to deliver a speech* (26)

ōrátor, ōrātóris, m., *orator, speaker* (22)

órdior, ōrdírī, órsus sum, *to begin* (38)

ōrnāméntum, -ī, n., *decoration*; pl., *furnishings* (30)

ōrnátus, -a, -um, *decorated* (32)

Órpheus, -ī, m., *Orpheus (legendary singer and husband of Euryudice)* (VII)

ōs, óris, n., *mouth, face, expression* (38)

óvum, -ī, n., *egg* (32)

P

paedagógus, -ī, m., *tutor* (37)

paéne, adv., *almost* (30)

Palātínus, -a, -um, *on/belonging to the Palatine Hill* (24)

pálla, -ae, f., *palla* (10)

pállium, -ī, n., *cloak* (32)

pánis, pánis, gen. pl., **pánium**, m., *bread* (32)

párēns, paréntis, m./f., *parent* (11)

páreō, -ére, -uī + dat., *to obey* (39)

páriēs, paríetis, m., *wall (of a house or room)* (30)

párō, -áre, -ávī, -átus, *to prepare, get ready* (5, 20)

   parátus, -a, -um, *ready, prepared* (10)

   sē paráre, *to prepare oneself, get ready* (22)

pars, pártis, gen. pl., **pártium**, f., *part, direction, region* (13)

párvulus, -a, -um, *small, little* (26)

párvus, -a, -um, *small* (30, 34)

páscō, páscere, pávī, pástus, *to feed, pasture* (31)

pássum, -ī, n., *raisin-wine* (33)

páter, pátris, m., *father* (6, 11)

pátior, pátī, pássus sum, *to suffer, endure* (38)

patrónus, -ī, m., *patron* (25)

pátruus, -ī, m., *uncle* (22)

paúcī, -ae, -a, *few* (34)

paulátim, adv., *gradually, little by little* (34)

paulísper, adv., *for a short time* (20)

paúlum, adv., *little* (35)

paúlum, -ī, n., *a small amount, a little* (37)

paúper, paúperis, *poor* (42)

péctō, péctere, péxī, péxus, *to comb* (28)

pecúnia, -ae, f., *money* (21)

pécus, pécoris, n., *livestock, sheep and cattle* (33)

péior, péior, péius, gen., **peióris**, *worse* (34)

   péius, adv., *worse* (35)

per, prep. + acc., *through, along* (6, 9)

   per iócum, *as a prank/joke* (16)

percútiō, percútere, percússī, percússus, *to strike* (35)

perīculósus, -a, -um, *dangerous* (17)

perículum, -ī, n., *danger* (14, 15)

pérna, -ae, f., *ham* (31)

pernóctō, -áre, -ávī, -ātúrus, *to spend the night* (17)

persuádeō, persuādére, persuásī, persuásus, *to make something* (acc.) *agreeable to someone* (dat.), *persuade someone of something; to persuade someone* (dat.) (36)

pertérritus, -a, -um, *frightened, terrified* (5)

pervéniō, pervenīre, pervénī, perventúrus + ad + acc., *to arrive (at), reach* (25)

pēs, pédis, m., *foot* (13)

péssimus, -a, -um, *worst* (34)

   péssimē, adv., *worst* (35)

pestiléntia, -ae, f., *plague* (33)

pétō, pétere, petívī, petítus, *to look for, seek, head for, aim at, attack* (5, 21)

pictúra, -ae, f., *picture* (1)

píla, -ae, f., *ball* (16)

   pílā lúdere, *to play ball* (16)

pínguis, -is, -e, *fat, rich* (31)

pīráta, -ae, m., *pirate* (21)

pírum, -ī, n., *pear* (33)

piscína, -ae, f., *fishpond* (3)

pīstrínum, -ī, n., *bakery* (37)

pláceō, -ére, -uī + dat., *to please* (34)

plácidē, adv., *gently, peacefully* (14)

plaústrum, -ī, n., *wagon, cart* (15)

plénus, -a, -um, *full* (11)

plúit, plúere, plúit, *it rains, is raining* (23)

plúrēs, plúrēs, plúra, gen., **plúrium**, *more* (34)

plúrimus, -a, -um, *most, very much* (34)

   plúrimī, -ae, -a, *most, very many* (34)

   plúrimum, adv., *most* (35)

plūs, plúris, n., *more* (35)

   plūs vínī, *more wine* (34)

plūs, adv., *more* (35)

Plútō, Plūtónis, m., *Pluto (king of the underworld)* (32)

póculum, -ī, n., *cup, goblet* (33)

poéna, -ae, f., *punishment, penalty* (40)

   poénās dáre, *to pay the penalty, be punished* (40)

poéta, -ae, m., *poet* (25)

Pompéiī, -órum, m. pl., *Pompeii*

pónō, pónere, pósuī, pósitus, *to put, place* (10, 21)

pōns, póntis, gen. pl., **póntium**, m., *bridge* (23)

popína, -ae, f., *eating-house, bar* (33)

pórcus, -ī, m., *pig, pork* (28, 33)

pórta, -ae, f., *gate* (11)

pórtō, -áre, -ávī, -átus, *to carry* (6)

póscō, póscere, popóscī, *to demand, ask for* (34)

póssum, pósse, pótuī, irreg., *to be able; I can* (5, 14, 21)

post, prep. + acc., *after* (20)

post, adv., *after(ward)* (39)

　múltīs post ánnīs, *many years afterward* (39)

pósteā, adv., *afterward* (33)

póstis, póstis, gen. pl., **póstium**, m., *door-post* (25)

póstquam, conj., *after* (20)

postrídiē, adv., *on the following day* (26)

praecípitō, -áre, -ávī, -átus, *to hurl* (18)

　sē praecipitáre, *to hurl oneself, rush* (18)

praeclárus, -a, -um, *distinguished, famous* (13)

praecúrrō, praecúrrere, praecúrrī,
　praecursúrus, *to run ahead* (18)

praédō, praedónis, m., *robber* (26)

praéferō, praeférre, praétulī, praelátus, irreg. +
　acc. and dat., *to carry X (acc.) in front of Y*
　(dat.) (37)

praéter, prep. + acc., *except* (21)

praetéreā, adv., *besides, too, moreover* (15)

praetéreō, praeteríre, praetériī or **praeterívī,**
　praetéritus, irreg., *to go past* (15)

praetéxta, tóga, -ae, f., *toga with purple border* (10)

prásinus, -a, -um, *green* (27)

prétium, -ī, n., *price* (31)

prídiē, adv. + acc., *on the day before* (36)

prímus, -a, -um, *first* (21, 38)

　prímā lúce, *at dawn* (21)

　prímō, adv., *first, at first* (40)

　prímum, adv., *first, at first* (23)

　cum prímum, conj., *as soon as* (40)

　quam prímum, adv., *as soon as possible* (40)

prínceps, príncipis, m., *emperor* (7)

príus, adv., *earlier, previously* (33)

procácitās, procācitátis, f., *insolence* (39)

prócāx, procácis, *insolent*; as slang, *pushy* (31)

prōcédō, prōcédere, prōcéssī, prōcessúrus, *to go
　forward* (33)

prócul, adv., *in the distance, far off, far* (15)

Prō dī immortálēs! *Good heavens!* (42)

profícíscor, profícíscī, proféctus sum, *to set out,
　leave* (36, 37)

prófugus, -a, -um, *exiled, fugitive* (39)

prōmíttō, prōmíttere, prōmísī, prōmíssus, *to
　promise* (9)

prónus, -a, -um, *face down* (35)

própe, prep. + acc., *near* (5, 9)

própter, prep. + acc., *on account of, because of* (26)

próximus, -a, -um, *nearby* (33)

prúdēns, prūdéntis, *wise, sensible* (34)

　prūdénter, adv., *wisely, sensibly* (34, 35)

puélla, -ae, f., *girl* (1)

púer, púerī, m., *boy* (3)

púgiō, pūgiónis, m., *dagger* (42)

púlcher, púlchra, púlchrum, *beautiful, pretty,*
　handsome (28)

　pulchérrimus, -a, -um, *most/very*
　beautiful (32)

　púlchrē, adv., *finely, excellently* (35)

púllus, -ī, m., *chicken* (32)

púlvis, púlveris, m., *dust* (15)

púniō, -íre, -ívī, -ítus, *to punish* (21)

púrgō, -áre, -ávī, -átus, *to clean* (6)

Q

quā dē caúsā, *for this reason* (32)

quadrátus, -a, -um, *squared* (25)

quaérō, quaérere, quaesívī, quaesítus, *to seek,
　look for, ask (for)* (30)

Quális...? Quális...? Quále...? *What sort of...?* (4)

Quam...! adv., *How...! What a...!* (13, 29, 36)

Quam...? adv., *How...?* (36)

quam, adv., *than, as* (34, 36)

　quam, adv. + superlative adj. or adv.,
　as...as possible (35, 36)

　quam celérrimē, adv., *as quickly as possible* (34)

　quam prímum, adv., *as soon as possible* (40)

Quam ob caúsam...? *For what reason...?* (28)

quámquam, conj., *although* (11)

Quándō...? adv., *When...?* (12, 21)

Quántus, -a, -um...? *How big...? How much...?*
　(41)

　Quántī...? *How much (in price)...?* (31)

　Quántum...! adv., *How much...!* (41)

quártus, -a, -um, *fourth* (38)

quártus décimus, -a, -um, *fourteenth* (38)

quáttuor, *four* (15, 38)

quattuórdecim, *fourteen* (38)

-que, enclitic conj., *and* (36)

quī, quae, quod, *who, which, that* (1, 3, 14, 28, 29, 36)

Quī...? Quae...? Quod...? interrog. adj., *What...? Which...?* (29)

Quid ágis? *How are you?* (18)

quídam, quaédam, quóddam, *a certain* (10, 29)

quídem, adv., *indeed* (31)

　nē...quídem, adv., *not even* (34)

quíēs, quiétis, f., *rest* (23)

　sē quiétī dáre, *to rest* (23)

quiéscō, quiéscere, quiévī, quietúrus, *to rest, keep quiet* (13, 23)

quíndecim, *fifteen* (38)

quīngentésimus, -a, -um, *five-hundredth* (38)

quīngéntī, -ae, -a, *five hundred* (15, 38)

quīnquāgésimus, -a, -um, *fiftieth* (38)

quīnquāgíntā, *fifty* (15, 38)

quínque, *five* (15, 38)

quíntus, -a, -um, *fifth* (26, 38)

quíntus décimus, -a, -um, *fifteenth* (38)

Quirīnális, -is, -e, *Quirinal (Hill)* (35)

Quis...? Quid...? *Who...? What...?* (1, 4, 29)

　Quid ágis? *How are you?* (18)

Quō...? adv., *Where...to?* (4)

quō...eō..., *the (more)...the (more)...* (36)

Quócum...? *With whom...?* (12, 26)

quod (see **quī, quae, quod**)

quod, conj., *because*; with verbs of feeling, *that* (1, 13, 29)

Quō īnstrūméntō...? *With what instrument...? By what means...? How...?* (12)

Quómodo...? adv., *In what manner...? In what way...? How...?* (12)

quóniam, conj., *since* (42)

quóque, adv., *also* (2, 13)

Quot...? *How many...?* (15, 38)

Quótus, -a, -um...? *What/Which (in numerical order)...?* (38)

　Quóta hóra est? *What time is it?* (38)

R

raéda, -ae, f., *carriage* (10)

raedárius, -ī, m., *coachman, driver* (10)

rámus, -ī, m., *branch* (4)

rápiō, rápere, rápuī, ráptus, *to snatch, seize* (40)

récitō, -áre, -ávī, -átus, *to read aloud, recite* (29)

　recitándī, *of reciting* (39)

réctus, -a, -um, *right, proper* (35)

　réctē, adv., *rightly, properly* (31, 35)

recúmbō, recúmbere, recúbuī, *to recline, lie down* (29)

recúperō, -áre, -ávī, -átus, *to recover* (21)

　ánimum recuperáre, *to regain one's senses, be fully awake* (21)

réddō, réddere, réddidī, rédditus, *to give back, return* (29)

rédeō, redíre, rédiī or redívī, reditúrus, irreg., *to return, go back* (7, 23)

　rédiēns, redeúntis, *returning* (39)

réditus, -ūs, m., *return* (25)

redúcō, redúcere, redúxī, redúctus, *to lead back, take back* (42)

refíciō, reficere, refécī, reféctus, *to remake, redo, restore* (32)

rēgína, -ae, f., *queen* (38)

régnum, -ī, n., *kingdom* (32)

regrédior, régredī, regréssus sum, *to go back, return* (36, 37)

relínquō, relínquere, relíquī, relíctus, *to leave behind* (16, 21)

remóveō, removére, remóvī, remótus, *to remove, move aside* (21)

rénovō, -áre, -ávī, -átus, *to renew, revive* (38)

repéllō, repéllere, réppulī, repúlsus, *to drive off, drive back* (5, 40)

reprehéndō, reprehéndere, reprehéndī, reprehénsus, *to blame, scold* (6, 31)

rēs, réī, f., *thing, matter, situation, affair* (19, 25)

　rem explicáre, *to explain the situation* (19)

　rēs urbánae, rérum urbānárum, f. pl., *affairs of the city/town* (33)

resístō, resístere, réstitī + dat., *to resist* (42)

respóndeō, respondére, respóndī, respōnsúrus, *to reply* (5, 21)

respónsum, -ī, n., *reply* (38)

retíneō, retinére, retínuī, reténtus, *to hold back, keep* (31)

révocō, -áre, -ávī, -átus, *to recall, call back* (7)

rídeō, rīdére, rísī, rísus, *to laugh (at), smile* (3, 21)

rīmósus, -a, -um, *full of cracks, leaky* (23)

rísus, -ūs, m., *smile, laugh* (13, 25)

rívus, -ī, m., *stream* (5)

ríxa, -ae, f., *quarrel* (29)

rogátiō, rogātiónis, f., *question* (40)

rógō, -áre, -ávī, -átus, *to ask* (12)

  sē rogáre, *to ask oneself, wonder* (21)

Róma, -ae, f., *Rome* (7)

  Rómae, *in Rome* (39)

  Rómam, *to Rome* (7)

Rōmánus, -a, -um, *Roman* (1)

  Rōmánī, -órum, m. pl., *the Romans* (III)

rósa, -ae, f., *rose* (34)

róta, -ae, f., *wheel* (15)

ruína, -ae, f., *collapse, ruin* (38)

rúmpō, rúmpere, rúpī, rúptus, *to burst* (29)

rúrsus, adv., *again* (36)

rūs, rúris, n., *country, country estate* (39)

  rúre, *from the country* (39)

  rúrī, *in the country* (39)

  rūs, *to the country* (39)

russátus, -a, -um, *red* (27)

rústica, vílla, -ae, f., *country house and farm* (1)

rústicus, -ī, m., *peasant* (13)

S

sácculus, -ī, m., *small bag (used for holding money)* (34)

saépe, adv., *often* (2, 13, 35)

  saépius, adv., *more often* (35)

  saepíssimē, adv., *most often* (35)

saévus, -a, -um, *fierce, savage* (39)

sal, sális, m., *salt, wit* (34)

saltátrīx, saltātrícis, f., *dancer* (21)

sáltō, -áre, -ávī, -átúrus *to dance* (21)

sálūs, salútis, f., *greetings* (36)

  salútem dícere, *to send greetings* (36)

salútem plúrimam dícere, *to send fondest greetings* (36)

salútō, -áre, -ávī, -átus, *to greet, welcome* (7)

Sálvē!/Salvéte! *Greetings! Hello!* (7)

sálvus, -a, -um, *safe* (5)

sánē, adv., *certainly, of course* (36)

sánguis, sánguinis, m., *blood* (33)

sátis, adv., *enough* (23)

  sátis témporis, *enough time* (23)

scápha, -ae, f., *small boat, ship's boat* (40, 42)

sceléstus, -a, -um, *wicked* (10)

scíndō, scíndere, scídī, scíssus, *to cut, split, carve* (33)

scíō, -íre, -ívī, -ítus, *to know* (16)

scriblíta, -ae, f., *tart or pastry with cheese filling* (37)

scríbō, scríbere, scrípsī, scríptus, *to write* (1, 24)

sē, *himself, herself, oneself, itself, themselves* (11)

secúndus, -a, -um, *second* (9, 38)

  secúndae ménsae, -árum, f. pl., *second course, dessert* (33)

secúrus, -a, -um, *carefree, unconcerned* (35)

sed, conj., *but* (2)

sédecim, *sixteen* (38)

sédeō, sedére, sédī, sessúrus, *to sit* (1, 21)

sélla, -ae, f., *sedan chair, seat, chair* (28)

sēmisómnus, -a, -um, *half-asleep* (9)

sémper, adv., *always* (4, 13)

senátor, senātóris, m., *senator* (7)

senátus, -ūs, m., *Senate* (25)

sénex, sénis, m., *old man* (I)

séniō, sēniónis, m., *the six (in throwing knucklebones)* (34)

sepéliō, sepeíre, sepelívī, sepúltus, *to bury* (39)

séptem, *seven* (15, 38)

Septémber, Septémbris, Septémbre, *September* (36)

septéndecim, *seventeen* (38)

septentriōnális, -is, -e, *northern* (39)

séptimus, -a, -um, *seventh* (13, 38)

séptimus décimus, -a, -um, *seventeenth* (38)

septuāgésimus, -a, -um, *seventieth* (IX)

sepúlcrum, -ī, n., *tomb* (22)

séquor, séquī, secútus sum, *to follow* (36, 37)

  séquēns, sequéntis, *following* (25)

sérō, adv., *late* (21, 35)

  sérius, adv., *later* (35)

  sēríssimē, adv., *latest* (35)

sérvō, -áre, -ávī, -átus, *to save* (26, 30)

sérvus, -ī, m., *slave* (3)

seu = síve, conj., *or if* (34)

sex, *six* (15, 38)

séxtus, -a, -um, *sixth* (37, 38)

séxtus décimus, *sixteenth* (38)

sī, conj., *if* (5)

  sī vīs, *if you wish, please* (26)

sīc, adv., *thus, in this way* (38, 39)

Sicília, -ae, f., *Sicily* (38)

sígnum, -ī, n., *signal* (27)

siléntium, -ī, n., *silence* (15)

sílva, -ae f., *woods, forest* (5)

símilis, -is, -e, *similar* (34)

símul, adv., *together, at the same time* (9, 13)

símulac, conj., *as soon as* (24)

símulō, -áre, -ávī, -átus, *to pretend* (21)

síne, prep. + abl., *without* (26)

sínō, sínere, sívī, sítus, *to allow* (34)

sīs = sī vīs, *if you wish, please* (36)

sítus, -a, -um, *located, situated* (33)

sólea, -ae, f., *sandal* (32)

sóleō, solére, sólitus sum + infin., *to be accustomed (to), be in the habit of* (10, 40)

sōlitúdō, sōlitúdinis, f., *solitude* (39)

sollícitus, -a, -um, *anxious, worried* (4)

sólus, -a, -um, *alone* (3)

sómnium, -ī, n., *dream* (21)

sómnus, -ī, m., *sleep* (21)

sónitus, -ūs, m., *sound* (21, 25)

sórdidus, -a, -um, *dirty* (19)

sóror, soróris, f., *sister* (11)

S.P.D. = salútem plúrimam dícit (36)

spectáculum, -ī, n., *sight, spectacle* (30)

spectátor, spectatóris, m., *spectator* (27)

spéctō, -áre, -ávī, -átus, *to watch, look at* (7)

spéculum, -ī, n., *mirror* (28)

státim, adv., *immediately* (5, 13)

státua, -ae, f., *statue* (3)

stéla, -ae, f., *tombstone* (33)

stércus, stércoris, n., *dung, manure* (21)

stértō, stértere, stértuī, *to snore* (25)

stílus, -ī, m., *pen* (25)

stō, stáre, stétī, statúrus, *to stand* (10, 22)

stóla, -ae, f., *stola (a woman's outer garment)* (10)

strátum, -ī, n., *sheet, covering* (32)

strénuus, -a, -um, *active, energetic* (2)

  strénuē, adv., *strenuously, hard* (6, 13, 35)

strépitus, -ūs, m., *noise, clattering* (23, 25)

stríngō, stríngere, strínxī, stríctus, *to draw* (26)

  gládium stríngere, *to draw a sword* (26)

stúdeō, -ére, -uī + dat., *to study* (39)

stúdium, -ī, n., *enthusiasm, study* (41)

stúltus, -a, -um, *stupid, foolish* (23)

stúpeō, -ére, -uī, *to be amazed, gape* (23)

suávis, -is, -e, *sweet, delightful* (34)

sub, prep. + abl., *under, beneath* (1, 9)

súbitō, adv., *suddenly* (3, 13)

Subúra, -ae, f., *Subura (a section of Rome off the Forum, known for its night life)* (35)

súī (see **sē**)

sum, ésse, fúī, futúrus, irreg., *to be* (1, 14, 20, 21)

súmmus, -a, -um, *greatest, very great, the top of…* (35)

  súmmā celeritáte, *with the greatest speed, as fast as possible* (29)

súmō, súmere, súmpsī, súmptus, *to take, take up, pick out* (22)

súperī, -órum, m. pl., *the gods above* (39)

súperō, -áre, -ávī, -átus, *to overcome* (42)

súprā, prep. + acc., *above* (23)

súprā, adv., *above, on top* (21)

súrgō, súrgere, surréxī, surrēctúrus, *to get up, rise* (6, 21)

súus, -a, -um, *his, her, its, their (own)* (9, 27)

T

tabellárius, -ī, m., *courier* (13)

tabérna, -ae, f., *shop* (25)

tablínum, -ī, n., *study* (26)

tabulátum, -ī, n., *story, floor* (30)

táceō, -ére, -uī, -itus, *to be quiet* (9)

tácitē, adv., *silently* (9, 13)

taédet, taedére, taésum est, *it bores* (16)

tálī, -órum, m. pl., *knucklebones* (34)

tális, -is, -e, *such, like this, of this kind* (23)
    tália, tálium, n. pl., *such things* (41)

tam, adv., *so* (30)

támen, adv., *however, nevertheless* (6, 13)

támquam, conj., *just as if* (33)

tándem, adv., *at last, at length* (2, 13)

tántus, -a, -um, *so great, such a big* (24)
    tántum, adv., *only* (15)

tárdus, -a, -um, *slow* (15)

tē (from **tū**) (4)

téla, -ae, f., *web, fabric* (41)

temerárius, -a, -um, *rash, reckless, bold* (5)

tempéstās, tempestátis, f., *storm* (38)

témplum, -ī, n., *temple* (40)

témptō, -áre, -ávī, -átus, *to try* (9)

témpus, témporis, n., *time* (2, 8, 12, 15)
    ad témpus, *on time* (37)

téneō, tenére, ténuī, téntus, *to hold* (9, 25)
    memóriā tenére, *to remember* (37)

térgum, -ī, n., *back, rear* (35)

térra, -ae, f., *earth, ground, land* (26, 38)

térreō, -ére, -uī, -itus, *to frighten, terrify* (4)

terríbilis, -is, -e, *frightening* (39)

térritus, -a, -um, *frightened* (39)

térror, terróris, m., *terror, fear* (22)

tértius, -a, -um, *third* (25, 36, 38)

tértius décimus, -a, -um, *thirteenth* (38)

testāméntum, -ī, n., *will, testament* (IX)

téxō, téxere, téxuī, téxtus, *to weave* (41)

Thrácia, -ae, f., *Thrace (country northeast of Greece)* (39)

tímeō, -ére, -uī, *to fear, be afraid (to/of)* (5)

tímidus, -a, -um, *afraid, fearful, timid* (21)

tímor, timóris, m., *fear* (35)

tóga, -ae, f., *toga* (8)
    tóga praetéxta, -ae, f., *toga with purple border* (10)
    tóga virílis, tógae virílis, f., *toga of manhood, plain white toga* (10)

tórus, -ī, m., *couch* (38)

tótus, -a, -um, *all, the whole* (21)

trádō, trádere, trádidī, tráditus, *to hand over* (7, 22)

tráhō, tráhere, tráxī, tráctus, *to drag, pull* (6, 12, 25)
    lánam tráhere, *to spin wool* (6)

trāns, prep. + acc., *across* (39)

trédecim, *thirteen* (38)

trémō, trémere, trémuī, *to tremble* (21)

trēs, trēs, tría, *three* (13, 15, 38)

trīclínium, -ī, n., *dining room* (31)

trístis, -is, -e, *sad* (36)

Tróia, -ae, f., *Troy* (I, 38)

Troiánus, -a, -um, *Trojan* (I)
    Troiánī, -órum, m. pl., *the Trojans* (I)

tū, *you* (sing.) (4, 27)

túlī (see **férō**)

tum, adv., *at that moment, then* (4, 13)

tumúltus, -ūs, m., *uproar, commotion* (25)

túnica, -ae, f., *tunic* (8)

túrba, -ae, f., *crowd, mob* (23)

túus, -a, -um, *your* (sing.) (9, 27)

U

Úbi…? adv., *Where…?* (10, 12)

úbi, adv., conj., *where, when* (1, 5, 13)

Ulíxēs, Ulíxis, m., *Ulysses, Odysseus (Greek hero of the Trojan War)* (38)

úlulō, -áre, -ávī, -átus, *to howl* (33)

úmbra, -ae, f., *shadow, shade (of the dead)* (31, 33)

úmquam, adv., *ever* (31)

únā, adv., *together* (33)

únda, -ae, f., *wave* (42)

Únde…? *From where…?* (12)

úndecim, *eleven* (38)

ūndécimus, -a, -um, *eleventh* (17, 38)

ūndēvīcésimus, -a, -um, *nineteenth* (38)

ūndēvīgíntī, *nineteen* (38)

úndique, adv., *on all sides, from all sides* (23)

unguéntum, -ī, n., *ointment, perfume* (34)

únus, -a, -um, *one* (15, 38)
    únā, adv., *together* (33)

urbánus, -a, -um, *of the city/town* (33)
    rēs urbánae, rérum urbānárum, f. pl., *affairs of the city/town* (33)

urbs, úrbis, gen. pl., **úrbium**, f., *city* (7)

ut, conj., *as* (16)

útilis, -is, -e, *useful* (37)

úva, -ae, f., *grape, bunch of grapes* (33)

úxor, uxóris, f., *wife* (11)

V

váldē, adv., *very, very much, exceedingly* (19)

váleō, -ére, -uī, -itúrus, *to be strong, be well* (40)

 Válē!/Valéte! *Goodbye!* (9)

valētúdō, valētúdinis, f., *health (good or bad)* (39)

-ve, enclitic conj., *or* (34)

véhemēns, veheméntis, *violent* (35)

 veheménter, adv., *very much, violently, hard* (19)

vehículum, -ī, n., *vehicle* (13, 15)

vel, conj., *or* (37)

vélle (see **vólō**)

véndō, véndere, véndidī, vénditus, *to sell* (28)

vénetus, -a, -um, *blue* (27)

véniō, veníre, vénī, ventúrus, *to come* (7, 20)

véntus, -ī, m., *wind* (42)

Vénus, Véneris, f., *Venus (the goddess of love); the highest throw of the knucklebones* (34)

venústus, -a, -um, *charming* (34)

vérberō, -áre, -ávī, -átus, *to beat, whip* (11)

verbósus, -a, -um, *talkative* (26)

vérbum, -ī, n., *word, verb* (39)

véreor, verérī, véritus sum, *to be afraid, fear* (37)

Vergílius, -ī, m., *Vergil (Roman poet)* (37)

versipéllis, versipéllis, gen. pl., **versipéllium,** m., *werewolf* (33)

vérsus, -ūs, m., *verse, line (of poetry)* (29)

vértō, vértere, vértī, vérsus, *to turn* (16)

vérus, -a, -um, *true* (40)

 Íta vérō! *Yes! Indeed!* (3, 13)

 Mínimē vérō! *No indeed! Not at all!* (31)

 véra dícere, *to tell the truth* (40)

 vérō, adv., *truly, really, indeed* (31)

vésperī, *in the evening* (18)

véster, véstra, véstrum, *your (pl.)* (22, 27)

vēstígium, -ī, n., *track, footprint, trace* (12, 15)

vestiméntum, -ī, n., *clothing;* pl., *clothes* (33)

véstis, véstis, gen. pl., **véstium,** f., *clothing, garment* (29)

vétō, vetáre, vétuī, vétitus, *to forbid, tell not to* (26)

vétus, véteris, *old* (34)

véxō, -áre, -ávī, -átus, *to annoy* (3)

 vexátus, -a, -um, *annoyed* (28)

vía, -ae, f., *road, street* (10)

 Vía Áppia, -ae, f., *Appian Way* (11)

viátor, viātóris, m., *traveler* (18)

vīcésimus, -a, -um, *twentieth* (38)

vīcínus, -a, -um, *neighboring, adjacent* (1)

víctor, victóris, m., *conqueror, victor* (27)

vídeō, vidére, vídī, vísus, *to see* (4, 21)

 vidétur, *(he/she/it) seems* (21)

vígilō, -áre, -ávī, -ātúrus, *to stay awake* (19)

vīgíntī, *twenty* (36, 38)

vílicus, -ī, m., *overseer, farm manager* (11)

vílla, -ae, f., *country house* (1)

 vílla rústica, -ae, f., *country house and farm* (1)

víncō, víncere, vícī, víctus, *to conquer, win* (27)

vínea, -ae, f., *vineyard* (12)

vínum, -ī, n., *wine* (25)

 vínō ábstinēns, *refraining from wine, abstemious* (34)

vir, vírī, m., *man, husband* (3, 11)

 vir óptime, *sir* (20)

vírga, -ae, f., *stick, rod, switch* (13)

virílis, -is, -e, *of manhood* (23)

 tóga virílis, tógae virílis, f., *toga of manhood, plain white toga* (10)

vīs, acc., **vim,** abl., **vī,** f., *force, amount* (30)

vísitō, -áre, -ávī, -átus, *to visit* (23)

vítō, -áre, -ávī, -átus, *to avoid* (13)

vívō, vívere, víxī, victúrus, *to live* (39)

vix, adv., *scarcely, with difficulty, only just* (24)

vócō, -áre, -ávī, -átus, *to call, invite* (28)

vólō, vélle, vóluī, irreg., *to wish, want, be willing* (5, 17, 20, 21)

 sī vīs, *if you wish, please* (36)

vōs, *you (pl.)* (8, 27)

vōx, vócis, f., *voice* (4)

vúlnerō, -áre, -ávī, -átus, *to wound* (33)

vúlnus, vúlneris, n., *wound* (35)

vult (from **vólō**) (5, 17)

ENGLISH TO LATIN VOCABULARY

Verbs are usually cited in their infinitive form. For further information about the Latin words in this list, please consult the Latin to English Vocabulary list.

A

able, to be, **pósse**
about, **dē**
above, **súprā**
absent, to be, **abésse**
abstemious, **vīnō ábstinēns**
accidentally, **cásū**
accomplish, to, **cōnfícere**
accuse, to, **accūsáre**
accustomed (to), to be, **solére**
across, **trāns**
active, **strénuus**
add, to, **áddere**
adjacent, **vīcínus**
adopt, to, **adoptáre**
advise, to, **monére**
Aeneas, **Aenéās**
Aeneid, the, **Aenéis**
affair, **rēs**
affairs of the city/town, **rēs urbánae**
affected, **afféctus**
afraid, **tímidus**
afraid, to be, **verérī**
afraid (to/of), to be, **timére**
Africa, **África**
after, **póstquam**
after(ward), **post**
afterward, **pósteā**
again, **íterum, rúrsus**
again and again, **idéntidem**
against, **in**
ago, **abhínc**
aim at, to, **pétere**

Alas! **Éheu!**
Alba Longa, of, **Albánus**
all, **cúnctī, ómnis, tótus**
All right! **Éstō!**
allow, to, **sínere**
allowed, it is, **lícet**
allowed, we are, **lícet nóbīs**
almost, **paéne**
alone, **sólus**
along, **per**
Alps, the, **Álpēs**
already, **iam**
also, **átque, étiam, quóque**
although, **quámquam**
always, **sémper**
amazed, to be, **stupére**
among, **in, ínter**
amount, **vīs**
amphitheater, **amphitheátrum**
amuse, to, **dēlectáre**
ancient, **antíquus**
and, **ac, átque, et, -que**
and...not, **néque**
and so, **ítaque**
anger, **íra**
angry, **īrátus**
annoy, to, **vexáre**
annoyed, **vexátus**
annoying, **moléstus**
another, **álius, álter**
anxious, **sollícitus**
apartment building, **ínsula**
apologize, to, **sē excūsáre**
appear, to, **appārére**
Appian Way, **Vía Áppia**
apple, **málum**
appoint, to, **creáre**
approach, to, **appropinquáre**
April, **Aprílis**

aqueduct, **aquaedúctus**
arch, **árcus**
arise, to, **cooríri**
armed, **armátus**
arms, **árma**
around, **círcum**
aroused, **excitátus**
arrive (at), to, **adveníre, perveníre**
as, **quam, ut**
as…as possible, **quam** + superl. adj. or adv.
as fast as possible, **súmmā celeritáte**
as long as, **dum**
as quickly as possible, **quam celérrimē**
as soon as, **cum prímum, símulac**
as soon as possible, **quam prímum**
as yet, **adhúc**
Asia Minor, **Ásia**
ask, to, **rogáre**
ask (for), to, **póscere, quaérere**
ask oneself, to, **sē rogáre**
asparagus, **aspáragus**
astonished, **attónitus**
astounded, **attónitus**
at, **ad**
at the house of, **ápud**
Athens, **Athénae**
atrium, **átrium**
attack, to, **adoríri, pétere**
attentively, **atténtē**
August, **Augústus**
Augustus, **Augústus**
avoid, to, **vītáre**
awake, to be fully, **ánimum recuperáre**
away, to be, **abésse**

B

back, **térgum**
bad, **málus**
badly, **mále**
bag (used for holding money), small, **sácculus**
bakery, **pīstrínum**
ball, **píla**

banquet, **convívium**
bar, **popína**
bark, a, **lātrátus**
bark, to, **lātráre**
barking, **lātrátus**
be, to, **ésse**
be done, to, **fíerī**
be made, to, **fíerī**
Be of good mind! **Bónō ánimō es!/éste!**
bear, to, **férre**
beat, to, **verberáre**
beautiful, **cándidus, púlcher**
beautiful, most/very, **pulchérrimus**
because, **quod**
because of, **própter**
become, to, **fíerī**
bed, **léctus**
bed, to go to, **cúbitum íre**
bedroom, **cubículum**
before, **ánte, ánteā, ántequam, ápud**
beg, to, **obsecráre**
began, I, **coépī**
beggar, **mendícus**
begin, to, **ōrdírī**
believe, to, **crédere**
beneath, **sub**
beseech, to, **obsecráre**
besides, **praetéreā**
besiege, to, **obsidére**
best, **óptimē, óptimus**
better, **mélior, mélius**
between, **ínter**
beware, to, **cavére**
bid, to, **iubére**
big, **mágnus**
big, such a, **tántus**
bigger, **máior**
biggest, **máximus**
bind up, to, **ligáre**
Bithynia, **Bīthýnia**
black, **níger**
blame, **cúlpa**
blame, to, **reprehéndere**
blood, **sánguis**

blue, **vénetus**
boat, small/ship's, **scápha**
body, **córpus**
bold, **aúdāx, temerárius**
book, **líber**
bores, it, **taédet**
born, to be, **náscī**
both...and, **et...et**
box, cylindrical, **fritíllus**
boy, **púer**
branch, **rámus**
brand, to, **inúrere**
brave, **fórtis**
bravely, **fórtiter**
bravely, most/very, **fortíssimē**
bread, **pánis**
breakfast, **iēntáculum**
bridge, **pōns**
briefly, **bréviter**
bring, to, **addúcere, afférre,**
    dúcere, férre
Bring help! **Fer/Férte auxílium!**
bring in, to, **afférre, īnférre**
bring out, to, **efférre**
bring to, to, **afférre**
Britain, **Británnia**
British, **Británnicus**
brother, **fráter**
Brundisium, **Brundísium**
Brundisium, at, **Brundísiī**
Brundisium, from, **Brundísiō**
Brundisium, to, **Brundísium**
build, to, **aedificáre**
building, **aedifícium**
bulk, huge, **mólēs**
bunch of grapes, **úva**
burden, **ónus**
burn, to, **incéndere**
burst, to, **rúmpere**
burst in, to, **irrúmpere**
bury, to, **sepelíre**
busy, **occupátus**
but, **at, aútem, sed**
butcher, **lánius**

buy, to, **comparáre, émere**
by, **ā** or **ab**
By Hercules! **Mehércule!**
bystanders, **adstántēs**

C

Caesar, **Caésar**
Caligula, **Calígula**
call, to, **appelláre, vocáre**
call back, to, **revocáre**
call together, to, **convocáre**
call upon, to, **invocáre**
can, I, **póssum**
candelabrum, **candēlábrum**
cane, **férula**
captain, **magíster**
captive, **captívus**
capture, to, **cápere**
care, **cúra**
carefree, **sēcúrus**
careful, to be, **cavére**
carefully, **dīligénter**
careless, **néglegēns**
carelessly, **neglegénter**
carelessness, **neglegéntia**
carriage, **raéda**
carriage, light two-wheeled, **císium**
carry, to, **férre, portáre**
carry away, to, **auférre**
carry out, to, **efférre**
carry X in front of Y, to, **praeférre**
cart, **plaústrum**
Carthage, **Carthágō**
carve, to, **scíndere**
castanet, **crótalum**
cat, **félēs**
catch, to, **cápere, excípere**
catch sight of, to, **cōnspícere**
catch up to, to, **cónsequī**
Cerberus, **Cérberus**
certain, **cértus**
certain, a, **quídam**

certainly, **cértē, sánē**
chair, **sélla**
chance, by, **cásū, fórte**
chariot-racing, **lúdī circénsēs**
charioteer, **auríga**
charming, **venústus**
Charon, **Chárōn**
Cheer up! **Bónō ánimō es!/éste!**
chest, **císta**
chicken, **púllus**
child, young, **ínfāns**
children, **líberī**
circus, in the, **circénsis**
Circus Maximus, **Círcus Máximus**
citizen, **cívis**
city, **urbs**
city, of the, **urbánus**
clattering, **strépitus**
clean, to, **pūrgáre**
client, **clíēns**
climb, to, **ascéndere**
climb down, to, **dēscéndere**
climb into (a carriage), to, **ascéndere**
cloak, **pállium**
closed, **claúsus**
closely, **atténtē**
clothes, **vestīménta**
clothing, **vestīméntum, véstis**
cloud, **núbēs**
club, **fústis**
coachman, **raedárius**
cobweb, **aránea**
cold, **frígidus**
collapse, **ruína**
collapse, to, **collábī**
comb, to, **péctere**
come, to, **veníre**
come down, to, **dēscéndere**
come near (to), to, **appropinquáre**
Come on! **Áge!/Ágite!**
come upon, to, **inveníre**
commands, **iússa**
commotion, **tumúltus**
companion, **cómes**

company (of charioteers), **fáctiō**
complete, to, **complére**
conceal, to, **cēláre**
concerning, **dē**
conquer, to, **víncere**
conqueror, **víctor**
consul, **cónsul**
consult, to, **cōnsúlere**
contrary, on the, **ímmō vérō**
conversation, **collóquium**
converse, to, **cólloquī**
cook, **cóquus**
cook, to, **cóquere**
cool, **frígidus**
Cornelius, belonging to, **Cornēliánus**
cottage, **cása**
couch, **léctus, tórus**
count, to, **numeráre**
country, **rūs**
country, from the, **rúre**
country, in the, **rúrī**
country, to the, **rūs**
country estate, **rūs**
country house, **vílla**
country house and farm, **vílla rústica**
courier, **tabellárius**
course, first, **gustátiō**
course, second, **secúndae ménsae**
courteously, **cómiter**
covered, **aspérsus**
covering, **strátum**
cow, **bōs**
cowardly, **ignávus**
cracks, full of, **rīmósus**
crash, **frágor**
Cremona, **Cremóna**
Crete, **Créta**
crowd, **multitúdō, túrba**
crown, **coróna**
crown, to, **corōnáre**
cruel, **crūdélis**
crushed, **oppréssus**
cry, to, **lacrimáre**
cudgel, **fústis**

cultivate, to, **cólere**
cup, **póculum**
Cupid, **Cupídō**
cut, to, **scíndere**

D

dagger, **púgiō**
daily, **cotídiē**
dance, to, **saltáre**
dancer, **saltátrīx**
danger, **perículum**
dangerous, **perīculósus**
dare (to), to, **audére**
dark, it gets, **advesperáscit**
daughter, **fília**
dawn, at, **prímā lúce**
day, **díēs**
day, by, **intérdiū**
day, during the, **intérdiū**
day, early in the, **máne**
day, every, **in díēs**
day, it is, **lúcet**
day before, on the, **prídiē**
day by day, **in díēs**
dead, **mórtuus**
dearest, **cāríssimus**
death, **mors**
December, **Decémber**
decide, to, **cōnstitúere**
decorated, **ōrnátus**
decoration, **ōrnāméntum**
decrease, to, **minúere**
dedicate, to, **dēdicáre**
deep, **áltus**
deep, the, **áltum**
defend, to, **dēféndere**
delay, to, **cessáre, morárī**
delight, to, **dēlectáre**
delightful, **suávis**
deliver a speech, to, **ōrātiónem habére**
Delos, **Délos**
demand, to, **póscere**
denarius (silver coin), **dēnárius**

depart, to, **discédere**
dependent, **clíēns**
desire, to, **cúpere, dēsīderáre**
dessert, **secúndae ménsae**
destroy, to, **dēlére**
detestable, **abōminándus**
devour, to, **dēvoráre**
Dido, **Dídō**
die, to, **mórī**
difficult, **difficílis**
difficulty, **difficúltās**
difficulty, with, **vix**
diligent, **díligēns**
din, **frágor**
dine, to, **cēnáre**
dining room, **trīclínium**
dinner, **céna**
dinner, to eat, **cēnáre**
direction, **pars**
dirty, **sórdidus**
disgusting, **foédus**
dish, **férculum**
dissimilar, **dissímilis**
distance, in the, **prócul**
distant, to be, **abésse**
distinguished, **praeclárus**
ditch, **fóssa**
divide, to, **dīvídere**
divine, **dīvínus**
do, to, **ágere, fácere**
do harm (to), to, **nocére**
doctor, **médicus**
dog, **cánis**
done, to be, **fíerī**
Don't…! **Nólī/Nōlíte** + infinitive
door, **iánua**
doorkeeper, **iánitor**
door-post, **póstis**
dormouse, **glīs**
doubt, **dúbium**
down from, **dē**
drag, to, **tráhere**
drag out, to, **extráhere**
drain, to, **hauríre**

draw, to, **stríngere**
draw a sword, to, **gládium stríngere**
dream, **sómnium**
drink, to, **bíbere**
drinking party, **commissátiō**
drive, to, **ágere, incitáre**
drive back, to, **repéllere**
drive off, to, **repéllere**
drive out, to, **expéllere**
drive to and fro, to, **iactáre**
driver, **raedárius**
drunk, **ébrius**
dung, **stércus**
dust, **púlvis**
dwell, to, **habitáre**

E

each, **ómnis**
eager, **inténtus**
earlier, **príus**
early in the day, **máne**
earth, **térra**
easily, **fácile**
easy, **fácilis**
eat, to, **ésse**
eat dinner, to, **cēnáre**
eating-house, **popína**
egg, **óvum**
eight, **óctō**
eighteen, **duodēvīgíntī**
eighteenth, **duodēvīcésimus**
eighth, **octávus**
either…or, **aut…aut**
elegant, **élegāns**
eleven, **úndecim**
eleventh, **ūndécimus**
embrace, **compléxus**
emperor, **Caésar, prínceps**
end, **fínis**
endure, to, **pátī**
energetic, **strénuus**
enough, **sátis**
enough time, **sátis témporis**

enter, to, **íngredī, iníre, intráre**
enthusiasm, **stúdium**
envoy, **lēgátus**
epistle, **lítterae**
eruption, **ērúptiō**
escape, to, **aufúgere, effúgere, ēvádere**
establish, to, **cóndere**
Eurydice, **Eurýdicē**
even, **étiam**
even if, **etiámsī**
evening, in the, **vésperī**
ever, **úmquam**
every, **ómnis**
every day, **cotídiē, in díēs**
evil, **málus**
examine, to, **īnspícere**
exceedingly, **váldē**
excellent, **óptimus**
excellently, **óptimē, púlchrē**
except, **nísi, praéter**
exclaim, to, **exclāmáre**
excuse, to, **excūsáre**
exiled, **prófugus**
expel, to, **expéllere**
explain, to, **explicáre**
explain the situation, to, **rem explicáre**
expression, **ōs**
extinguish, to, **exstínguere**
eye, **óculus**

F

fabric, **téla**
face, **ōs**
face down, **prónus**
fact, in, **ímmō vérō**
fair-skinned, **cándidus**
faithful, **fidélis**
fall, to, **cádere**
fall down, to, **concídere**
fame, **glória**
famous, **céleber, praeclárus**
famous, that, **ílle**
far, **lóngē, prócul**

far off, **prócul**
farm, **fúndus**
farm manager, **vílicus**
fast, very, **celérrimē, celérrimus**
fast as possible, as, **súmmā celeritáte**
fastest, **celérrimus**
fat, **obésus, pínguis**
fate, **fátum**
father, **páter**
fault, **cúlpa**
favor, to, **favére**
fear, **métus, térror, tímor**
fear, to, **timére, verérī**
fearful, **tímidus**
feast, **convívium**
February, **Februárius**
feed, to, **páscere**
few, **paúcī**
field, **áger**
fierce, **férōx, saévus**
fiercely, **feróciter**
fifteen, **quíndecim**
fifteenth, **quíntus décimus**
fifth, **quíntus**
fiftieth, **quinquāgésimus**
fifty, **quīnguāgíntā**
fill, to, **complére**
filthy, **foédus**
find, to, **inveníre**
finely, **púlchrē**
finish, to, **cōnfícere, finíre**
fire, **ígnis, incéndium**
fire, to set on, **incéndere**
first, **prímus**
first, (at), **prímō, prímum**
first course, **gustátiō**
first day in the month, **Kaléndae**
fishpond, **piscína**
five, **quínque**
five hundred, **quīngéntī**
five-hundredth, **quīngentésimus**
flame, **flámma**
flee, to, **effúgere, fúgere**
flesh, **cárō**

floor, **tabulátum**
flower, **flōs**
follow, to, **séquī**
following, **séquēns**
following day, on the, **postrídiē**
food, **cíbus**
foolish, **stúltus**
foot, **pēs**
footprint, **vēstígium**
for, **énim, nam**
for a short time, **paulísper**
forbid, to, **vetáre**
force, **vīs**
forehead, **frōns**
forest, **sílva**
forgetful, **ímmemor**
forgive, to, **excūsáre**
former, the, **ílle**
Forum, the, **Fórum**
found, to, **cóndere**
four, **quáttuor**
fourteen, **quattuórdecim**
fourteenth, **quártus décimus**
fourth, **quártus**
frail, **īnfírmus**
free, **grátīs**
freedman, **lībértus**
freedom, **lībértās**
friend, **amíca, amícus, hóspes**
friendly way, in a, **cómiter**
frighten, to, **terrére**
frightened, **pertérritus, térritus**
frightening, **terríbilis**
from, **ā, ab, ē, ex**
front of, in, **ánte, ápud**
fugitive, **prófugus**
full, **plénus**
furnishings, **ōrnāménta**

G

Gades, **Gádēs**
game, **lúdus**
games, **lúdī**

gape, to, **stupére**
garden, **hórtus**
garland, **coróna**
garment, **véstis**
garum, **liquámen**
gate, **pórta**
Gaul, **Gállia**
gently, **plácidē**
get, to, **accípere**
get ready, to, **paráre**
get up, to, **súrgere**
get well, to, **convaléscere**
girl, **puélla**
give, to, **dáre, dōnáre**
give back, to, **réddere**
give favor (to), to, **favére**
give trust (to), to, **cōnfídere**
glad, **laétus**
glad, to be, **gaudére**
gladly, **libénter**
glory, **glória**
go, to, **íre**
go around, to, **circumíre**
go away, to, **abíre, discédere**
go back, to, **redíre, régredī**
go down, to, **dēscéndere**
go forward, to, **prōcédere**
go in, to, **íngredī**
go into, to, **iníre, intráre**
go out, to, **égredī, exíre**
go past, to, **praeteríre**
goal, **méta**
goblet, **póculum**
god, **déus**
gods above, the, **súperī**
gold, **aúrum**
golden, **aúreus**
good, **bónus**
good, very, **óptimus**
Good heavens! **Dī immortálēs! Prō dī immortálēs!**
Goodbye! **Válē/Valéte!**
Goodness me! **Mehércule!**
goods, **bóna**

grab, to, **corrípere**
grab hold of, to, **arrípere**
graciously, **cómiter**
gradually, **paulátim**
grape, **úva**
gratitude, **grátia**
great, **mágnus**
great, so, **tántus**
great, very, **máximus, súmmus**
greater, **máior**
greatest, **máximus, súmmus**
greatest speed, with the, **súmmā celeritáte**
greatly, **magnópere, múltum**
Greece, **Graécia**
Greek, **Graécus**
Greeks, the, **Graécī**
green, **prásinus**
greet, to, **salūtáre**
greetings, **sálūs**
Greetings! **Ávē!/Avéte! Sálvē!/Salvéte!**
greetings, to send, **salútem dícere**
grief, **dólor**
groan, to, **gémere**
ground, **térra**
ground, on the, **húmī**
grunt, to, **grunníre**
guard, **cústōs**
guard, to, **custōdíre**
guest, **hóspes**
guest (at a banquet), **convíva**

H

habit of, to be in the, **solére**
Hail! **Ávē!/Avéte!**
hair, **crínēs**
half-asleep, **sēmisómnus**
ham, **pérna**
hand, **mánus**
hand over, to, **trádere**
handsome, **púlcher**
happen, to, **fíerī**
happens, it, **áccidit**
happily, **fēlíciter, laétē**

happy, **laétus**
hard, **strénuē**
hare, **lépus**
harm, to, **nocére**
have, to, **habére**
he, **is**, **ílle**
head, **cáput**
head for, to, **pétere**
health (good or bad), **valētúdō**
hear, to, **audíre**
"heart," **ánima**
heat, **aéstus**
heaven, **caélum**
heavy, **grávis**
Hello! **Sálvē!/Salvéte!**
help, **auxílium**
Help! **Fer/Férte auxílium!**
help, to, **adiuváre**
her (own), **súus**
Hercules, **Hérculēs**
here, **hīc, hūc**
here, to, **hūc**
here and there, **hūc illúc**
herself, **ípsa, sē**
Hesperia, **Hespéria**
Hey! **Ého!**
hide, to, **cēláre, obscūráre**
high, **áltus**
highest throw of the knucklebones, the, **Vénus**
hill, **cóllis, mōns**
himself, **ípse, sē**
hinder, to, **impedíre**
hire, to, **condúcere**
his (own), **súus**
hit, to, **feríre**
hold, to, **habére, tenére**
hold back, to, **retinére**
hold out, to, **exténdere**
holiday, celebrating a, **fēriátus**
home, **dómum, dómus**
home, at, **dómī**
home, from, **dómō**
homeward, **dómum**
honor, **hónor**

Horace, **Horátius**
horrible, **abōminándus**
hors d'oeuvre, **gustátiō**
horse, **équus**
host, **hóspes**
hour, **hóra**
house, **dómus**
house of, at the, **ápud**
How…! **Quam…!**
How…? **Quam…?, Quō īnstrūméntō…?, Quōmodo…?**
How are you? **Quid ágis?**
How big…? **Quántus…?**
How many…? **Quot…?**
How much…? **Quántus…?**
How much…! **Quántum…!**
How much (in price)…? **Quántī…?**
however, **aútem, támen**
howl, to, **ululáre**
huge, **íngēns**
humble, **húmilis**
hundred, a, **céntum**
hundredth, **centésimus**
hungry, to be, **ēsuríre**
hurl, to, **praecipitáre**
hurl oneself, to, **sē praecipitáre**
Hurray! **Eúge!/Eúgepae!**
hurry, to, **festīnáre**
husband, **cóniūnx, vir**
hut, **cása**

I

I, **égo**
Ides, the, **Ídūs**
idle, to be, **cessáre**
if, **sī**
if…not, **nísi**
ignorant, to be, **ignōráre, nescíre**
ill, **aéger**
ill, to be, **aegrōtáre**
immediately, **státim**
immortal, **immortális**
Immortal Gods! **Dī immortálēs!**

important, it is, **ínterest**
in, **in**
in front of, **ápud**
in return, **cóntrā**
in vain, **frústrā**
Indeed! **Íta vérō!**
indeed, **quídem**, **vérō**
infant, **ínfāns**
inhabitant, **íncola**
inn, **caupóna**
innkeeper, **caúpō**
innocence, **innocéntia**
inside, **íntrā**
insolence, **procácitās**
insolent, **prócāx**
instruction, **mandátum**
instrument…, With what, **Quō īnstrūméntō…?**
intend, to, **in ánimō habére**
intent, **inténtus**
interrupt, to, **interpelláre**
into, **in**
invite, to, **invītáre, vocáre**
invoke, to, **invocáre**
irritability, **īrācúndia**
irritable, **īrācúndus**
island, **ínsula**
it, **ílle, is**
Italy, **Itália**
Ithaca, **Íthaca**
its (own), **súus**
itself, **ípse, sē**
ivy, **hédera**

J

January, **Iānuárius**
joke, **iócus**
joke, as a, **per iócum**
journey, **íter**
joy, **gaúdium**
July, **Iúlius**
June, **Iúnius**
Juno, **Iúnō**
just as if, **támquam**

K

Kalends, the, **Kaléndae**
keen, **ácer**
keep, to, **retinére**
kill, to, **necáre**
kind, of this, **tális**
kingdom, **régnum**
kitchen, **culína**
know, not to, **ignōráre, nescíre**
know, to, **scíre**
known, **nótus**
knucklebones, **tálī**

L

lack, to, **carére**
ladle, small, **cýathus**
lady of the house, **dómina**
lamp-stand, **candēlábrum**
land, **áger, térra**
language, **língua**
lantern, **lantérna**
large, **mágnus**
large, very, **máximus**
last, at, **tándem**
last laugh, to get the, **dērīdére**
late, **sérō**
later, **sérius**
latest, **sēríssimē**
Latin, **Latínus**
Latium, **Látium**
latter, the, **hic**
laugh, **rísus**
laugh (at), to, **dērīdére, rīdére**
laughter, **cachínnus**
Lavinium, of, **Lāvínius**
lay down, to, **dēpónere**
lazy, **ignávus**
lead, to, **dúcere**
lead back, to, **redúcere**
lead on, to, **addúcere**
leaky, **rīmósus**
leap down, to, **dēsilíre**

learn, to, **díscere**
learned, **ērudítus**
least, **mínimē**
leave, to, **égredī**, **proficíscī**
leave behind, to, **relínquere**
leave out, to, **omíttere**
length, at, **tándem**
less, **mínus**
lessen, to, **minúere**
letter, **epístula**, **lítterae**
letter (of the alphabet), **líttera**
letters, **lítterae**
lie, to, **iacére**
lie down, to, **recúmbere**
light, **lūx**
light, it is, **lúcet**
like, **símilis**
like, to, **amáre**
like this, **tális**
line (of poetry), **vérsus**
listen to, to, **audíre**
literature, **lítterae**
litter, **lectíca**
litter-bearer, **lectīcárius**
little, **párvulus**
little, a, **paúlum**
little by little, **paulátim**
live, to, **habitáre**, **vívere**
livestock, **pécus**
load, **ónus**
located, **sítus**
long, **lóngus**
long for, to, **dēsīderáre**
long time, for a, **díū**
longer, **diútius**
longest, **diūtíssimē**
Look (at)...! **Écce...!**
look after, to, **cūráre**
look at, to, **spectáre**
look for, to, **pétere**, **quaérere**
look out for, to, **exspectáre**
loud (voice, laugh), **mágnus**
love, **ámor**
love, to, **amáre**

luckily, **fēlíciter**
lucky, **félīx**
lying down, to be, **iacére**

M

made, to be, **fíerī**
magnificent, **magníficus**
main room in a house, **átrium**
make, to, **fácere**
make something (acc.) agreeable to someone (dat.),
        to, **persuādére**
man, **hómō**, **vir**
manhood, of, **virílis**
manner...?, In what, **Quómodo...?**
Mantua, **Mántua**
manure, **stércus**
many, **múltī**
many, very, **plúrimī**
many years afterward, **múltīs post ánnīs**
March, **Mártius**
mark, **méta**
marvelous, **mírus**
mass, **mólēs**
master, **árbiter**, **dóminus**, **magíster**
master of the drinking, **árbiter bibéndī**
matter, **rēs**
may, we, **lícet nóbīs**
me, **mē**
me, with, **mécum**
means...?, By what, **Quō īnstrūméntō...?**
meanwhile, **intéreā**
measure (of wine), **cýathus**
meat, **cárō**
meet, to, **occúrrere**
Megara, **Mégara**
members of the family of Cornelius,
        the, **Cornéliī**
memory, **memória**
merchant, **mercátor**
Mercury, **Mercúrius**
messenger, **núntius**
method, **módus**
mid-, **médius**

middle of, **médius**
midnight, **média nox**
Milan, **Mediolánum**
mind, **ánimus**
mindful, **mémor**
mine, **méus**
mirror, **spéculum**
miserable, **míser, miserábilis**
miss, to, **dēsīderáre**
mistaken, to be, **erráre**
mistress, **dómina**
mix, to, **miscére**
mob, **túrba**
moment, at that, **tum**
money, **pecúnia**
month, **ménsis**
mood, in a bad, **īrācúndus**
moon, **lúna**
more, **mágis, plū́rēs, plūs**
more wine, **plūs vī́nī**
moreover, **aútem, praetéreā**
morning, in the, **mā́ne**
most, **máximē, plū́rimī, plū́rimum,**
    plū́rimus
mother, **mā́ter**
motionless, **immóbilis**
Mount Vesuvius, **Mōns Vesúvius**
mountain, **mōns**
mouse, **mūs**
mouth, **ōs**
move, to, **commovére, movére**
move aside, to, **removére**
move one's home, to, **migráre**
move toward, to, **admovére**
moved, **commótus**
much, **múltum, múltus**
much, too, **nímis**
much, very, **máximē, plū́rimus**
mud, **lútum**
murmur, **múrmur**
Muse, **Mū́sa**
mushroom, **bōlétus**
mutter, to, **mussáre**
my, **méus**

N

name, **nṓmen**
name, to, **appelláre**
napkin, **máppa**
Naples, **Neápolis**
narrator, **nārrátor**
nation, **génus**
near, **ad, própe**
near, to be, **adésse**
nearby, **próximus**
necessary, **necésse**
need, to, **carére**
neighboring, **vīcínus**
neither...nor, **néque...néque**
neither...nor...anything,
    néque...néque...quídquam
never, **númquam**
nevertheless, **támen**
new, **nóvus**
next, **deínde**
night, **nox**
night, happening during the, **noctúrnus**
nine, **nóvem**
nineteen, **ūndēvīgíntī**
nineteenth, **ūndēvīcésimus**
ninth, **nónus**
no, **nū́llus**
No! **Mínimē (vḗrō)!**
No indeed! **Mínimē vḗrō!**
no longer, **nōn iam**
no one, **némō**
noise, **frágor, strépitus**
none, **nū́llus**
Nones, **Nṓnae**
noon, at, **merídiē**
northern, **septentriōnális**
nose, **nā́sus**
not, **nōn**
Not at all! **Mínimē vḗrō!**
not even, **nē...quídem**
not yet, **nóndum**
nothing, **níhil, nīl**
nothing, for, **grátīs**

nothing, to do, **cessáre**
notice, to, **animadvértere**
November, **Novémber**
now, **iam, nunc**
nowhere, **núsquam**
number, **númerus**

O

obey, to, **pārére**
obtain, to, **comparáre**
October, **Octóber**
Odysseus, **Ulíxēs**
of course, **sánē**
often, **saépe**
often, more, **saépius**
often, most, **saepíssimē**
oil, **óleum**
ointment, **unguéntum**
old, **vétus**
old man, **sénex**
olive, **olíva**
olive grove, **olīvétum**
omit, to, **omíttere**
on, **in**
on account of, **ob, própter**
on time, **ad témpus**
once (upon a time), **ólim**
one, **únus**
one (of two), **álter**
one...another, **álius...álius**
one...the other, the, **álter...álter**
oneself, **sē**
only, **módo, tántum**
only just, **vix**
open, to, **aperíre**
open space, **área**
or, **aut, -ve, vel**
or if, **seu**
oration, **ōrátiō**
orator, **ōrátor**
order, **mandátum**
order, to, **iubére**
orders, **iússa**

Orpheus, **Órpheus**
other, **álius**
other (of two), the, **álter**
others, the, **céterī**
otherwise, **áliter**
ought, **debére**
our, **nóster**
out of, **ē, ex**
outside, **éxtrā, fórās**
overcome, **afféctus**
overcome, to **superáre**
overseer, **vílicus**
overtake, to, **cónsequī**
overturn, to, **ēvértere**
overwhelm, to, **opprímere**
owe, to, **debére**
owner, **dóminus**
ox, **bōs**

P

painstaking, **díligēns**
Palatine Hill, belonging to the, **Palātínus**
palla, **pálla**
parent, **párēns**
parsley, **ápium**
part, **pars**
pastry with cheese filling, **scriblíta**
pasture, to, **páscere**
patron, **patrónus**
pay the penalty, to, **poénās dáre**
peacefully, **plácidē**
pear, **pírum**
peasant, **rústicus**
pen, **stílus**
penalty, **poéna**
people, **hóminēs**
perfume, **unguéntum**
perhaps, **fortásse**
person related to one of another city by ties of
      hospitality, **hóspes**
persuade, to, **persuādére**
persuade someone of something, to, **persuādére**
pest, **moléstus**

pick out, to, **súmere**

picture, **pictúra**

pig, **pórcus**

pirate, **pīráta**

place, **lócus**

place, to, **pónere**

place, to that, **illúc**

plague, **pestiléntia**

play, to, **lúdere**

play ball, to, **pílā lúdere**

please, **sī vīs, sīs**

please, to, **placére**

pleasing to someone to do something, it is, **líbet**

Pluto, **Plútō**

poet, **poéta**

Pompeii, **Pompéiī**

poor, **paúper**

pork, **pórcus**

possessions, **bóna**

pour out, to, **effúndere**

praise, to, **laudáre**

prank, **iócus**

prank/joke, as a, **per iócum**

prepare, to, **paráre**

prepare oneself, to, **sē paráre**

prepared, **parátus**

present, to be, **adésse**

presently, **mox**

pretend, to, **simuláre**

pretty, **púlcher**

prevent, to, **impedíre**

previously, **abhínc, ánte, ánteā**

price, **prétium**

prisoner, **captívus**

promise, to, **prōmíttere**

proper, **réctus**

properly, **réctē**

pull, to, **tráhere**

punish, to, **pūníre**

punished, to be, **poénās dáre**

punishment, **poéna**

pupil, **discípulus**

pure, **mérus**

pushy, **prócāx**

put, to, **pónere**

put aside, to, **dēpónere**

put on, to, **indúere**

put out, to, **exstínguere**

Q

quarrel, **ríxa**

queen, **rēgína**

question, **rogátiō**

quickly, **celériter**

quickly, more, **celérius**

quickly, very, **celérrimē**

quiet, to be, **tacére**

quiet, to keep, **quiéscere**

Quirinal (Hill), **Quirīnális**

R

race, **génus**

race track, **currículum**

rain, **ímber**

raining, it is, **plúit**

rains, it, **plúit**

raisin-wine, **pássum**

rash, **temerárius**

rather, **ímmō**

reach, to, **adveníre, perveníre**

read, to, **légere**

read aloud, to, **recitáre**

ready, **parátus**

ready, to get, **comparáre, sē paráre**

really, **vérō**

rear, **térgum**

reason, **caúsa**

reason, for this, **quā dē caúsā**

reason…?, For what, **Quam ob caúsam…?**

rebuke, to, **castīgáre**

recall, to, **revocáre**

receive, to, **accípere, excípere**

recite, to, **recitáre**

reciting, of, **recitándī**

reckless, **temerárius**

recline, to, **recúmbere**

recline (at table), to, **accúmbere**

recognize, to, **agnóscere**

recover, to, **recuperáre**

red, **russátus**

redo, to, **refícere**

reduce, to, **minúere**

refraining from, **ábstinēns**

refraining from wine, **vínō ábstinēns**

refuse, to, **nólle**

regain one's senses, to, **ánimum recuperáre**

region, **pars**

reins, **habénae**

rejoice, to, **gaudére**

remain, to, **manére, morárī**

remake, to, **refícere**

remember, to, **memóriā tenére**

remembering, **mémor**

remove, to, **removére**

renew, to, **renováre**

repeatedly, **idéntidem**

reply, **respónsum**

reply, to, **respondére**

reprimand, to, **castīgáre**

rescue, to, **ērípere**

resist, to, **resístere**

rest, **quiés**

rest, the, **céterī**

rest, to, **sē quiétī dáre, quiéscere**

restore, to, **refícere**

return, **réditus**

return, to, **réddere, redíre, régredī**

returning, **rédiēns**

revive, to, **renováre**

rich, **díves, pínguis**

right, **réctus**

rightly, **réctē**

rise, to, **súrgere**

rise up, to, **coorírī**

road, **vía**

robber, **praédō**

rod, **vírga**

Roman, **Rōmánus**

Romans, the, **Rōmánī**

Rome, **Róma**

Rome, in, **Rómae**

Rome, to, **Rómam**

room, **cubículum**

rose, **rósa**

rouse, to, **excitáre**

route, **íter**

ruin, **ruína**

rumble, **múrmur**

run, to, **cúrrere**

run about, to, **concursáre**

run ahead, to, **praecúrrere**

run away, to, **aufúgere, effúgere**

run to and fro, to, **concursáre**

run together, to, **concúrrere**

run toward/up to, to, **accúrrere**

rush, to, **sē praecipitáre**

rush up, to, **concúrrere**

S

sad, **trístis**

sad, to be, **dolére**

safe, **sálvus**

safe and sound, **incólumis**

said, (he/she), **ínquit**

said, (he/she/it) is, **dícitur**

sail, to, **nāvigáre**

salt, **sal**

same, the, **ídem**

same as, the, **ídem ac**

same time, at the, **símul**

sandal, **sólea**

savage, **saévus**

save, to, **serváre**

say, to, **dícere**

says, (he/she), **ínquit**

scarcely, **vix**

scent of, to catch the, **olfácere**

scholarly, **ērudítus**

school, **lúdus**

schoolmaster, **magíster**

scold, to, **reprehéndere**

scrap, **frústum**

sea, **áltum, máre**

seat, **sélla**
second, **secúndus**
second, a/the, **álter**
second time, a, **íterum**
secretly, **clam**
sedan chair, **sélla**
see, to, **vidére**
seek, to, **pétere, quaérere**
seems, (he/she/it), **vidétur**
seize, to, **arrípere, corrípere, occupáre, rápere**
-self, **ípse**
sell, to, **véndere**
Senate, **senátus**
Senate House, **Cúria**
senator, **senátor**
send, to, **míttere**
send fondest greetings, to, **salútem plúrimam dícere**
send for, to, **arcéssere**
send greetings, to, **salútem dícere**
send out, to, **ēmíttere**
sensible, **prúdēns**
sensibly, **prūdénter**
September, **Septémber**
serious, **grávis**
set down, to, **dēpónere**
set out, to, **proficíscī**
seven, **séptem**
seventeen, **septéndecim**
seventeenth, **séptimus décimus**
seventh, **séptimus**
seventieth, **septuāgésimus**
several, **complúrēs**
shade (of the dead), **úmbra**
shadow, **úmbra**
shaky, **īnfírmus**
she, **éa, ílla**
she-wolf, **lúpa**
sheep and cattle, **pécus**
sheet, **strátum**
ship, **návis**
ships's boat, **scápha**
shop, **tabérna**
shore, **lítus, óra**

short, **brévis**
short time, for a, **paulísper**
shout, **clámor**
shout, to, **clāmáre**
shout out, to, **exclāmáre**
shouting, **clámor**
show, to, **dēmōnstráre, mōnstráre**
shut, **claúsus**
shut, to, **claúdere**
Sicily, **Sicília**
sides, from/on all, **úndique**
sight, **spectáculum**
signal, **sígnum**
silence, **siléntium**
silent, to become, **conticéscere**
silently, **tácitē**
similar, **símilis**
since, **cum, quóniam**
sing, to, **cánere, cantáre**
sir, **vir óptime**
sister, **sóror**
sit, to, **sedére**
sit down, to, **cōnsídere**
situated, **sítus**
situation, **rēs**
six, **sex**
sixteen, **sédecim**
six (in throwing knucklebones), the, **séniō**
sixteenth, **séxtus décimus**
sixth, **séxtus**
skill, **ars**
sky, **caélum**
slave, **sérvus**
slave-woman, **ancílla**
sleep, **sómnus**
sleep, to, **dormíre**
sleep, to go to, **obdormíre**
sleepy, to be, **dormitáre**
slender, **grácilis**
slow, **léntus, tárdus**
slowly, **léntē**
small, **párvulus, párvus**
small, very, **mínimus**
small amount, a, **paúlum**

small boat, **scápha**
smaller, **mínor**
smallest, **mínimus**
smell, to, **olfácere**
smile, **rísus**
smile, to, **rīdére**
smoke, **fúmus**
snatch, to, **arrípere, rápere**
snatch from, to, **ērípere**
snore, to, **stértere**
so, **íta, tam**
So be it! **Éstō!**
soldier, **míles**
solitude, **sōlitúdō**
some, **áliquī**
some…others…, **áliī…áliī…**
something, **áliquid**
sometimes, **nōnnúmquam**
son, **fílius**
soon, **mox**
sorry, to be, **dolére**
sort of…?, What, **Quális…?**
soul, **ánima**
sound, **sónitus**
space, open, **área**
Spain, **Hispánia**
speak, to, **lóquī**
speak together, to, **cólloquī**
speaker, **ōrátor**
spectacle, **spectáculum**
spectator, **spectátor**
speech, **ōrátiō**
speed, **celéritās**
speed, with the greatest, **súmmā celeritáte**
spend the night, to, **pernoctáre**
spill, to, **effúndere**
spin wool, to, **lánam tráhere**
split, to, **scíndere**
spur on, to, **incitáre**
squared, **quadrátus**
staff, **báculum**
stand, to, **stáre**
standing out, **éxstāns**
statue, **státua**

stay, to, **manére, morárī**
stay awake, to, **vigiláre**
stealthily, **fúrtim**
stick, **báculum, vírga**
stick, to, **haerére**
still, **adhúc**
stock, **génus**
stola, **stóla**
stone, **lápis**
stone, of, **lapídeus**
stony, **lapídeus**
storm, **tempéstās**
story, **fábula, tabulátum**
story, funny, **iócus**
strange, **mírus**
stream, **rívus**
street, **vía**
strenuously, **strénuē**
strike, to, **feríre, percútere**
strong, to be, **valére**
stronger, to grow, **convaléscere**
study, **stúdium**
study (room), **tablínum**
study, to, **studére**
stupid, **fátuus, stúltus**
Subura, **Subúra**
such, **tális**
such things, **tália**
suddenly, **súbitō**
suffer, to, **pátī**
summer, **aéstās**
summon, to, **arcéssere**
support, to, **favére**
surname, **cognómen**
sweet, **suávis**
swift, **céler**
swim, to, **natáre**
switch, **vírga**
sword, **gládius**

T

table, **ménsa**
tail, **caúda**

take, to, **cápere, dúcere, súmere**
take away (from), to, **adímere, auférre**
take back, to, **redúcere**
take care of, to, **cūráre**
take off, to, **exúere**
take out, to, **extráhere**
take up, to, **súmere**
talk, to, **lóquī**
talkative, **verbósus**
tall, **áltus**
tart with cheese filling, **scriblíta**
tasteful, **élegāns**
teach, to, **docére**
teacher, secondary school, **grammáticus**
tell, to, **dícere**
tell (a story), to, **nārráre**
tell not to, to, **vetáre**
tell the truth, to, **véra dícere**
temper, bad, **īrācúndia**
temple, **témplum**
ten, **décem**
tenant, **íncola**
tenth, **décimus**
terrified, **pertérritus**
terrify, to, **terrére**
territory, **áger**
terror, **térror**
test, to, **experírī**
testament, **testāméntum**
than, **quam**
thanks, **grátia**
Thank you! **Grátiās tíbi ágō!**
that, **is, ílle, quī, quod**
that famous, **ílle**
that place, to, **éō**
the (more)…the (more), **quō…éō…**
their (own), **súus**
themselves, **ípsī, sē**
then, **deínde, índe, tum**
there, **éō, íbi, illúc**
there, from, **índe**
therefore, **ígitur, ítaque**
thing, **rēs**
think, to, **cōgitáre**

third, **tértius**
thirteen, **trédecim**
thirteenth, **tértius décimus**
this, **hic, is**
this way and that, **hūc illúc**
thorough, **díligēns**
thousand, a, **mílle**
thousandth, **mīllésimus**
Thrace, **Thrácia**
three, **trēs**
threshing-floor, **área**
through, **per**
throw, to, **conícere, iácere**
throw down, to, **dēícere**
throw of the knucklebones, the highest, **Vénus**
throw of the knucklebones, the lowest, **cánis**
throw out, to, **eícere**
thus, **íta, sīc**
time, **témpus**
time, on, **ad témpus**
time to time, from, **intérdum**
timid, **tímidus**
tired, **dēféssus**
to, **ad**
today, **hódiē**
toga, **tóga**
toga, plain white, **tóga virílis**
toga of manhood, **tóga virílis**
toga with purple border, **tóga praetéxta**
together, **símul, únā**
toil, **lábor**
told, **nārrátus**
tomb, **sepúlcrum**
tombstone, **stéla**
tomorrow, **crās**
tongue, **língua**
too, **praetéreā**
top, on, **súprā**
top of, the, **súmmus**
toss about, to, **iactáre**
toward, **ad**
towering, **éxstāns**
town, **óppidum**
town, of the, **urbánus**

trace, **vēstígium**
track, **vēstígium**
travel, to, **íter fácere**
traveler, **viátor**
tray, **férculum**
tree, **árbor**
tremble, to, **trémere**
Trojan, **Troiánus**
Trojans, the, **Troiáni**
troublesome, **moléstus**
Troy, **Tróia**
true, **vérus**
truly, **vérō**
trunk, **císta**
trust, to, **cōnfídere, crédere**
try, to, **cōnárī, experírī, temptáre**
tunic, **túnica**
turn, to, **vértere**
turn aside, to, **dēvértere**
turning post, **méta**
tutor, **paedagógus**
twelfth, **duodécimus**
twelve, **duódecim**
twentieth, **vīcésimus**
twenty, **vīgíntī**
two, **dúo**
two-wheeled carriage, light, **císium**

U

Ulysses, **Ulíxēs**
uncle, **pátruus**
unconcerned, **sēcúrus**
under, **sub**
underworld, the, **ínferī**
unforgetting, **mémor**
unhappy, **míser**
unhurt, **incólumis**
unless, **nísi**
unspeakable, **īnfándus**
until, **dónec, dum**
unwilling, **invítus**
unwilling, to be, **nólle**
uproar, **tumúltus**

upset, to, **commovére, ēvértere**
urge on, to, **incitáre**
us, **nōs**
useful, **útilis**

V

vegetable, **hólus**
vehicle, **vehículum**
Venus, **Vénus**
verb, **vérbum**
Vergil, **Vergílius**
verse, **vérsus**
very, **ípse, máximē, váldē**
very much, **váldē, veheménter**
victor, **víctor**
vineyard, **vínea**
violent, **véhemēns**
violently, **veheménter**
visit, to, **vīsitáre**
voice, **vōx**

W

wagon, **plaústrum**
wait, to, **manére**
wait for, to, **exspectáre**
wake (someone) up, to, **excitáre, expergíscī**
wakened, **excitátus**
walk, to, **ambuláre**
wall, **múrus, páriēs**
walls, **moénia**
wander, to, **erráre**
want, to, **cúpere, vélle**
war, **béllum**
warm, **cálidus**
warn, to, **monére**
wash, to, **laváre**
wash overboard, to, **ēícere**
watch, to, **observáre, spectáre**
watch out for, to, **cavére**
water, **áqua**
wave, **únda**
way, **módus**

way, in this, **íta, sīc**
way...?, In what, **Quómodo...?**
way and that, this, **hūc illúc**
we, **nōs**
weak, **īnfírmus**
weapons, **árma**
wear, to, **gérere**
weave, to, **téxere**
web, **téla**
weep, to, **lacrimáre**
welcome, to, **accípere, excípere, salūtáre**
well, **béne, fēlíciter**
well, to be, **valére**
well, very, **óptimē**
werewolf, **versipéllis**
What...? **Quī...?, Quid...?**
What a...! **Quam...!**
What time is it? **Quóta hóra est?**
What/Which (in numerical order)...? **Quótus...?**
wheel, **róta**
When...? **Quándō...?**
when, **cum, úbi**
where, **úbi**
Where...? **Úbi...?**
where...?, From, **Únde...?**
Where...to? **Quō...?**
which, **quī**
Which...? **Quī...?**
which (in numerical order)...? **Quótus...?**
while, **dum**
whip, to, **verberáre**
white, **albátus, cándidus**
who, **quī**
Who...? **Quis...?**
whole, the, **ómnis, tótus**
whom...?, With, **Quócum...?**
Whose...? **Cúius...?**
Why...? **Cūr...?**
wicked, **sceléstus**
wife, **cóniūnx, úxor**
will, **testāméntum**
willing, to be, **vélle**
win, to, **víncere**

wind, **véntus**
window, **fenéstra**
wine, **vínum**
wine, undiluted, **mérum**
wine sweetened with honey, **múlsum**
winter, **híems**
wise, **prúdēns**
wisely, **prūdénter**
wish, to, **vélle**
wish, if you, **sī vīs, sīs**
wish, not to, **nólle**
wit, **sal**
with, **ápud, cum**
with difficulty, **vix**
without, **síne**
wolf, **lúpus**
woman, **fémina, múlier**
woman's outer garment, **stóla**
wonder, to, **sē rogáre**
wonderful, **mírus**
woods, **sílva**
wool, **lána**
word, **vérbum**
work, **lábor**
work, to, **labōráre**
worried, **sollícitus**
worse, **péior, péius**
worst, **péssimē, péssimus**
wound, **vúlnus**
wound, to, **vulneráre**
wretched, **míser, miserábilis**
write, to, **scríbere**

Y

year, **ánnus**
Yes! **Íta vérō!**
yesterday, **héri**
you, (sing.) **tū**, (pl.) **vōs**
young man, **aduléscēns**
your, (sing.) **túus**, (pl.) **véster**
youth, **aduléscēns**

INDEX OF GRAMMAR

INDEX OF CULTURAL INFORMATION

First Triumvirate, 79
Fish sauce, 54
Fleece, 94
Fleet, 79
Food, 54
Forum, 81, 124
    lists of names posted, 29
    new construction, 127

Galen, 140
Gallia Narbonensis, 81
Garden, 16
Garum, 54
Gaul, provinces, 79
Georgics (Vergil), 127
Germanic tribes, 28
Golden Age, 127
Gossip, 52
Gracchi brothers, 26–27
Gracchus
    Gaius Sempronius, 27
    Tiberius Sempronius, 26
Grammaticus, 113
Greece, 28, 79
Gustātiō, 54

Hair
    dressers, 7
    false, 7
    pins, 7
    styles, 6–8
Homelessness, 26
Horace
    Odes, 127
    Satires, 114
Hors d'oeuvre, 54

I came, I saw, I conquered, 80
Ides of March, 124
Iēntāculum, 39
Imperātor, 125
Imperium, 125
Imperium sine fīne, 127
Inheritance, rights of, 84

Ink, 137
Institutio oratoria (Quintilian), 115
Īnsulae, 17
Italy, 79

Jugurtha, King, 28
Julia, 79
Julian
    Emperor, 6
    reform, 81
Jupiter, 127
Justinian, Emperor, 84
Juvenal, *Satires*, 22, 55

Kitchen, 16
Knives, 39

Lamps, 39
Land
    allotments, 27
    grants, 79
Law, 114
    Roman, 84
    of the Twelve Tables, 84
Lectī, 39
Leftist, 26
Legal expressions, Latin, 84–85
Legal systems, modern, 84
Lēgātī, 126
Legislation, 26
Lepidus, 124
Letters (Pliny), 102, 114–115
Libanius, *Orations*, 104
Libraries, 138
    public, 138
Liquāmen, 54
Literary works, recitations, 138
Literature, Greek and Latin, 113
Livy, 127
Looms, 145–146
Lotions, hair, 8
Lūdus litterārius, 103, 113